Linguistic intersections of language and gender

Linguistic intersections of language and gender

Of gender bias and gender fairness

Edited by
Dominic Schmitz, Simon David Stein and Viktoria Schneider

We acknowledge support by the Open Access Publication Fund of the University and State Library Düsseldorf.

ISBN 978-3-11-138727-7
e-ISBN (PDF) 978-3-11-138869-4
e-ISBN (EPUB) 978-3-11-138877-9
DOI https://doi.org/10.1515/9783111388694

This work is licensed under the Creative Commons Attribution 4.0 International License. For details go to https://creativecommons.org/licenses/by/4.0.

Creative Commons license terms for re-use do not apply to any content that is not part of the Open Access publication (such as graphs, figures, photos, excerpts, etc.). These may require obtaining further permission from the rights holder. The obligation to research and clear permission lies solely with the party re-using the material.

Library of Congress Control Number: 2025934324

Bibliographic information published by the Deutsche Nationalbibliothek
The Deutsche Nationalbibliothek lists this publication in the Deutsche Nationalbibliografie; detailed bibliographic data are available on the internet at http://dnb.dnb.de.

© 2025 with the author(s), editing © 2025 Dominic Schmitz, Simon David Stein and Viktoria Schneider, published by Walter de Gruyter GmbH, Berlin/Boston, Genthiner Straße 13, 10785 Berlin. This book is published with open access at www.degruyter.com.

d | u | p düsseldorf university press is an imprint of Walter de Gruyter GmbH.

Cover image: agsandrew / iStock / Getty Images Plus

dup.degruyter.com
Questions about General Product Safety Regulation:
productsafety@degruyterbrill.com

Preface

This volume grew out of a conference of the same title organized by the Association for Diversity in Linguistics (Diversität in der Linguistik e.V.), members of the Department of English Language and Linguistics at Heinrich Heine University Düsseldorf, and FörderLinK e.V., held at Heinrich Heine University Düsseldorf from 20 to 21 July 2023. We are grateful to all contributors for the smooth collaboration, to all reviewers of abstracts and articles for invaluable feedback, and to our student assistants who proofread all contributions. Special thanks go to düsseldorf university press's Anne Sokoll and Jessica Bartz and to De Gruyter's Elisabeth Stanciu for a supportive and dedicated supervision of the publication process and to the Open-Access-Fonds of the University and State Library Düsseldorf for covering the publication costs.

Contents

Preface —— V

Dominic Schmitz, Simon David Stein and Viktoria Schneider
Linguistic intersections of language and gender: Introduction —— 1

Lena Völkening
What if -*in* is a new suffix? —— 11

Samira Ochs and Jan Oliver Rüdiger
Of stars and colons: A corpus-based analysis of gender-inclusive orthographies in German press texts —— 31

Jens Fleischhauer and Dila Turus
Women are sexy and men provoke – Gender stereotypes and the interpretation of the German adjective *aufreizend* —— 63

Sol Tovar
Understanding (mis)gender(ing) and pronouns from a politeness theory standpoint —— 83

Dominic Schmitz
Pronoun comprehension from a discriminative perspective: A proof of concept —— 95

Simon David Stein and Viktoria Schneider
Effects of English generic singular *they* on the gender processing of L1 German speakers —— 111

Dominic Schmitz, Julia Elisabeth Blessing-Plötner, Nazire Cinar, Nguyet Minh Dang, Henrike Hoffmanns, Aaron Luther, Imran Peksen, and Tomma Lilli Robke
Form identity and gendered associations: L2 English -*er* facilitates the bias of L1 German -*er* —— 127

Zaal Kikvidze
Gender-inclusive or not? Covert gender patterns in Georgian —— 145

Francesca Panzeri and Martina Abbondanza
Gender-inclusive language and male bias: Task matters! —— 157

Laura Vela-Plo and Marina Ortega-Andrés
Theoretical and empirical basis for gender-fair language use: The case of Spanish —— 173

Jeff Roxas
Teaching Spanish in the Philippines: A queer-decolonial pedagogy —— 199

D. Hunter
Morphosyntax and me: The reflections of a non-binary linguist on English gendered language —— 219

Notes on contributors —— 239

Index —— 241

Dominic Schmitz, Simon David Stein and Viktoria Schneider
Linguistic intersections of language and gender: Introduction

1 Setting the scene: Language and gender

"Stop teaching kids pronouns and start teaching them grammar!"
– Laverne Spicer, 13 September 2022[1]

This demand, emblematic of the backlash against efforts to make language more gender-inclusive, reveals its own contradiction: Pronouns are, after all, a fundamental part of grammar. Such calls underscore the confusion and emotional charge that often fuel resistance to linguistic change, particularly in regard to questions of gender. But what exactly is gender, and how do language and gender intersect?

Answering these questions requires a clear differentiation of related yet distinct terms. In most cultures, *sex* is a social distinction based on physiological – or, as often termed, 'biological' – characteristics. *Gender*, from a social science perspective, encompasses the social, psychological, cultural, and behavioral aspects of a given identity, such as that of a woman (Haig 2004). Gender includes social structures, such as gender roles and expressions (Lindqvist et al. 2021; Bates et al. 2022). Many cultures, particularly those of the global north, have traditionally adhered to a binary model of gender, wherein individuals are categorized into one of two groups (cf. Maddux and Winstead 2019). These categories are typically aligned with those defined by sex. However, individuals who are outside this binary challenge these traditional systems and often face discrimination based on their gender (e.g., Richards et al. 2016).

In linguistic research, the terms *grammatical gender* (*genus*), *natural gender* (*sexus*), *lexico-semantic gender*, and *conceptual gender* are commonly used to describe the intersections of sex, gender, and language (cf., e.g., Kotthoff and Nübling 2024). *Grammatical gender* refers to noun classes which are reflected in the behavior

---

[1] The original tweet on Twitter was deleted by Spicer. However, screenshots are still being circulated, see, for example, https://www.yahoo.com/lifestyle/21-incredible-replies-people-spouted-234602965.html, accessed: 07 February 2025.

Dominic Schmitz, Simon David Stein and Viktoria Schneider, Department of English Language and Linguistics, Heinrich Heine University Düsseldorf, e-mail of corresponding author: dominic.schmitz@uni-duesseldorf.de

∂ Open Access. © 2025 the author(s), published by De Gruyter. [CC BY] This work is licensed under the Creative Commons Attribution 4.0 International License.
https://doi.org/10.1515/9783111388694-001

of associated words (Hockett 1958), dividing nouns into two or more distinct classes (Siemund 2008). These classes often trigger the appearance of certain formal exponents in their syntactic surroundings (e.g., in articles, adjectives, pronouns; Corbett 1991). *Natural gender* aligns with the concept of sex as it appears in linguistic analysis. *Lexico-semantic gender* refers to the intrinsic sex-related characteristics in many words used to refer to animate beings, for instance, the class 'female' in *mother* or *sister* and the class 'male' in *father* or *brother*. Finally, *conceptual gender* relates to the association of words with gender stereotypes.

In languages with grammatical gender, nouns referring to animate beings often reflect their sex or gender both lexico-semantically and grammatically. For instance, the word for *mother* typically belongs to the grammatical gender class 'female', while *father* aligns with the 'male' class. This alignment, known as the *Genus-Sexus-Prinzip* ('genus-sexus principle'), demonstrates that, even though grammatical gender by no means always corresponds with gender or sexus, there is a tendency for genus and gender or sex to interlink. This phenomenon is also observable in cases in which genus and gender or sexus do not match; cases commonly characterized by derogatory intentions (Eisenberg and Schöneich 2020; Kopeke and Zubin 2020). For example, in Italian, *checca* 'fairy (a pejorative term for an effeminate gay man)' takes the feminine genus, while for women, the neuter genus is sometimes used in derogatory terms, such as the German *Frauenzimmer* 'wench' (Nübling 2020; Werner 2012). These mismatches underscore the interplay between grammatical gender and social constructs of gender, as their marked usage relies on the general expectation of alignment between genus and sex or gender. In other words, the genus-sexus principle and its violation clearly demonstrate that language and gender do indeed intersect.

Although this volume does not intend to make a political statement, the contributions in it certainly address language policy – a highly political and often contentious topic. Omitting this discussion would itself constitute a political stance. Thus, we emphasize that all contributions focus on analyzing the intersections between various notions of gender and language. Current language policies primarily consider how *gender-fair*, *gender-neutral*, or *gender-inclusive* a given term or phrase is. While we leave the choice and definition of these terms to the individual contributions, linguistic and psychological research across multiple languages brought forward empirical evidence that certain language features often exhibit a male bias (for French, e.g., Gygax et al. 2008; Kim et al. 2023; for German, e.g., Schunack and Binanzer 2022; Schmitz 2024; for Italian, e.g., Cacciari and Padovani 2007; Horvath et al. 2016; for Spanish, e.g., Andriychenko et al. 2024; Anaya-Ramírez et al. 2022). Consequently, language policies seek either to replace such features or, conversely, to preserve them, often by questioning the evidence of bias. The latter stance frequently claims that language and sex or gender are unconnected. However, as demonstrated by the genus-sexus principle, this claim cannot be universally upheld.

The contributions in this volume are concerned with uncovering, analyzing, and discussing further intersections of language and gender. They address questions such as how gender is encoded grammatically and how novel gender-inclusive grammatical structures might function (Chapter 2), and how gendered forms are distributed across a language (Chapter 3). They investigate how lexico-semantic and conceptual gender manifest in nouns and adjectives (Chapters 4 and 9), as well as how individuals outside the binary are linguistically represented and dealt with (Chapters 5 and 13). Further, they examine how differences between L1 and L2 gender systems affect the comprehension of gender (Chapters 6 and 7), and how pronoun comprehension may be modeled more generally (Chapter 8). They highlight the importance of task selection in studying language and gender (Chapter 10), and offer strategies for making classrooms (Chapter 12) and language as such more gender-inclusive (Chapter 11).

2 The articles in this volume

In what follows, we will provide a concise overview of the individual articles included in this volume. Each summary offers a glimpse into the unique contributions made by the authors, spanning various facets of linguistic inquiry. Collectively, the articles illustrate the multifaceted nature of gender linguistic research.

Our volume opens with the contribution *What if –*in is a new suffix?* by Lena Völkening. The chapter explores the emergence and current usage of gender-inclusive nouns in German that incorporate morphological structures beyond the grammarian tradition. The forms are analyzed from a constructionist perspective with regard to their phonological, morphosyntactic, and semantic properties, and it is argued that these forms feature variants of a new gender-inclusive suffix. Building on this comprehensive account of the novel gender-inclusive forms, it is concluded that the new suffix is gradually being integrated into the mental grammar of language users, reflecting a shift towards more gender-inclusive language practices.

With their contribution *Of stars and colons: A corpus-based analysis of gender-inclusive orthographies in German press texts*, Samira Ochs and Jan Oliver Rüdiger provide a quantitative baseline for the distribution of different gendered forms in German press texts. Based on a text corpus with more than one billion tokens from fifteen press sources, the authors accounted for the share of occurrences of generic masculines[2] and more gender-inclusive forms in a microdiachronic analysis. It was found that generic masculines are still the most frequent form by far, and that in the realm of more gender-inclusive forms those forms which reflect the gender-binary show decreasing numbers while those which include genders beyond the binary are on the rise. Notably, the political orientation of a pertinent source is reflected in the use of forms: Gender-inclusive forms beyond the binary are found mostly in left-leaning sources. This contribution offers several insights: a quantitative baseline regarding the shares of gendered forms, an account on how the frequencies of more gender-inclusive forms develop microdiachronically, and a first glimpse into the role of political orientation regarding the choice of gendered forms.

The contribution *Women are sexy and men provoke – Gender stereotypes in use of the German adjective aufreizend* by Jens Fleischhauer and Dila Turus investigated the uses of the German adjective *aufreizend* in a corpus study. Many adjectives show a preference of referring either to female or male referents based on stereotypical attributes assigned to gender identities. That is, they hold conceptual gender information. For example, men are often described as *aggressive*, while women are often described as *emotional*. The adjective *aufreizend* may have one of two interpretations: *arousing* or *provocative*. The authors performed a corpus analysis to find attestations for *aufreizend* with female and male referents. Potentially influential factors like the syntactic and event structure were controlled for and entered the analysis together with the variable of interest, the referent's gender. Similar to other gender-biased adjectives, the sexual reading of the two, *arousing*, is mostly used for female referents whereas the other, *provocative*, is predominantly used for male referents. The study contributes to the findings that stereotypical gender-specific features influence language use.

Sol Tovar, in her contribution *Understanding (mis)gender(ing) and pronouns from a politeness theory standpoint*, presents a detailed qualitative case study of a German speech held in 2022 in the *Bundestag* (German Federal Parliament), discussing the practice of misgendering and other forms of gender-related linguistic wounding in light of politeness theory. German features grammatical, natural, lexico-semantic, and conceptual gender, and hence offers a variety of gendered forms which have wounding potential. The author examines the linguistic strategies by which Beatrix von Storch, cisgender woman and member of the far-right party AfD, attacks Tessa Ganserer, transgender woman and member of the center-left Greens. Tovar shows that von Storch capitalizes on the wounding potential of gendered language, for example by using discriminative and exclusionary identity

---

[2] Generic masculines are grammatically masculine role nouns which are used with the intention of conveying a gender-neutral meaning.

markers for Ganserer (misgendering, deadnaming). The author offers an interpretation of this in an impoliteness framework by conceptualizing such strategies as face-threatening acts to the interlocutor's *gender face*. In doing so, the contribution provides us with useful categories of analysis to be added to a methodological toolbox that can analyze the social functions of gendered language.

Dominic Schmitz's contribution *Pronoun comprehension from a discriminative perspective: A proof of concept* investigates the semantics and comprehension of pronouns in English. Focusing on *he*, *she*, plural *they* and generic singular *they*, an array of computational methods is used to shed light on these pronouns' semantic interrelations and comprehension features. Naive discriminative learning was used to compute vector representations of the semantics of English words excluding pronouns. Vector representations of pronoun semantics were computed based on the mean of the vectors of the words surrounding a pronoun, rendering the semantics of each pronoun token context-sensitive. Using vector representations of all words, including those for pronouns, linear discriminative learning was implemented to extract measures on pronoun comprehension. Comparing the measures of the four pronoun types to each other, it was found that generic singular *they* shows characteristics distinct from *he* and *she* on the one and plural *they* on the other hand. The contribution offers a new perspective for the investigation of pronoun semantics and comprehension.

Simon David Stein and Viktoria Schneider, in their article *Effects of English generic singular they on the gender processing of L1 German speakers*, breathe new life into the short story approach, an experimental method which can test for the gender-neutrality of pronouns, role nouns, or other gendered forms in a well-disguised way. To illustrate this approach, the authors test which of the English pronouns *their* and *his* is interpreted as more gender-neutral by L1 German speakers when these pronouns are used generically. They asked their L1 German participants to write a short story following one of two versions of the sentence *On [pronoun] first day at school, a pupil is usually very nervous*, with either *their* or *his* as pronoun. Using this method, they first replicate the male bias for *his* known from other studies, with *his* being associated with significantly more male protagonists than female protagonists in the stories. Stein and Schneider then find some support for the idea that generically used singular *they* can reduce this bias. Given that the authors investigated L1 German learners of English, this tells us that linguistic gender bias can carry over to learners of languages with semantic gender assignment who speak languages with predominantly morphosyntactic gender assignment systems, hinting at possible transfer effects.

With their contribution *Form identity and gendered associations: L2 English –er activates the bias of L1 German –er*, Dominic Schmitz, Julia Blessing-Plötner, Nazire Cinar, Nguyet Minh Dang, Henrike Hoffmanns, fNadja Khadouj, Aaron Luther, Imran Peksen, and Tomma Robke take inspiration from the short story approach revived by Simon David Stein and Viktoria Schneider. To answer the question whether the male bias found in German generic masculines ending in the *-er* suffix is transferred to English role nouns ending in *-er*, participants had to write a short story in German, their L1, following three prompts in English, their L2. Irrespective of the stereotypicality of the role nouns in the English prompts, participants made use of mostly masculine forms as translations. To further investigate the role of the *-er* suffix, in a subsequent translation task, the same participants were asked to translate role nouns from English to German. The authors found that the *-er* suffix does indeed facilitate the transfer of the male bias from L1 German to L2 English. These findings present novel evidence for the transfer of biases between L1s and L2s and the first evidence of the relevance of form identity in this process.

The contribution *Gender inclusive or not? Covert gender patterns in Georgian* by Zaal Kikvidze presents work on the gender-inclusiveness of occupational nouns in Georgian. This contribution stands out, as Georgian is a genderless language. That is, in contrast to grammatical gender languages like Spanish or German and notional gender languages like English, Georgian does not mark gender. Why, then, is gender-inclusiveness a topic in Georgian? A language without gender marking surely is gender-inclusive, as it, for example, lacks the typical bias of masculine defaults. This quick assumption is shown to be premature and incorrect by the results of a questionnaire on occupational nouns lacking morphological and semantic information on gender. Participants had to provide two names for fictional characters for each occupation and, even though the target words are, from a structural perspective, gender-neutral, participants selected typical male names for several occupations and typical female names for others. This contribution hence takes a different perspective on the intersections of language and gender: Even with a structurally gender-neutral language, gender-inclusiveness is not achieved, as societal stereotypes in the form of conceptual gender information overwrite gender-neutral notions.

In the contribution *Gender-inclusive language and male bias: Task matters!*, Francesca Panzeri and Martina Abbondanza examine the impact of generic masculines on the perception of inclusiveness in various contexts. The study involved 245 participants who evaluated job offers and advertisements in Italian presented using three different linguistic strategies: generic masculines, feminization, and neutralization. Their findings showed that the use of generic masculines in comparison to feminization or neutralization did not make participants feel less motivated, connected, included, or satisfied, regardless of the context. Further, the study found no significant difference between the feminization and neutralization strategies. While at first glance, these results challenge the notion that the use of masculine generics inherently contradicts gender-inclusiveness, at second glance it demonstrates the importance of experimental paradigm choice. That is, this contribution illustrates that more metalinguistic tasks, which access participants' conscious reflection on language, may provide different evidence on gender bias than more implicit tasks, which access participants' subconscious language perception and comprehension. Overall, the present findings highlight the complexity of gender representation in language and the research thereof.

Laura Vela and Marina Ortega give an overview about the discussion on gender-fair language in their contribution *Theoretical and empirical basis for gender-fair language use: The case of Spanish*. Arguments in favor and against the use of gender-fair language are compared by example of Spanish, a grammatical gender language in which the grammatical masculine is the standard strategy to refer to referents independent of their gender. In Spanish, several different options to use gender-fair language, which can be divided in two broader categories, are under debate. First, a symmetrical use of gender-inclusive strategies like neutralization, gender-neutral pronouns, neo-pronouns, elided nominals, and the use of special symbols. Second, the explicit inclusion of women used in pair coordination, abbreviated forms with slashes or grammatically female forms instead of grammatical masculine forms to refer to a gender-mixed group of referents. Apart from the different gender strategies, the authors discuss several different approaches to feminist language reforms, enriching the main discussion of gender-fair language in general with a political component. The authors use real language examples from Spanish to show that gender-fair language is not only possible in Spanish, but also shows a positive effect on language attitudes and behavior. That is, the use of gender-fair language maps to a social change which can be fortified and is visible in language use.

The chapter *Teaching Spanish in the Philippines: A queer-decolonial pedagogy* by Jeff Roxas presents an autoethnographic exploration of implementing gender-inclusive language and queer-affirming pedagogies in the context of teaching Spanish in the Philippines. Drawing from experiences as a queer Spanish professor, the author addresses the challenges posed by the gendered structure of the Spanish language, which often conflicts with the more gender-neutral L1s of Filipino students. Through a historical overview and a sociolinguistic analysis, the contribution advocates for a decolonized approach to language instruction that promotes social justice and gender equality. The importance of developing teaching materials and practices that validate and celebrate diverse gender identities is underlined, arguing that such inclusivity is a fundamental human right and essential for enriching the educational experience of Filipino students.

The contribution *Morphosyntax and me: The reflections of a non-binary linguist on English gendered language* by D. Hunter provides novel insight into the remnants of gendered elements in English. As a first, this essay combines self-reflection and distributed morphology. Introspective self-reflection is used to investigate how different gendered terms cause varying levels of dysphoria for non-binary individuals. Then, the theoretical framework of distributed morphology is used to find an explanation as to why some terms are more distressing than others, proposing that the level of dysphoria is related to where and how gender attaches to words. The contribution provides not only a novel perspective on gender in English, for which gender linguistic research typically focuses on pronouns, but also food for thought for the everyday use of English.

3 Conclusion

In sum, the diverse contributions in this volume illustrate the thematic and methodological versatility of gender linguistics as an area of linguistic research. The collection of articles demonstrates that the intersections of language and gender are a meaningful topic for all languages, no matter whether they show a grammatical gender system, a notional gender system, or no gender system at all. Further, the contributions illustrate that the field of gender linguistics is explorable by a variety of different methods, from corpus analysis to experimental investigations to computational modeling. While these methods were illustrated by but a sample of different languages – English, Georgian, German, Italian, and Spanish – they may and should be used for similar investigations in other languages to further our knowledge of the interrelations of language and gender as a whole.

The ongoing public and also linguistic debate on efforts to make language more gender-inclusive is reflected in many of the contributions. The articles of the present volume tackle issues surrounding this discussion from different perspectives and offer insights to advance the debate. Most importantly, though, the contributions do not deviate from the descriptive nature of modern linguistics.

As editors, we not only believe that the volume at hand will be a valuable contribution to the area of gender linguistics, but also are convinced that language users may gain novel insights into the topic of gender-inclusive language and with that may reflect on their beliefs and opinions on the matter. In the ideal case, such reflection will do away with some of the opinionated sentiments surrounding gender-inclusive language in favor of scientifically informed opinion.

References

Anaya-Ramírez, Alejandro, John Grinstead, Melissa Nieves Rivera, David Melamed and Asela Reig-Alamillo. 2022. The interpretation of Spanish masculine plural NPs: Are they perceived as uniformly masculine or as a mixture of masculine and feminine? *Applied Psycholinguistics* 43(6). 1257–1274. https://doi.org/10.1017/S0142716422000352.

Andriychenko, Yuliia, Nataliia Popova, Nataliia Chorna and Olena Bratel. 2024. Linguistic representation of gender stereotypes in Spanish. *JURNAL ARBITRER* 11(2). 160–171. https://doi.org/10.25077/ar.11.2.160-171.2024.

Bates, Nancy, Marshall Chin and Tara Becker. 2022. *Measuring sex, gender identity, and sexual orientation*. Washington, D.C.: National Academies Press. https://doi.org/10.17226/26424.

Cacciari, Cristina and Roberto Padovani. 2007. Further evidence of gender stereotype priming in language: Semantic facilitation and inhibition in Italian role nouns. *Applied Psycholinguistics* 28(2). 277–293. https://doi.org/10.1017/S0142716407070142.

Corbett, Greville G. 1991. *Gender*. Cambridge: Cambridge University Press. https://doi.org/10.1017/CBO9781139166119.

Eisenberg, Peter and Rolf Schöneich. 2020. *Grundriss der deutschen Grammatik: Der Satz*. Stuttgart: J.B. Metzler. https://doi.org/10.1007/978-3-476-05094-6.

Gygax, Pascal, Ute Gabriel, Oriane Sarrasin, Jane Oakhill and Alan Garnham. 2008. Generically intended, but specifically interpreted: When beauticians, musicians, and mechanics are all men. *Language and Cognitive Processes* 23(3). 464–485. https://doi.org/10.1080/01690960701702035.

Haig, David. 2004. The inexorable rise of gender and the decline of sex: Social change in academic titles, 1945–2001. *Archives of Sexual Behavior* 33. 87–96. https://doi.org/10.1023/B:ASEB.0000014323.56281.0d.

Hockett, Charles F. 1958. *A course in modern linguistics*. New York: The Macmillan Company. https://doi.org/10.1111/j.1467-1770.1958.tb00870.x.

Horvath, Lisa K., Elisa F. Merkel, Anne Maass and Sabine Sczesny. 2016. Does gender-fair language pay off? The social perception of professions from a cross-linguistic perspective. *Frontiers in Psychology* 6. 2018. https://doi.org/10.3389/FPSYG.2015.02018.

Kim, Jonathan, Sarah Angst, Pascal Gygax, Ute Gabriel and Sandrine Zufferey. 2023. The masculine bias in fully gendered languages and ways to avoid it: A study on gender neutral forms in Québec and Swiss French. *Journal of French Language Studies* 33(1). 1–26. https://doi.org/10.1017/S095926952200014X.

Kopeke, Klaus-Michael and David Zubin. 2020. Prinzipien für die Genuszuweisung im Deutschen. In Ewald Lang and Gisela Zifonun (eds.), *Deutsch - typologisch*, 473–491. De Gruyter. https://doi.org/10.1515/9783110622522-021.

Kotthoff, Helga and Damaris Nübling. 2024. *Genderlinguistik: Eine Einführung in Sprache, Gespräch und Geschlecht*. 2nd edn. Tübingen: Narr.

Lindqvist, Anna, Marie Gustafsson Sendén and Emma A. Renström. 2021. What is gender, anyway: A review of the options for operationalising gender. *Psychology & Sexuality* 12. 332–344. https://doi.org/10.1080/19419899.2020.1729844.

Maddux, James E. and Barbara A. Winstead. 2019. *Psychopathology: Foundations for a contemporary understanding*. 5th edn. New York: Routledge. https://doi.org/10.4324/9780429028267.

Nübling, Damaris. 2020. Geschlecht in der Grammatik: Was Genus, Deklination und Binomiale uns über Geschlechter(un)ordnungen berichten. *Muttersprache* 130(1). 17–33.

Richards, Christina, Walter Pierre Bouman, Leighton Seal, Meg John Barker, Timo O. Nieder and Guy T'Sjoen. 2016. Non-binary or genderqueer genders. *International Review of Psychiatry* 28. 95–102. https://doi.org/10.3109/09540261.2015.1106446.

Schmitz, Dominic. 2024. Instances of bias: The gendered semantics of generic masculines in German revealed by instance vectors. *Zeitschrift für Sprachwissenschaft* 43(2). 295–325. https://doi.org/10.1515/zfs-2024-2010.

Schunack, Silke and Anja Binanzer. 2022. Revisiting gender-fair language and stereotypes – A comparison of word pairs, capital I forms and the asterisk. *Zeitschrift für Sprachwissenschaft* 41(2). 309–337. https://doi.org/10.1515/ZFS-2022-2008.

Siemund, Peter. 2008. *Pronominal gender in English: A study of English varieties from a cross-linguistic perspective*. London: Routledge.

Werner, Martina. 2012. *Genus, Derivation und Quantifikation. Zur Funktion der Suffigierung und verwandter Phänomene im Deutschen*. Berlin, Boston: De Gruyter.

Lena Völkening
What if -*in is a new suffix?

Abstract: This paper provides a synchronic constructionist analysis and discusses the diachronic emergence of German gender-inclusive nouns containing a gender star (e.g., *Linguist*innen* 'linguists [of any gender]'), as well as other special characters such as the gender gap (e.g., *Linguist_innen*) and the capital *I* (e.g., *LinguistInnen*). These nouns feature a new suffix -*in (with -_in, -In, etc. as variants) rather than the feminine suffix -in. Consequently, it is this new suffix, rather than the gender star etc., that conveys gender-inclusive meaning. The new suffix and its derivatives are analyzed from a constructionist perspective, which allows for modeling the phonological, morphosyntactic, and semantic level together. The syntactic level is also considered, with an outline of the structure of definite noun phrases containing a gender star (e.g., *der*die Linguist*in*).

Keywords: construction grammar, construction morphology, gender-fair, gender-inclusive, gender-neutral, gender star, grammatical gender, noun phrases

1 Introduction

For more than 40 years, German language users have employed gender-inclusive forms with a capital *I* (e.g., *LinguistInnen*)[1] to avoid using generic masculines (e.g., *Linguisten*). For 20 years, people have made use of the gender gap (e.g., *Linguist_innen*),[2] and for at least 15 years, nouns with a gender star[3] have been used

---

1 It is assumed that the first person to use forms with a capital *I* was the author Christoph Busch, who, in his book *Was Sie schon immer über Freie Radios wissen wollten, aber nie zu fragen wagten!*, published in 1981, employed the new form *HörerInnen* 'listeners' (Kotthoff and Nübling 2018: 217). This new noun then also appeared in the Swiss newspaper *Die Wochenzeitung (WOZ)* (Okamura 2012: 415) and was subsequently adopted in other German newspapers like *Die Tageszeitung (taz;* Scott 2006: 163).
2 The gender gap was presumably first mentioned in 2003 by philosopher Steffen Kitty Herrmann in an article for the leftist journal *arranca!*. Hornscheidt (2012: 311) assumes that this may only have been the first publication about this new form and that it might have already been used in certain communities.
3 The term *gender star* is used in this chapter and in the chapter by Schmitz et al., while Ochs & Rüdiger in their chapter refer to the same concept as *asterisk*.

Lena Völkening, Department of German Studies, Carl von Ossietzky Universität Oldenburg, e-mail: lena.voelkening@uni-oldenburg.de

∂ Open Access. © 2025 the author(s), published by De Gruyter. [CC BY] This work is licensed under the Creative Commons Attribution 4.0 International License.
https://doi.org/10.1515/9783111388694-002

(e.g., *Linguist*innen*).⁴ New linguistic forms ought to be described and analyzed. However, these gender-inclusive nouns with special characters are often discussed in linguistic literature and science communication without providing detailed information about their assumed structure. An in-depth, well-founded analysis of the form of these nouns is a crucial prerequisite for investigating and discussing their meaning, their use in texts, and, furthermore, their consistency with the regularities of the language system.

In this paper, I will discuss previous perspectives on this topic presented by other authors and subsequently outline a constructionist analysis.⁵ In Section 2, gender-inclusive nouns containing a gender star will be analyzed. Sections 3 and 4 focus on spoken language: In Section 3, the prosodic structure of the suffix –**in* [ʔm] is examined. In Section 4, the question whether or not the glottal stop is optional in the pronunciation of these nouns is discussed. In Section 5, then, it will be demonstrated that the analysis developed in the previous sections also applies to nouns containing other special characters, such as the gender gap and the capital *I*. Section 6 addresses the question of the grammatical gender of these nouns with special characters and of the underlying structures of their syntactic use.

I will adopt a usage-based constructionist perspective (cf., e.g., Goldberg 1995, 2006; Lakoff 1987): Words and noun phrases formed and employed by language users are analyzed with the aim of understanding the underlying cognitive structures. These structures are modeled in the form of constructions, that is, formalizations intended to represent the linguistic knowledge these language users apply as accurately as possible, based on the assumption that linguistic knowledge can be thoroughly modeled through constructions (cf. Hilpert 2011: 60). Constructions are defined to be conventionalized pairings (Goldberg 2006: 3) of form and meaning (Lakoff 1987: 467). Therefore, they are not innate, but learned patterns. The more a person uses a pattern in their language reception and production, the more the pattern becomes entrenched in their mental language system (Hilpert and Diessel 2017: 57). The mental lexicon and the mental grammar are not thought to be different modules. Instead, fully specified (e.g., words and idioms) and (partly and fully) schematic constructions are stored together mentally. The latter are generalizations

---

4 The earliest publication I could find mentioning nouns with the gender star is a guide to gender-sensitive language from 2009 (cf. Fischer and Wolf 2009: 5). According to Haider (2024: 60–61), the star was imported from English-speaking countries, where it was used in forms like *trans**. In Germany, the adjective *trans** and compounds such as *Trans*-Mensch* 'transgender person' had already been used in the mid-1990s (Regh 2002: 191–192).
5 The present paper is derived from my PhD thesis, which is still being developed and will contain a more comprehensive discussion of this analysis.

the language user makes about various linguistic structures they encounter that share similarities (Ziem and Lasch 2013: 103–104).

2 Gender-inclusive nouns do not include the feminine suffix -*in* (anymore)

It is often assumed that gender-inclusive nouns with a gender star contain the feminine derivational suffix –*in*, which regularly transforms masculine forms (e.g., *Linguist*) into their grammatically feminine counterparts (e.g., *Linguistin*) and conveys the meaning component 'female'. The structure of the gender-inclusive nouns, then, would be as follows (cf., e.g., Pusch 2014; Zifonun 2021):

(1) [*Linguist*] [*] [–*in*]

The linguistic material to the left of the *, then, could be a derivational base (cf. Kotthoff and Nübling 2018: 218) or a masculine form (cf. Krome 2020: 71, Zifonun 2021: 46, Eisenberg 2021). Usually, both options are isomorphic in written language (e.g., **Linguistin** – **Linguist**). However, sometimes their forms differ (e.g., *Ärztin* – *Arzt* 'physician' and **Kundin** – **Kunde** 'customer'). Hence, if language users form words like *Ärzt*innen* and *Kund*innen* (instead of *Arzt*innen* and *Kunde*innen*, for instance), this can be taken as evidence that their mental representation of the structure of these words includes a derivational base, rather than a masculine form.

The morphological structure of gender-inclusive nouns with special characters should therefore be investigated using corpus data. To date, only one investigation of this kind has been published: In a corpus study, Müller-Spitzer et al. (2024) have found that on the website of the city of Hamburg, only four percent of the gender-inclusive forms that contain special characters, such as the gender star, cannot be analyzed as containing only a stem to the left of the * (e.g., *den Anwohnern*innen*, cf. *den Anwohnerinnen*, 'female residents'). Müller-Spitzer et al. classify these as ungrammatical exceptions.

If –*in* is analyzed as the feminine derivational suffix, as shown in (1), the morphological status of the gender star remains unclear. Nouns containing a gender star have been shown to evoke different, more gender-inclusive meanings compared to feminine and masculine forms (Körner et al. 2022; Zacharski and Ferstl 2023; see also Section 5). This raises the question of whether it is the star that conveys this gender-inclusive meaning, either partially or entirely. Zifonun (2021: 47) discusses the possibility that the star is not a linguistic sign, but a *gestural sign* that interrupts the word and operates on a metalinguistic level. Ferstl and Nübling (2024: 266–267) discuss an analysis of the gender star as an *ideogram*, that is, a sign with semantic content – and hence, a morpheme. They compare the star in gender-inclusive nouns to the star in spellings like **1970* which means 'born in 1970' and state that the meaning of the gender star is already quite conventionalized.

However, a few decades ago, when the use of the star within the internal structure of nouns was new and unfamiliar, their gender-inclusive meaning must have been achieved at least partly through pragmatic inference. The star might then have disrupted the usual structure of words derived from the suffix *–in* which would partially align with Zifonun's analysis. Even today, language users who have rarely encountered texts that contain nouns with gender stars might still perceive the star as an interruption of familiar feminine word forms and infer the meaning. For language users and communities that regularly use gender-inclusive nouns, on the other hand, the star may have acquired a fixed meaning through conventionalization, and thus become a morpheme.

The question then remains whether the morphological structure of gender-inclusive nouns outlined in (1) is correct, namely, whether language users derive these nouns through suffixation with a morpheme *–** and then with the feminine suffix *–in*. Indeed, derived nouns that contain the feminine suffix *–in* as their final element would be assigned the feminine grammatical gender, assuming the word formation operates regularly and considering that the suffix *–in* regularly transforms nouns into feminine nouns (cf. Eisenberg 2021). However, instead, language users often employ new structures in order to form noun phrases (cf. also, for this observation, Schneider 2021: 30, Zifonun 2021: 50, Ferstl and Nübling 2024: 274):

(2) *Die Listenstimme darf nur an eine Partei gehen, die* **den*die Wahlkreiskandidat*in** *unterstützt, für den* **der*die Wähler*in** *optiert* [emphasis added].[6]
'The list vote may only go to a party that supports **the constituency candidate** for which **the voter** has opted.'

In (2), the complex nouns *Wahlkreiskandidat*in* and *Wähler*in* are not syntactically treated as though they were feminine, which would be reflected in the form of the definite article.[7] If they contain the suffix *–in*, this suffix, in these forms, has lost its property of turning the complex noun it forms into a feminine one. In other words, its grammatical function has changed, differentiating it from the original suffix *–in*.

---

6 Source: Article on the website of the German newspaper *taz*, https://taz.de/Vor-den-Wahlen-in-Italien/!5872786, accessed: 07 February 2025.
7 If the nouns *Wahlkreiskandidat*in* and *Wähler*in* had been assigned feminine grammatical gender, the noun phrases would have been *die Wahlkreiskandidat*in*.ACCUSATIVE and die *Wähler*in*.NOMINATIVE. If they had been assigned masculine grammatical gender, it would have been: *den Wahlkreiskandidat*in* and *der Wähler*in*.

The fact that gender-inclusive nouns containing special characters, such as the gender star, exhibit differences in their use, their form (cf. the following sections) and, crucially, their meaning has prompted some authors to propose that they contain a new suffix that is distinct from the established feminine suffix –*in* 'female'. Scott (2006) argues that in word forms like *HörerInnen*, *–In* is a new suffix that is added to the language system. Stefanowitsch (2018) suggests in a blog post that –**in* is a new suffix. Zifonun (2021: 47–48) discusses the implications of this analysis. Based on the common pronunciation of these nouns (cf. Section 3), Völkening (2022) analyzes –**in* as a new suffix. Ferstl and Nübling (2024: 267–269) discuss this analysis, as does Haider (2024, cf. Section 4). In these analyses, the gender star (as well as the gender gap or the capital *I*, respectively) is not a distinct element that evokes meaning on its own, but rather an integral part of the derivational suffix:

(3) [*Linguist*] [–**in*]

The new suffix, then, differs from feminine –*in* 'female' in its orthographic form. Notably, the two analyses outlined in (1) and (3) do not necessarily exclude each other. The morphological structure given in (1) might have been an intermediate step, shifting into the structure represented in (3) through a diachronic process. If the new suffix –**in* then combines with derivational bases, the grammatical properties and the meaning of the complex nouns it forms result from regular word-formation processes.

In a usage-based constructionist perspective, language users learn how to form nouns with a certain suffix by making a generalization about various nouns they encounter containing this suffix (cf. Booij 2010: 544). Gender-inclusive nouns containing a gender star all have in common that they include the character sequence **in*, which is preceded by varying linguistic material. It is therefore plausible that language users who have encountered many gender-inclusive nouns containing the sequence **in* make the generalization that **in* is a bound morpheme and store the pattern mentally. Following the constructionist analysis suggested by Booij (2010, 2015), suffixes are mentally stored as partially schematic constructions at the word level, since they are bound and unfold their meaning only in combination with the preceding linguistic material. For example, nouns containing the derivational suffix –*in* are instantiations of the construction $[[x]_N \ in]_N$. Consequently, language users who frequently encounter or form gender-inclusive nouns with a gender star mentally store the following construction, which is a generalization about these nouns:

(4) $[[x]_N \ *in]_N$

If these language users perceive the linguistic material to the left of the star as a derivational base, this information is stored in the construction as a requirement for the linguistic material that can fill the empty slot *x*. It seems that language users attach the new suffix –**in* to the same bases as they do with the feminine suffix *–in*. The construction outlined in (4) thus replicates the properties of the empty slot *x* from the construction [[x]$_N$ *in*]$_N$. Gender-inclusive nouns like *Wähler*innen* as well as *Wahlkreiskandidat*in* and *Ärzt*innen*, then are all instantiations of this word-formation pattern, and their feminine counterparts *Wählerinnen, Wahlkreiskandidatin* and *Ärztinnen* as instantiations of the construction [[x]$_N$ *in*]$_N$ contain the same bases. In fact, if we revisit this from a diachronic perspective, analogy likely played a role in the emergence of the new construction in (4). While the suffix may have developed through a process of coalescence, the bases used for the complex word might simply have been copied from feminine complex nouns derived from *–in*.

The same applies to a language user who learns to use the suffix –**in*: If they regularly engage with and produce gender-inclusive texts, they will come to perceive and use –**in* as a new suffix. However, the mental representation of this new suffix, as represented in (4), retains many properties of the construction [[x]$_N$ *in*]$_N$, that is, the mental representation of the suffix *–in* (cf. Völkening 2022: 69–70). Thus, someone who has encountered the word *Kund*innen* may form *Ärzt*innen* even if they have never seen the form *Ärzt*innen* before.

3 In spoken language, -**in* [ʔɪn] differs from -*in* [ɪn] in terms of its prosodic structure

A key argument supporting the analysis of –**in* as a new suffix is that, in a commonly encountered pronunciation of these nouns involving a glottal stop (e.g., *Wähler[ʔ]innen*), the morphophonological structure of the suffix –**in* [ʔɪn] significantly differs from that of the feminine suffix *–in* [ɪn] (Völkening 2022). The latter is consistently syllabified with the stem. For example, in *Wählerinnen*, the final consonant of the stem, /r/, is incorporated into the onset of the following syllable during pronunciation: [vɛː.lə.ʁɪnən]. This is because in German, onset-less syllables are generally avoided, and because the morphological boundary between the base and the suffix does not coincide with a break for syllabification. This, in turn, is due to the fact that the domain for syllabification in German is the phonological word, and vowel-initial suffixes typically do not form separate phonological words. Instead, they are integrated into the preceding phonological word (cf. Wiese 2000: 65–67).

However, the new suffix –**in* [ʔɪn] does constitute its own phonological word, just like consonant-initial suffixes in German typically do (cf. Wiese 2000: 67, Raffelsiefen 2000: 55). Thus, there is a break for syllabification between the stem and the suffix [ʔm], cf. (6), but not between the stem and the feminine suffix [m], nor between the two suffixes and the following vowel-initial inflectional suffix *-en*:

(5) (*Wählerinnen*)ω

(6) (*Wähler*)ω([ʔ]*innen*)ω

Due to the prosodic boundary between the two phonological words, in *Wähler[ʔ]innen*, the final consonant of the stem is not incorporated into the onset of the following syllable; instead, it can undergo syllable-final processes such as vocalization in (7) and final-obstruent devoicing in (8):

(7) *Wähler[ʔ]innen* [vɛː.lɐ.ʔm̩ən],
 cf. *Wählerinnen* [vɛː.lə.ʁm̩ən]

(8) *Freund[ʔ]innen* [fʁɔɪ̯nt.ʔm̩ən],
 cf. (*Freundinnen* [fʁɔɪ̯n.dm̩ən]

Thus, the forms of the two suffixes *-*in* [ʔm] and *-in* [m] differ considerably in spoken language; the former constitutes a phonological word, whereas the latter does not, which is reflected in the syllabification of the complex nouns. The construction presented in (4) can therefore be extended by incorporating a formalization of the prosodic structure that is mentally stored alongside the morphosyntactic information:

(9) phonology /ω(x)ω ω(ʔm)ω/
 morphosyntax [[x]_N **in*]_N

The construction outlined in (9) is based on a notation given by Booij (2023, preprint). It represents the linguistic knowledge of a language user who frequently encounters and uses gender-inclusive nouns with a gender star and a glottal stop, respectively.

Diachronically, the pronunciation of the suffix as a phonological word might have originated from gender-inclusive nouns with a capital *I* – the oldest version of the different spellings with special characters. Scott (2006: 169–170) assumes that gender-inclusive nouns derived from the suffix *-In* are normally pronounced the same way as feminine forms derived by means of suffixation with *-in*, but he also already mentions the possibility of pronouncing it with a glottal stop. In German, capital letters are regularly used for nouns, proper names, formal pronouns, etc., all of which constitute separate phonological words. They also appear in certain compound spellings, such as in *BahnCard* 'train card', where they mark both the morphological boundary (Kopf 2017: 179) and the boundary between two phonological words, e.g., (*Bahn*)ω(*Card*)ω. Gender-inclusive nouns with a capital *I* initially only appeared in written language, such as in books and newspapers. When language users began reading these words aloud, the prosodic structure illustrated in (9) might have been applied by analogy.

Additionally, the subsequently developed writing variants (cf. Section 5) containing the gender gap, the gender star, etc. can be compared to linking elements (e.g., *Verfall-s-datum* 'expiration date') that mark and strengthen the boundaries of (weak) phonological words (cf. Nübling and Szczepaniak 2013: 75).

4 Since -**in* [ʔɪn] differs from -*in* [ɪn] in terms of its prosodic structure, the glottal stop might be optional

The analysis of –**in* [ʔɪn] as a phonological word now raises the question of whether the glottal stop is obligatory in its pronunciation. In Völkening (2022: 73–74), I argue that the glottal stop might be a consequence of the fact that the gender-inclusive suffix is a vowel-initial phonological word, and hence consists of a syllable that would otherwise have an empty onset in the pronunciation of the derived nouns. According to Wiese (2000: 58), the glottal stop "should not be analysed [sic] as a phoneme of Modern Standard German" because: (1) Its distribution is predictable, and (2) its presence is optional. Wiese (2000: 59) argues that the glottal stop can be optionally inserted into the otherwise empty onset of vowel-initial syllables that form the first (or only) syllable of a foot. As the suffix –**in* [ʔɪn] constitutes a phonological word, it also constitutes a foot, cf. the prosodic hierarchy assumed by Wiese (2000: 83) given in Figure 1.

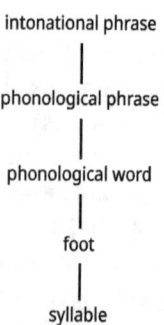

Fig. 1: Prosodic hierarchy following Wiese (2000: 83).

The prosodic structure of gender-inclusive words with a glottal stop therefore includes two feet directly dominated by a phonological word, as in [(Wähler)_F]ω [([ʔ]innen)_F]ω. This is also true for the singular forms, as in [(Wähler)_F]ω [([ʔ]in)_F]ω. Thus, the glottal stop in this suffix occurs in its regular position. Given the prosodic structure outlined above, its presence is predictable and therefore, it might be optional.

However, Haider (2024) argues that (only) in gender-inclusive nouns, the glottal stop has become a phoneme and that –*in [ʔɪn] should be analyzed as a consonant-initial suffix. He justifies this by stating that the glottal stop would have gained a distinctive function, distinguishing feminine –in and the new suffix –*in in spoken language. As a structural domain, the phonological word, according to Haider, cannot have such a distinctive function.[8]

Whether language users consistently include the glottal stop in the pronunciation of gender-inclusive nouns or occasionally omit it while retaining the structure of the suffix as a phonological word is a question that needs to be answered empirically. However, a study by Friedrich et al. (2022) on the comprehensibility of gender-inclusive nouns in spoken language sheds some light on whether or not gendered nouns with a new suffix that is a phonological word but lacks a glottal stop are easily processed by listeners. In this study, participants watched a video recording of a PowerPoint slide presentation with commentary by a non-visible speaker. They were randomly assigned one of two versions of this video: In the audio track of the first version, all forms that were used were generic masculines (e.g., *Lehrer, Schulleiter*), while the second version featured a modified audio track with gender-inclusive forms. Subsequently, the participants were asked to fill out a questionnaire with several questions on whether they found the video comprehensible. The result: For the audio track containing the gender-inclusive nouns, there were no statistically relevant impairments on the comprehensibility (and only weak impairments on the subjective sentence difficulty and the aesthetic appeal). Thus, Friedrich et al. (2022: 10) state that participants "had no problems understanding the video in gender-fair language or got used to the corresponding form quickly."

In their paper, the authors report that they used gender-inclusive nouns with a glottal stop for the second, modified version of the audio track. They therefore apply their conclusion mentioned above to gender-inclusive nouns containing a glottal stop. However, the audio track they created did not actually include gender-inclusive nouns with a glottal stop. This is apparent from the description of how

---

[8] Haider also emphasizes that –*in [ʔɪn] would be the first and only vowel-initial suffix in German that is a separate phonological word, not taking into account bound morphemes like –artig, which is also not integrated into the preceding phonological word (cf. Ferstl and Nübling 2024: 268).

they created the second version of the audio track. First, the speaker "recorded the audio twice, once with masculine-only forms and once with feminine-only forms" (Friedrich et al. 2022: 7). The authors describe the following procedure:

> To create the version with the glottal stop and the ending "-innen", the ending "-innen" was copied from the recording with feminine-only forms for each manipulated word and appended to the respective words in the audio track with masculine-only forms, resulting in a short pause (of about 20 to 40 milliseconds) between the masculine stem and the feminine ending in order to mimic the sound of the glottal stop. (Friedrich et al. 2022: 7)

The fact that they did not insert a glottal stop – that is, a consonant, a voiceless plosive – in the audio track can be explained by their understanding of the glottal stop as "an abrupt and sustained closure of the vocal cords in the larynx" (Friedrich et al. 2022: 1). Thus, what the authors mean by glottal stop is, in fact, a pause.

Furthermore, the stems in the gender-inclusive nouns created for the second audio track are all isomorphic with masculine generics. All these forms end with the suffix *-er* (*Lehrer, Schulleiter, Sekundarschulleiter, Teilnehmer*), wherein the /r/ can be vocalized in syllable-final position, as mentioned earlier. The authors kindly sent me the modified audio track used for their experiment, and it could be confirmed by analyzing it in Praat (Boersma and Weenink 2024) that indeed, the /r/ was vocalized in these stems (e.g., [ʃuːllaɪ̯tɐmən]). It can also be confirmed through analysis in Praat that there was no glottal stop in these assembled nouns. In the example given in Figure 2, the form [ʃuːllaɪ̯tɐmən] is followed by the phonological word *und*, which is pronounced with a visible glottal stop, [ʔʊnt]. By contrast, the program does not detect the voiceless plosive in the onset of the suffix syllable. The suffix evidently is vowel-initial.

Since all of the gender-inclusive nouns in the modified audio track were assembled from masculine generics in the first audio track, combined with the ending *-innen*, it is clear that the suffix is never syllabified with the stem. Both the stem and the suffix are therefore pronounced as separate phonological words. For example, *Schulleiter* and *-innen* form two distinct phonological words in the example above.

The results of this experiment therefore suggest that participants were not irritated by gender-inclusive nouns consisting of two separate phonological words, one being a base isomorphic with a masculine form, and the other a vowel-initial suffix that is distinct from the feminine suffix *-in* only in that it constitutes a separate phonological word. They did not judge the video with this audio track less comprehensible, even despite the fact that the glottal stop was missing. Besides, it is unlikely that the participants mistook the gender-inclusive nouns for female forms, since they differed phonetically from these. The results of this study therefore support the hypothesis that in gender-inclusive nouns, the glottal stop is completely

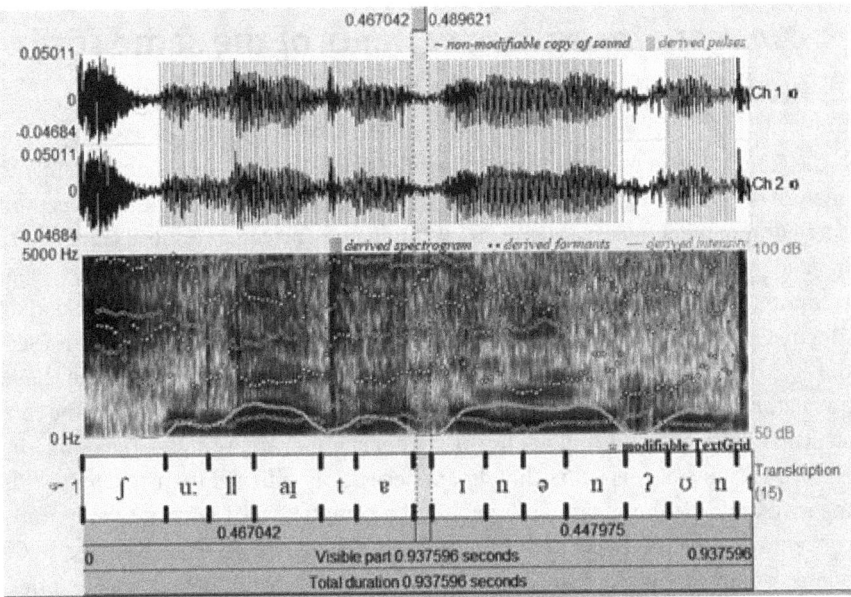

Fig. 2: Waveform and spectrogram of the word [ʃuːllaɪtɐɪnən] in Praat.

optional, a result of the empty onset of the vowel-initial suffix, and not a phoneme. Phonemes can, indeed, be omitted in speech. But they are seldom omitted in such an integral position within a lexeme or a derivational suffix (rather than within an inflectional morpheme) where they are lexically distinctive. /h/, for instance, as a consonant that shares some properties with [ʔ], might be omitted in *Faulheit* 'laziness' without causing difficulties for listeners in comprehending the word, as a suffix *-eit* does not exist and the suffix *-keit* is analyzed as a variant of *-heit* (Fleischer and Barz 2012: 209–210). But if *Haus* 'house' would be pronounced [au̯s] instead of [hau̯s], listeners could no longer distinguish it phonetically from the preposition *aus* 'out of, from'.

The defining feature of these gender-inclusive nouns, then, is not the glottal stop, but rather the fact that *-*in* is pronounced as a phonological word.[9]

---

[9] Furthermore, it is interesting to note that language users have a valid point when they talk about inserting "a pause" before the suffix, or if they refer to the glottal stop as "a pause". In gender-inclusive nouns, a pause is not necessary, but it is possible because the suffix is not syllabified with the stem. What language users are describing by these expressions is essentially the fact that the derivational base and the suffix are pronounced as two separate prosodic units.
Cf., for example, this statement in a guideline for gender-fair language on the website of the University of Leipzig: "Ärzt:in wird beispielsweise **Ärzt [kleine Pause] in** ausgesprochen. In gesproch-

5 -*in, -_in, -In, etc. are variants of the same suffix and do not necessarily differ in meaning

If the glottal stop is not a phoneme in gender-inclusive nouns, it is not possible to analyze the gender star – or any other special character in a gender-inclusive noun – as a grapheme that corresponds to this phoneme. Instead, the special characters in gender-inclusive nouns mark and strengthen the boundary between two separate phonological words. They prevent syllabification and therefore serve a similar function as German linking elements (cf. Nübling and Szczepaniak 2013: 75, and Section 3). Crucially, they do not carry semantic meaning (anymore); instead, they have a structural function. The semantic meaning is carried by the suffix, that is, the construction outlined in (9), and not by the gender star etc. Accordingly, -*in, -_in, -In, etc. are variants of this suffix that do not necessarily differ in their meaning.[10] As the suffix is new, the meaning it adds to the complex word may not yet be fully conventionalized (cf. Ferstl and Nübling 2024: 268). Language users who use these nouns usually intend them to be gender-inclusive. Meanwhile, it is crucial to differentiate whether the meaning of these words is intended to equally include people of different genders or to be gender-neutral.

Thus far, the meaning evoked by gender-inclusive nouns with special characters has been investigated by Körner et al. (2022) and by Zacharski and Ferstl (2023) for forms with a gender star in written language, and by Körner et al. (2024) for forms with a glottal stop in spoken language. The first two of these studies have found that the nouns with a gender star in written language activate more balanced or neutral mental concepts than generic masculines, whereas Körner et al. (2024) did not find the same effect for spoken language. However, the studies by Körner et al. (2022) and Körner et al. (2024) indicate a slight female bias in the mental concepts activated by the nouns, which is consistent with findings from experiments that test

---

ener Form ist die kleine **Pause, auch Glottisschlag genannt**, die phonetische Entsprechung des Gender-Doppelpunkts.", 'Ärzt is pronounced, for example, as **Ärzt [slight pause] in**. In spoken language, the slight **pause, also known as a glottal stop**, is the phonetic equivalent of the gender colon [translation and emphasis added by the author].' Source: https://www.uni-leipzig.de/chancengleichheit/doppelpunkt/geschlechtergerechte-sprache, accessed: 07 February 2025.

10 Plural forms ending in –*Innen* are often assumed to only refer to groups of men and women, excluding non-binary people. Nouns with a capital *I* may have once been used as abbreviations for double forms (e.g., *Linguistinnen und Linguisten*), but from a synchronic point of view, it is possible that they evoke the same mental concepts as nouns with a gender star etc. If they activate binary gender concepts, this is due to their metalinguistically achieved connotation rather than their structure per se.

the meanings evoked by gender-inclusive nouns with a capital *I* (e.g., Kusterle 2011; Heise 2000). This might be due to the resemblance of the suffix to the feminine suffix –*in* and to the fact that the construction in (9) that represents them shares many of the morphosyntactic properties of the construction [[x]$_N$ *in*]$_N$ that represents the feminine suffix –*in*. That is, the suffix is attached to the same bases, the result being a noun to which the same inflectional suffixes are added. Nonetheless, the meaning evoked by gender-inclusive nouns is not the same as that of feminine nouns ending in –*in*, which are usually used for female-only groups (if they are not used as feminine generics). The experiment by Zacharski and Ferstl (2023) confirms this, as female forms were also tested and led to different results than the forms with the gender star. For instance, pictures of men were accepted more quickly after the gender star form than after feminine forms, which indicates a more balanced mental representation of the genders. The construction in (9) can now be modified: Language users who regularly use and process the new suffix mentally store a certain meaning, as illustrated in the construction in (10).

(10) phonology   /ω(x)ω ω(ɪn)ω/
      morphosyntax   [[x]$_N$ **in*]$_N$
      semantics   'N: any gender' or 'N: gender not specified'

As with the other layers of the construction, the semantic layer represents a generalization that the language user has made about many gender-inclusive nouns they have encountered in various contexts.

6 On the syntactic level, gender-inclusive nouns give rise to a new paradigmatic construction

In German, every noun is regularly assigned to one of three grammatical genders. As the suffix –**in* is new, and as grammatical gender can, but does not necessarily, coincide with reference to gender categories (cf. Kotthoff and Nübling 2018), complex words derived from –**in* could, in principle, be categorized as feminine, masculine, or neuter.[11] However, as mentioned in Section 2, language users often do not adopt this simple solution. Instead, they often employ new structures to form noun phrases, such as the one reported in (2).

The grammatical gender of nouns like those in this example is considered unclear or "open" by Zifonun (2021: 50), whereas Schneider (2021: 28) states that

---

[11] Ferstl and Nübling (2024: 269) thus recommend their use as feminine nouns.

they would encounter the limitations of the current language system. A description based on grammatical categories might be adaptable by introducing a new category, but it fails to precisely describe the changes the linguistic material undergoes. It focuses on the eventual result of a nuanced process, the grammatical category, and might even lead to a normative judgment, as the pre-existing categories simply do not seem to fit. This is why this kind of traditional analysis inevitably fails in the case of gender-inclusive noun phrases like those given in (2).

Although constructionist approaches usually still make use of abstract grammatical categories, it is possible to use constructions to model very precisely and systematically what grammatical categories like grammatical gender are at their core: (usually very abstract) meanings that are assigned to sets of specific forms which are paradigmatically organized (cf. Diewald 2020; Diewald and Politt 2020). This allows the model to also capture gradual changes in both form and meaning (cf. Coussé et al. 2018). The underlying structures of noun phrases with gender stars, such as those in (2), are a combination of the constructions that language users employ to form feminine and masculine noun phrases:

(11) $[der\ [x]_N]_{NP}$ 'N: definite; N: male[12]'

(12) $[die\ [x]_N]_{NP}$ 'N: definite; N: female'

(13) $[[x]\ en]_N$ 'N: plural'

The constructions in (11) and (12) represent the schemas instantiated by masculine and feminine definite noun phrases, respectively (cf. Flick 2019). Each of these schemas has a paradigmatic axis: They represent one cell among eight that define the structure of definite noun phrases for each grammatical case in singular and plural. The construction in (13) represents the plural morpheme (cf. Booij 2010: 552–553) and is part of a paradigmatic construction that represents the inflectional paradigm of feminine nouns formed by suffixation with *–in* which is also used to inflect gender-inclusive nouns with *–*in*. Noun phrases like those in (2) may initially have been formed by combining these three mentally stored constructions. The gender-inclusive meaning of the noun phrase may then have been achieved pragmatically.

However, a language user who repeatedly processes or forms noun phrases such as *den*die Wahlkreiskandidat*in*, etc. is very likely to mentally store a new paradigmatic construction (cf. Völkening 2025, for a more detailed discussion):

---

12 As masculine grammatical gender is optionally associated to male gender representations, the meaning 'N: male' is optional in instantiations of this construction. The same applies to the construction in (12) and the meaning 'N: female', as feminine forms can be used as feminine generics.

(14)   [*der*die* [x]$_N$]$_{NP}$ 'N: definite; N: any gender' (or: 'N: gender not specified')

Crucially, language users seem to only fill the empty slot *x* of this construction with gender-inclusive nouns. The construction in (11) is used with masculine nouns, and this information is stored in the construction in (11) as a requirement for the linguistic material that can fill the empty slot *x*. The construction in (12), on the other hand, is used exclusively with feminine nouns, and this information is similarly stored as a requirement within the construction. And if the construction in (14) is used solely with gender-inclusive nouns, this information must also be mentally stored. The construction in (14) represents a generalization that a language user has made over many instances of gender-inclusive nouns.[13] Along with the form given in (14), the gender-inclusive meaning is stored as well. Thus, it is no longer achieved pragmatically, that is, spontaneously, but becomes increasingly entrenched in the language user's mind.

Translated back into grammatical categories, this means that these gender-inclusive noun phrases are instances of change in this language user's mental grammatical gender system: They are assigned to a fourth grammatical gender. Initially, this change only affects the mental language system of language users and communities who frequently use and process gender-inclusive noun phrases. The construction might not yet be strongly entrenched, as language users are not likely to encounter gender-inclusive noun phrases very often. Only with frequent use of the construction in (14) may become strongly entrenched in the minds of language users and eventually become increasingly conventionalized.

7 Conclusion

It has been shown that, from a synchronic point of view, gender-inclusive nouns containing a gender star do not necessarily include the feminine suffix *-in* 'female' (anymore). Language users who frequently process and form these nouns do so by means of the new suffix *-*in* instead. It is this new suffix, or respectively the construction [[x]$_N$ **in*]$_N$, that conveys gender-inclusive meaning, rather than the gender star alone. Consequently, *-_in*, *-In*, etc. are variants of the new suffix and do not necessarily differ in meaning. In particular, the meaning of nouns containing a capital *I* does not necessarily only include men and women.

In spoken language, the glottal stop is not the defining feature of the new gender-inclusive suffix and, consequently, should not be analyzed as a phoneme.

---

13 Thus far, this generalization appears to be limited to written language.

Instead, the suffix –*in* [ʔɪn] and the feminine suffix –*in* [ɪn] are distinguished by their prosodic structure: –*in* [ʔɪn] is a phonological word, whereas –*in* [ɪn] is not. The insertion of the glottal stop is a consequence of the suffix syllable having an empty onset due to the prosodic boundary between the two phonological words; it is optional. Correspondingly, in written language, the gender star, the gender gap, the capital *I*, etc. do not represent the glottal stop. Instead, they serve a structural function; they mark and strengthen the boundary between two phonological words.

The form and meaning of complex words derived from the new suffix –*in* have been modeled through a construction intended to represent the linguistic knowledge applied by language users who frequently use and process these words. The constructionist perspective adopted in this paper allows for considering the different linguistic levels, and thus the layers of linguistic material, together. As a result, the prosodic, morphosyntactic, and semantic structure of the gender-inclusive nouns with special characters are modeled through a single multi-layered construction. Whether this analysis is adequate still needs to be empirically verified.

Lastly, an analysis of the structure underlying gender-inclusive definite noun phrases such as *der*die Wähler*in* has been outlined. It has been suggested that language users form these noun phrases by means of a new paradigmatic construction [*der*die* [x]$_N$]$_{NP}$ that is associated with a new, gender-inclusive meaning. This analysis also still needs to be empirically verified; namely, it would be crucial to investigate whether language users only fill the empty slot *x* of this construction with gender-inclusive nouns such as words derived from the suffix –*in* as well as nominalized participles (*der*die Studierende*) and adjectives (*der*die Neue*). If this is the case, these noun phrases are not formed by a combination of the constructions that form feminine and masculine noun phrases, but by means of a new construction. Consequently, they should be analyzed as neither masculine nor feminine, nor as a combination of both, nor as lacking grammatical gender altogether. Instead, they might be assigned to a new grammatical gender category: Language users, then, convey gender-inclusive meaning not only through word-formation by means of a new suffix-construction, but also through the syntactic properties of this suffix, that is by means of a new syntactic construction.

References

Boersma, Paul and David Weenink. 2024. Praat: Doing phonetics by computer.
Booij, Geert. 2010. Construction morphology. *Language and Linguistics Compass* 4(7). 543–555. https://doi.org/10.1111/j.1749-818X.2010.00213.x.
Booij, Geert. 2015. Word-formation in construction grammar. In Peter Müller, Ingeborg Ohnheiser, Susan Olsen and Franz Rainer (eds.), *Word-formation. An international handbook of the languages of Europe*, vol. 1, 188–202. Berlin, Boston: De Gruyter.
Booij, Geert. 2023. Parallel architecture and the orthography of Dutch. https://www.researchgate.net/publication/370659638_Parallel_Architecture_and_the_orthography_of_Dutch. Preprint, published on ResearchGate in May 2023. Accessed: 27 July 2024.
Coussé, Evie, Peter Andersson and Joel Olofson. 2018. Grammaticalization meets construction grammar. Opportunities, challenges and potential incompatibilities. In Evie Coussé, Peter Andersson and Joel Olofson (eds.), *Grammaticalization meets construction grammar*, 3–19. Amsterdam: Benjamins.
Diewald, Gabriele. 2020. Paradigms lost – paradigms regained: Paradigms as hyper-constructions. In Lotte Sommerer and Elena Smirnova (eds.), *Nodes and networks in diachronic construction grammar*, 277–315. Amsterdam: Benjamins.
Diewald, Gabriele and Katja Politt. 2020. Grammatical categories as paradigms in construction grammar. *Belgian Journal of Linguistics* 34. 42–51.
Eisenberg, Peter. 2021. Unter dem Muff von hundert Jahren. Faz.net, 08.01.2021. https://www.faz.net/aktuell/feuilleton/debatten/der-duden-und-der-unsinn-der-gegenderten-sprache-17135087.html. Accessed: 26 July 2024.
Ferstl, Evelyn and Damaris Nübling. 2024. Sonderzeichen als typographische Kennzeichnung geschlechtersensiblen Sprachgebrauchs. In Sabine Krome, Mechthild Habermann, Henning Lobin and Angelika Wöllstein (eds.), *Orthographie in Wissenschaft und Gesellschaft. Schriftsystem – Norm – Schreibgebrauch*, 259–284. Berlin, Boston: De Gruyter.
Fischer, Beatrice and Michaela Wolf. 2009. *Leitfaden zum geschlechtergerechten Sprachgebrauch. Zur Verwendung in Lehrveranstaltungen und in wissenschaftlichen Arbeiten*. University of Vienna.
Fleischer, Wolfgang and Irmhild Barz. 2012. *Wortbildung der deutschen Gegenwartssprache*. Berlin, Boston: De Gruyter. https://doi.org/10.1515/9783110256659.
Flick, Johanna. 2019. "Alte" Daten, neue Methoden. Die Konstruktionalisierung von [Definitartikel + N] im Althochdeutschen. *Jahrbuch für Germanische Sprachgeschichte* 10(1). 151–175.
Friedrich, Marcus, Jennifer Muselick and Elke Heise. 2022. Does the use of gender-fair language impair the comprehensibility of video lectures? – An experiment using an authentic video lecture manipulating role nouns in German. *Psychology Learning & Teaching* 21(3). 296–309. https://doi.org/10.1177/14757257221107348.
Goldberg, Adele. 1995. *Constructions. A construction grammar approach to argument structure*. Chicago, London: University of Chicago Press.
Goldberg, Adele. 2006. *Constructions at work. The nature of generalization in language*. Oxford: Oxford University Press.
Haider, Hubert. 2024. Phonematisierung des glottalen Plosivs aufgrund politischer Korrektheit? In Ewa Trutkowski and André Meinunger (eds.), *Gendern – auf Teufel*in komm raus?*, 59–71. Berlin: Kulturverlag Kadmos.

Heise, Elke. 2000. Sind Frauen mitgemeint? Eine empirische Untersuchung zum Verständnis des generischen Maskulinums und seiner Alternativen. *Sprache & Kognition* 19. 3–13. https://doi.org/10.1024//0253-4533.19.12.3.

Hilpert, Martin. 2011. Was ist Konstruktionswandel? In Alexander Lasch and Alexander Ziem (eds.), *Konstruktionsgrammatik III: Aktuelle Fragen und Lösungsansätze*, 59–75. Tübingen: Stauffenburg.

Hilpert, Martin and Holger Diessel. 2017. Entrenchment in construction grammar. In Hans-Jörg Schmid (ed.), *Entrenchment and the psychology of language learning. How we reorganize and adapt linguistic knowledge*, 57–74. Berlin, Boston: De Gruyter.

Hornscheidt, Lann. 2012. *Feministische w_orte: ein lern-, denk- und handlungsbuch zu sprache und diskriminierung, gender studies und feministischer linguistik*. Frankfurt am Main: Brandes, Apels.

Kopf, Kristin. 2017. Fugenelement und Bindestrich in der Compositions-Fuge. Zur Herausbildung phonologischer und graphematischer Grenzmarkierungen in (früh)neuhochdeutschen N+N-Komposita. In Nanna Fuhrhop, Renata Szczepaniak and Karsten Schmidt (eds.), *Sichtbare und hörbare Morphologie*, vol. 565 Linguistische Arbeiten, 177–204. Berlin, Boston: De Gruyter.

Kotthoff, Helga and Damaris Nübling. 2018. *Genderlinguistik: Eine einführung in Sprache, Gespräch und Geschlecht*. 1st edn. Tübingen: Narr.

Krome, Sabine. 2020. Zwischen gesellschaftlichem Diskurs und Rechtschreibnormierung: Geschlechtergerechte Sprache als Herausforderung für gelungene Textrealisation. *Muttersprache* 130(1). 64–78.

Kusterle, Karin. 2011. *Die Macht der Sprachformen. Der Zusammenhang von Sprache, Denken und Genderwahrnehmung*. Frankfurt: Brandes, Apels.

Körner, Anita, Bleen Abraham, Ralf Rummer and Fritz Strack. 2022. Gender representations elicited by the gender star form. *Journal of Language and Social Psychology* 41. 553–571. https://doi.org/10.1177/0261927X221080181.

Körner, Anita, Sarah Glim and Rals Rummer. 2024. Examining the glottal stop as a mark of gender-inclusive language in German. *Applied Psycholinguistics* 45. 156–179. https://doi.org/10.1017/S0142716424000018.

Lakoff, George. 1987. Case study 3. There-constructions. In *Women, fire, and dangerous things. What categories reveal about the mind*, 462–585. Chicago, London: University of Chicago Press.

Müller-Spitzer, Carolin, Samira Ochs and Jan Oliver Rüdiger. 2024. Auf der Suche nach Genderzeichen: Die Hamburger Volksinitiative "Schluss mit Gendersprache in Verwaltung und Bildung" und die Verwendung von Genderzeichen auf der Webseite der Stadt Hamburg. https://lingdrafts.hypotheses.org/2671. Accessed: 26 July 2024.

Nübling, Damaris and Renata Szczepaniak. 2013. Linking elements in German: Origin, change, functionalization. *Morphology* 23(1). 67–89. https://doi.org/10.1007/s11525-013-9213-9.

Okamura, Saburo. 2012. Sprachliche Lösungsmöglichkeiten der Genderproblematik im Japanischen und Deutschen. In Susanne Günthner, Dagmar Hüpper and Constanze Spieß (eds.), *Genderlinguistik. Sprachliche Konstruktionen von Geschlechtsidentität*, 413–432. Berlin, Boston: De Gruyter. https://doi.org/10.1515/9783110272901.413.

Pusch, Luise. 2014. *Feministische Linguistik und Queer Theory. Teil 1: Brauchen wir den Unterstrich?* Göttingen: Wallstein Verlag.

Raffelsiefen, Renate. 2000. Evidence for word-internal phonological words in German. In Rolf Thieroff, Matthias Tamrat, Nanna Fuhrhop and Oliver Teuber (eds.), *Deutsche Grammatik in Theorie und Praxis*, 43–56. Tübingen: Niemeyer.

Regh, Alexander. 2002. Transgender in Deutschland zwischen Transsexuellen-Selbsthilfe und Kritik an der Zweigeschlechterordnung. In Polymorph – Arbeitsgruppe zur Kritik der

Zweigeschlechtlichen Ordnung (ed.), *(K)ein Geschlecht oder viele? Transgender in politischer Perspektive*, 185–203. Berlin: Querverlag.

Schneider, Jan Georg. 2021. Zum prekären Status sprachlicher Verbindlichkeit: Gendern im Deutschen. In Jürgen Raab and Justus Heck (eds.), *Prekäre Verbindlichkeiten. Studien an den Problemschwellen normativer Ordnungen*, 17–43. Wiesbaden: Springer Fachmedien. https://doi.org/10.1007/978-3-658-34227-2_2.

Scott, Alan. 2006. Das Suffix -In. Eine Ergänzung zum deutschen Wortbildungssystem. *Zeitschrift für Dialektologie und Linguistik* 17. 161–175.

Stefanowitsch, Anatol. 2018. Gendergap und Gendersternchen in der gesprochenen Sprache. http://www.sprachlog.de/2018/06/09/gendergap-und-gendersternchen-inder-gesprochenen-sprache. Accessed: 27 July 2024.

Völkening, Lena. 2022. Ist Gendern mit Glottisverschlusslaut ungrammatisch? Ein Analysevorschlag für das Suffix [ʔɪn] als phonologisches Wort. *Zeitschrift für Wortbildung / Journal of Word Formation* 6(1). 58–80. https://doi.org/10.3726/zwjw.2022.01.02.

Völkening, Lena. 2025. Gendern entlang der Beschränkungen des Sprachsystems. Nominalphrasen mit Genderstern aus konstruktionsgrammatischer Perspektive. In Paul Meuleneers, Lisa Zacharski, Evelyn Ferstl and Damaris Nübling (eds.), *Genderbezogene Personenreferenzen: Routinen und Innovationen*, Linguistische Berichte (special issue) 36, 157–175. Hamburg: Helmut Buske.

Wiese, Richard. 2000. *The phonology of German*. Oxford: Clarendon Press.

Zacharski, Lisa and Evelyn Ferstl. 2023. Gendered representations of person referents activated by the nonbinary gender star in German: A word-picture matching task. *Discourse Processes* 60(4–5). 294–319. https://doi.org/10.1080/0163853X.2023.2199531.

Ziem, Alexander and Alexander Lasch. 2013. *Konstruktionsgrammatik. Konzepte und Grundlagen gebrauchsbasierter Ansätze*. Berlin, New York: De Gruyter.

Zifonun, Gisela. 2021. Eine Linguistin denkt nach über den Genderstern. *Sprachreport* 37(2). 46–51. https://doi.org/10.14618/sr-2-2021-zifo.

Samira Ochs and Jan Oliver Rüdiger

Of stars and colons: A corpus-based analysis of gender-inclusive orthographies in German press texts

Abstract: New gender-inclusive orthographies such as the asterisk or the colon are widely debated in various German public spheres, including areas of academia. However, little is known about the frequency and distribution of these neographies. This study presents a microdiachronic analysis of binary (i.e., including only men and women) and non-binary (i.e., inclusive of all genders) variants of gender-inclusive orthographies from 2015 to 2023. Using the German Reference Corpus (DeReKo), we assembled a subcorpus of press texts from 15 sources, comprising approximately 1.2 billion tokens. Our corpus-driven approach reveals that the non binary variants asterisk (*Schüler*innen* 'pupils') and colon (*Schüler:innen*) have become dominant after the 2019 change of the German civil status law to encompass a third positive gender option, *divers*. Binary forms, especially the capital *I* (as in *SchülerInnen*), have been in decline since. The non-binary forms are unevenly distributed across sources and lexemes, a pattern further explored through a lexicon-based search. We examined 131 pre-selected personal nouns with systematic gender differentiation to compare binary and non-binary variants to regular masculine and feminine forms. The results show that masculine forms remain dominant, followed by feminine forms, with both maintaining stable frequencies over time. In contrast, binary and non-binary forms remain marginal. These quantitative baselines enhance the linguistic understanding of how sources, lexemes, and extralinguistic events shape the use of gender-inclusive language. Our study thus offers a foundation for more objective discussions on the subject.

Keywords: corpus analysis, gender-inclusive language, gender symbols, German Reference Corpus (DeReKo), language change, neographies, non-binary language, press texts

---

Samira Ochs, Leibniz Institute for the German Language (IDS), e-mail: ochs@ids-mannheim.de
Jan Oliver Rüdiger, Leibniz Institute for the German Language (IDS), e-mail: ruediger@ids-mannheim.de

 Open Access. © 2025 the author(s), published by De Gruyter. This work is licensed under the Creative Commons Attribution 4.0 International License.
https://doi.org/10.1515/9783111388694-003

1 Introduction

The efforts to develop more (gender-)inclusive linguistic forms in German date back to the emergence of feminist linguistics in the 1970s. During this time, scholars like Pusch (1979) and Trömel-Plötz (1978) began to critically examine the pervasive dominance of masculine forms and called for greater linguistic visibility of women. Among the resulting proposals – many of which were rooted in a binary understanding of gender – was the practice of explicitly including both masculine and feminine forms within a noun phrase, such as *Bürgerinnen und Bürger* ('female and male citizens') instead of using only the generically intended masculine *Bürger* ('[male] citizens').

However, concepts of social gender – its performativity and fluid nature – have evolved significantly since then (cf., for example, Butler 1988). Today, gender is commonly understood as a continuum that includes not only male and female but also non-binary, genderfluid, or agender identities, among others (Jourian 2015; Lev 2004; Thorne et al. 2019). This shift is also reflected on the legal level: In 2019, the German civil status law was amended to include the gender category *divers* for intersex, non-binary or genderfluid individuals[1]. While binary forms of person reference sufficed for feminist linguistic efforts, emerging queer realities call for linguistic forms that have the potential to encompass a wider spectrum – or even the entirety – of gender identities.

Binary as well as gender-neutral linguistic forms (e.g., *die Person* 'the person', *der Mensch* 'the human being') are widely accepted by the German population as strategies for gender-inclusive language, as evidenced by a recent poll conducted by the German broadcaster WDR (2023). Because these forms are part of the standard language system, they are often not even explicitly perceived as gender-inclusive language (Zacharski 2024: 230). In contrast, innovative linguistic forms that are intended to include all genders frequently interfere with standard German orthography – for instance, through the insertion of typographic characters within words – and are therefore highly debated, both in the public sphere and within academia (for a comprehensive overview of the content of these debates, cf. Acke 2023: 47–51).

To date, gender-inclusive language has primarily been investigated from psycholinguistic perspectives, focusing on aspects such as comprehensibility (Braun et al. 2007; Friedrich et al. 2021; Pabst and Kollmayer 2023; Tross 2023) and men-

---

[1] https://www.antidiskriminierungsstelle.de/EN/about-discrimination/grounds-for-discrimination/gender-and-gender-identity/third-option/third-option-node.html, accessed: 25 March 2024. In Austria, a similar law allowing a third gender entry was introduced in 2019. Switzerland followed in 2022.

tal representations (Keith et al. 2022; Körner et al. 2022; Kurz and De Mulder 2023; Zacharski and Ferstl 2023). These efforts are complemented by sociolinguistic studies examining attitudes and opinions towards gender-inclusive language (Adler and Plewnia 2019; Jäckle 2022; Kotthoff 2023; Löhr 2021, 2022). Quantitative, corpus-based analyses of gender-inclusive German in written texts have recently become another focus of research (Link 2024; Müller-Spitzer et al. 2024c,b; Müller-Spitzer and Ochs 2023; Sökefeld 2021, forthcoming; Waldendorf 2023). Our study contributes to this emerging field by investigating the actual use and distribution of gender-inclusive orthographies in German press texts. We analyze data from 15 sources available in the German Reference Corpus (DeReKo), comprising a total of 1.2 billion tokens and covering the period from 2015 to 2023.

Our analysis is structured along two perspectives: First, we examine the frequency of various gender-inclusive orthographies relative to one another. We highlight changes from binary to non-binary usages, especially following the amendment of the German civil status law in 2019. Second, we conduct a detailed analysis of a preselected set of personal nouns, comparing gender-inclusive variants with regular masculine and feminine forms. By providing these quantitative baselines, we aim to enhance the linguistic understanding of how sources, lexemes, and extralinguistic events shape the use of gender-inclusive language. Additionally, we seek to contribute valuable insights to ongoing discussions about gender-inclusive language.

In Section 2, we briefly outline the grammatical gender system of German, the so-called *masculine generic*, and various strategies for gender-inclusive language. Section 3 introduces the study design, including a description of the corpus and the data. The results of our analyses are presented and discussed in Section 4, followed by concluding remarks in Section 5.[2]

2 Gender-inclusive German

2.1 Grammatical gender and the masculine generic

German is a grammatical gender language with three genders: masculine, feminine, and neuter. Gender assignment is largely arbitrary but can, in some cases – particularly for monosyllabic nouns – be predicted by morphophonological criteria (Hellinger and Bußmann 2003: 143; cf. Kupisch et al. 2022 for examples of further

---

[2] Datasets, Python scripts and Supplementary Material are available in the OSF at https://osf.io/9mzab, accessed: 20 February 2025.

predictable structures). Personal nouns, which refer to human beings, represent a unique nominal domain where lexical-semantic factors often influence grammatical gender assignment (Hellinger and Bußmann 2003: 146). In simple terms, this means that feminine forms are typically used to refer to women, while masculine forms refer to men – for instance, the word for 'mother' (*die Mutter*) is feminine, whereas the word for 'father' (*der Vater*) is masculine. Exceptions to this pattern are sometimes systematic, such as the derogatory use of feminine nouns to describe men who deviate from traditional gender norms (Kotthoff and Nübling 2018: 85).

In this context, the concept of the masculine generic is central. In many natural and grammatical gender languages (Hellinger and Bußmann 2001), the masculine form is used not only to refer to specific men but also to groups of people whose gender is either unknown or irrelevant, as well as to mixed-gender groups (Diewald 2018: 286). In German, only personal nouns with systematic gender differentiation are affected by the ambiguity of the masculine form – specifically, masculine personal nouns from which feminine forms can be derived. Feminine derivations are typically created by adding the suffix *-in* to the masculine base (Doleschal 1992), as in *Wissenschaftlerin* 'female scientist' derived from *Wissenschaftler* 'male scientist'. This suffix is highly productive and attaches to nearly all masculine derivation bases (Fleischer and Barz 2012: 236–237). The suffixation with *-in* transforms "grammatically masculine, semantically male human nouns into grammatically feminine, semantically female ones" (Stefanowitsch and Middeke 2023: 293). Thus, referential gender is specified through morphological means (Hellinger and Bußmann 2003: 152–153). Within such pairs, the masculine form serves a dual purpose: It can be used either gender-specifically or generically. For example, consider the noun phrase *ein Wissenschaftler und zwei Wissenschaftlerinnen* ('one male and two female scientists'): Here, the masculine form is used gender-specifically, contrasting with the feminine form and creating a semantic minimal pair. In contrast, in the phrase *Sieben Wissenschaftler diskutierten* ('seven scientists.MASC.PL were discussing'), the masculine form is ambiguous. It may refer exclusively to men or to a mixed-gender group, with the exact reference determined only by context (Müller-Spitzer et al. 2024c: 3). Other types of personal nouns, such as epicene or lexical gender nouns[3], are not subject to the concept of masculine generics.

The generic use of the masculine is often linked to androcentrism and the notion of 'male as norm' (Bailey et al. 2019), which is why it is frequently criticized in (queer-)feminist contexts as exclusive of non-male gender identities (Kotthoff and

---

3 Epicene nouns do not specify referential gender via grammatical gender, i.e., they can be used to refer to people of any gender (e.g., *die Person*.FEM 'the person', *der Mensch*.MASC 'the human being'). Lexical gender nouns have referential gender encoded in their lexical meaning; grammatical gender usually aligns with this (e.g., *die Mutter*.FEM 'the mother' vs. *der Vater*.MASC 'the father').

Nübling 2024: 135–144). Therefore, the adequacy of the masculine generic as a form to denote all genders is a topic of ongoing controversy in both society and academia (for a selection of perspectives, see Müller-Spitzer 2022; Pusch 1984; Simon 2022; Trutkowski and Weiß 2023). Advocates of non-discriminatory language typically reject it as a truly gender-neutral way of person reference (e.g., Acke 2019; Hellinger and Bußmann 2003). In contrast, opponents of new gender-inclusive forms argue that the masculine generic is inherently gender-neutral (e.g., Eisenberg 2020; Meineke 2023; Trutkowski and Weiß 2023). However, a growing body of psycholinguistic studies demonstrates that the masculine generic consistently carries a male bias (e.g., Glim et al. 2023; Gygax et al. 2008; Körner et al. 2022; Zacharski and Ferstl 2023). As Glim et al. put it, it "does not represent men and women equally well" (2023: 2) but instead favors the (mental) representation of men. This is supported by evidence from computational linguistics and discriminative learning, which shows that masculine generics are semantically very close to gender-specific masculines in actual language use (Schmitz et al. 2023; Schmitz 2024). It is therefore not only questionable whether women are adequately represented by the masculine generic, but also whether it can account for identities beyond the gender binary. Such limitations are at the heart of current debates on gender-inclusive language.

2.2 Strategies of gender-inclusive language in German

As the adequacy of the masculine generic as a gender-neutral form is increasingly questioned, alternative, more inclusive ways of person reference are being explored. In German, two broad categories of gender-inclusive language can be distinguished: implicit and explicit strategies.

Implicit strategies, sometimes referred to as gender-neutral strategies, aim to make gender linguistically 'invisible'. This is achieved through neutralizing forms such as epicenes, collective nouns, and the nominal use of plural participles and adjectives (Eisenberg 2020). Paraphrasing with pronouns, relative clauses, or passive constructions also falls into this category. These strategies are generally unobtrusive – indeed, a recent poll by the German broadcaster WDR (2023) found that most respondents held positive attitudes toward gender-neutral formulations.

Explicit strategies, by contrast, make gender visible in language, either in a binary or non-binary way. Binary forms are particularly common in political and journalistic context. Fully-fledged pair forms such as *Lehrerinnen und Lehrer* ('female and male teachers') or *Bürgerinnen und Bürger* ('female and male citizens') are widely used there (Bast et al. 2024; Müller-Spitzer et al. 2022, 2024a; Rosar 2022; Truan 2019). Shortened versions of the pair form include those using a forward slash (*Lehrer/Lehrerinnen, Lehrer/innen, Lehrer/-innen*), parentheses (*Lehrer(innen)*), or the capitalised *I* (called *Binnen-I* 'capital *I*', as in *LeherInnen*). Notably, fully-fledged binary pair forms like *Lehrerinnen und Lehrer* have the highest acceptance rates in the WDR poll and are not perceived as intrusive ways to represent gender in language (Müller-Spitzer et al. 2022; Zacharski 2024). This suggests that feminist efforts to increase the visibility of women in language and normalize such visibility have been relatively successful.

However, current research indicates that binary forms are seen as reinforcing the gender binary and are neither representative of nor accepted by the queer community (Motschenbacher 2013; Siegenthaler 2024). In fact, when asked for acceptability judgments, queer respondents rate masculine generics higher than pair forms or the capital *I* (Löhr 2021, 2022). This underscores the limitations of binary strategies in addressing the linguistic needs of non-binary and gender-diverse individuals. Gender is increasingly understood as a spectrum rather than a purely binary concept. This change is also evident in the legal sphere, as Germany's civil status law was revised to introduce the gender category *divers* in 2019, providing recognition for gender-nonconforming individuals. As a result of these societal changes, gender-queer and other marginalized communities are seeking linguistic forms that represent this expanded understanding of gender, leading to the emergence of new gender-inclusive forms.

Similar to shortened binary forms like the capital *I*, forward slashes, or parentheses, these new forms operate on the word-internal level: A typographic character is inserted between the masculine base and the feminine suffix, thereby creating a new suffix (Völkening 2022, and in this volume). The characters currently in use in German include the asterisk (*Lehrer*innen*)[4], the colon (*Lehrer:innen*), and the underscore (*Lehrer_innen*). It is possible that additional symbols, such as the mediopoint (*Lehrer·innen*) already used in French, could be adopted in the future (Diewald and Steinhauer 2020: 127). However, our analysis focuses on the characters already in use today.[5]

---

[4] The term *asterisk* is used in this chapter, while Völkening and Schmitz et al. in their chapters refer to the same concept as *gender star*.

[5] We also do not consider proposals falling under so-called *exit gender* strategies, which advocate for more radical linguistic innovations. These include introducing entirely new suffixes, such as *-x* or *-ecs*, to create gender-neutral personal nouns like *Lehrx* instead of the gender-marked forms *Lehrer*.MASC and *Lehrerin*.FEM (AG Feministisch Sprachhandeln 2014: 22). Another example is the systematic use of the neuter for gender-neutral designations, combined with the elimination of the feminine suffix *-in*. This would result in paradigms such as *der Lehrer*.MASC.SG – *die Lehrer*.FEM.SG – *das Lehrer*.NEUT.SG (Pusch 1984). However, the feasibility of such innovations is questionable, as they would require profound changes to grammatical structures (Kotthoff and Nübling 2018: 221). Moreover, the lack of corresponding corpus annotations makes it impossible to identify and an-

The symbolic meanings of these characters vary, with the asterisk and underscore carrying the most interpretive weight (Kotthoff 2017: 11). The asterisk, for instance, might function as a placeholder (akin to its use in programming languages), or symbolize gender diversity through its radiating form. The underscore, by contrast, may signify a 'gap' to be filled by new gender identities or the fluidity between male and female. The colon, while lacking this level of symbolic association, shares with the others a common goal: to represent gender identities beyond the binary (Diewald and Steinhauer 2020; Friedrich et al. 2021; Genderleicht 2024; Körner et al. 2022). Both psycholinguistic (Zacharski and Ferstl 2023) and sociolinguistic research (Löhr 2021, 2022) suggests that forms with gender symbols are more inclusive – not only in terms of mental representations but also in their acceptability among members of queer communities.

To illustrate the differences between all strategies, consider the sentence 'All teachers were in school' and its various realizations in Examples (1-a) to (1-f). It is important to note, however, that not all masculine generics can be replaced by every option shown here. In particular, the availability of epicenes is not always guaranteed:

(1)   a.   Masculine generic:
Alle Lehrer waren an der Schule.
       b.   Implicit strategy (epicene):
Alle Lehrkräfte waren an der Schule.
       c.   Implicit strategy (paraphrase):
Alle, die unterrichten, waren an der Schule.
       d.   Explicit strategy (binary):
Alle Lehrerinnen und Lehrer waren an der Schule.
       e.   Explicit strategy (shortened binary):
Alle Lehrer/-innen waren an der Schule.
       f.   Explicit strategy (non-binary):
Alle Lehrer*innen waren an der Schule.

Gender symbols such as in example (1-f) (also called *neographies*) represent an overt strategy of gender-inclusive language that intentionally challenges conventional orthography. This has made them a subject of debate within the *Rat für Deutsche Rechtschreibung* ('Council for German Orthography'), the primary international body regulating Standard German orthography. In its most recent resolution, the Council classified gender symbols as special characters, akin to the

---

alyze such forms systematically in corpus-linguistic studies, particularly in standard press texts. Consequently, these strategies fall outside the methodological scope of the present study.

paragraph (§) or percent (%) signs. This means they are not considered part of core orthography. Opponents of gender symbols often use this classification to argue that they constitute "incorrect" or "poor" German (Eisenberg 2022; Zifonun 2021). This reasoning has spurred a rise in petitions to prohibit gender symbols in certain regions, and restrictive regulations have been implemented in several German federal states (see Müller-Spitzer et al. 2024a for an overview of states and petitions). A common argument supporting such bans is that gender symbols render texts cumbersome, unreadable, and overly lengthy (Kurfer 2024; Meuleneers 2024; Pfalzgraf 2024). However, empirical research has repeatedly refuted these claims (Blake and Klimmt 2010; Friedrich et al. 2021, 2024; Pabst and Kollmayer 2023). Moreover, such criticisms would only be valid if the use of gender-inclusive forms caused substantial changes to text structure or content, which a recent study by Müller-Spitzer et al. (2024c) suggests not to be the case.

A key aspect often overlooked in the debate is the actual frequency of gender symbols: How often do we encounter them in everyday written language? Are they sufficiently frequent and widely distributed to warrant claims of being a significant intrusion into the language? Where are they most commonly used, and how has their usage evolved over time? Although these questions are important, the research landscape is still limited. Some studies have examined specific lexical items and their various realizations in corpora (Adler and Hansen 2020; Bast et al. 2024; Krome 2020, 2021). Other studies focus on highly specialized sources, such as university documents (Acke 2019; for French: Burnett and Pozniak 2021) or city websites (Müller-Spitzer et al. 2024b; Müller-Spitzer and Ochs 2023).

To date, only three larger-scale corpus studies on gender-inclusive language in German exist: Sökefeld (2021) compares press texts and blog posts, annotating all possible variants of personal nouns in her data. Her findings show that while the asterisk is increasing in frequency over time, masculine generics and gender-neutral forms still dominate. Waldendorf (2023) extracts different variants of gender-inclusive language from five German newspapers using computer-linguistic methods. She observes a rise in binary pair forms as well as non-binary variants such as the asterisk and colon, linking these trends to the political orientation of the newspapers. Most recently, Link's study (2024) examines the use of gender-inclusive language from a contrastive perspective. Analyzing six conservative and left-liberal newspapers from Germany, Austria, and Switzerland, she finds that Austria employs gender-inclusive forms significantly more frequently than the other two countries. The study also identifies a marked increase in the use across all three countries between 2017 and 2021, with trends diverging thereafter. Contrary to previous findings, Link states that the political orientation of the newspapers had no significant influence on the use of gender-inclusive language.

Our study builds on and extends these foundational efforts by analyzing gender-inclusive language across a considerably broader textual basis. In contrast to these previous studies, which often focus on broader patterns of gender-inclusive language use, we exclusively examine gender symbols. This means that pair forms like *Lehrerinnen und Lehrer* and gender-neutral nouns like *Lehrkräfte* are deliberately excluded from our analysis. Instead, the first part of our study systematically compares the relative frequencies of binary forms (capital *I*, parentheses, forward slash) and non-binary forms (asterisk, colon, underscore), providing a nuanced perspective on their use and distribution. We also focus on how the use of gender symbols changed after the 2019 amendment to the German civil status law, adding an extralinguistic dimension to our analysis that has not been considered in previous studies.

In the second part, we introduce an innovative approach by analyzing gender-inclusive orthographies at the lexical level. Using a preselected set of personal nouns, we compare the frequency of their gender-inclusive realizations to that of regular inflectional forms (i.e., masculine and feminine). Unlike previous studies, which often rely on anecdotal evidence or focus on single lexemes, our approach enables a comprehensive, data-driven analysis of the relationship between regular forms and gender symbols for a broader set of terms. Our diachronic perspective (2015–2023) allows us to trace remarkable changes in usage over time and offers insights into lexical dynamics that have so far been little discussed in the field.

3 Corpus and data

Our analysis employs two complementary corpus approaches: First, a corpus-driven investigation extracts all gender-inclusive orthographies (Section 4.1), and second, a lexicon-based search is conducted with a pre-selected set of lexemes (Section 4.1.1). Combining these two methods enables us to a) track the development of gender-inclusive orthographies across all personal nouns in the corpus, and b) analyze the full inflectional paradigm for a set of lexemes, allowing us to compare gender-inclusive to regular inflectional forms.

The corpus is a specifically compiled subcorpus of the German Reference Corpus (DeReKo; Kupietz et al. 2018, 2010). It comprises 15 different press sources, including newspapers, magazines, and the German Press Agency (*dpa*), from Germany, Switzerland, and Austria. These sources are all published on a national level and represent a variety of publishing houses, target different audiences, and reflect diverse political orientations, thus ensuring a broad spectrum of German-language media.⁶ For our analysis, we focused on texts published between 2015 and 2023, resulting in a total of approximately 2.3 million documents with 1.2 billion tokens.⁷ We decided on this time span as it covers the years just before the amendment of the German civil status law up until the most recent year available in DeReKo.

We used the raw data from DeReKo (IDS-I5/XCES, Lüngen and Sperberg-McQueen 2012) and analyzed it using the CorpusExplorer software (Rüdiger 2023). Frequency lists and N-gram tables⁸ were generated: Words with gender symbols were broken down into bi- or trigrams. For example, the word *Lehrer*innen* would be split into 1) *Lehrer* 2) *, and 3) *innen*, allowing these components to be extracted directly from the N-Gram table. Forms with a capital *I* were retrieved as bigrams. For example, *LehrerIn* would be represented as 1) *Lehrer*, and 2) *In*. The data was further filtered using a separate Python script.⁹ Following this, the corpus-driven data was manually reviewed and cleaned, especially to eliminate false positives. 10,187 types and 24,438 tokens were removed, which accounts for 31.51% of the originally retrieved types and 8.86% of the tokens. This included proper names like *LinkedIn* (false positive for the capital *I*) or trigrams in which punctuation marks were followed by the preposition *in* (e.g., *Berlin : In*). After data cleansing, a total of 22,600 types and 250,730 tokens remain in the corpus-driven dataset. Manual cleansing was not necessary for the lexicon-based search, which involved a pre-selected set of search terms, ensuring no false positives were retrieved.

While it is also possible to use regular expressions (Regex) for data extraction (Sökefeld forthcoming; Waldendorf 2023), we opted against this approach after testing it in a small preliminary study. We found that the tokenization of gender symbols in DeReKo is inconsistent. While forms such as the capital *I* are rather unproblematic, punctuation characters like the slash and colon are inconsistently to-

---

6 Table S1 in the Supplementary Material gives an overview of all sources and their category, main topics, target audience and political orientation. This information was retrieved either from the website of the source, specific media information platforms like AdAlliance, from the Wikipedia, or from the *Institut für Medien- und Kommunikationspolitik* (IfM).
7 Tables S2 and S3 in the Supplementary Material show the amounts of documents and tokens per source and year. Unfortunately, the zwi16 corpus (*ZEIT Wissen* from 2016) is not available in DeReKo.
8 N-grams are contiguous sequences of n items (typically words or characters) from a given text or speech corpus. For example, a bigram consists of two consecutive words, a trigram consists of three, and so on. N-gram tables provide a way to count and analyze the frequency of these sequences within a corpus, which helps in identifying patterns and structures in the data.
9 The scripts (annotated Jupyter notebooks) are provided in the OSF. We publish a simple version of the code which works well with smaller data. We also publish the version we used, which employs *Ray*. *Ray* is a Python package that enables a strong parallelization of tasks and performs well in big data scenarios. The datasets for both the corpus-driven and the lexicon-based approach can also be downloaded from the repository.

kenized. While it is possible to account for this with Regex, it increases complexity and leads to a high rate of false positives, particularly for non-binary forms. In contrast, N-grams offer a clearer, simpler solution that avoids these issues, while providing a computationally more efficient and easily parallelizable solution.

4 Results and discussion

4.1 Corpus-driven approach

To capture all personal nouns with gender-inclusive orthographies in our corpus, we conducted a corpus-driven search that covered both binary (capital *I*, parentheses, slash) and non-binary (asterisk, colon, underscore) strategies. This approach does not allow for comparisons with their corresponding regular inflectional forms (i.e., masculine and feminine forms), as the basic population of nouns detected by our search remains unknown. This limitation applies to personal nouns in general. In practical terms, this means we cannot determine whether gender-inclusive forms are becoming more frequent in relation to the unknown baseline population, or if the entire category of personal nouns is simply growing. Nevertheless, if we assume that the proportion of personal nouns in standard press texts does not change significantly over time, we can reasonably infer that gender-inclusive forms are indeed increasing in frequency. So far, only two studies have addressed the question of a quantitative baseline for personal nouns, both estimating their proportion at approximately 3% in their respective corpora (Müller-Spitzer et al. 2024c; Sökefeld et al. 2023). Large-scale diachronic studies on the frequency of personal nouns have yet to be conducted. Keeping this limitation in mind, our corpus-driven approach offers an overview of the development and source-specific distribution of various gender inclusive strategies.

4.1.1 Development over time

Figure 1 shows the development of all six gender-inclusive orthographies from 2015 to 2023 across all sources. The vertical line marks the year 2019, when the German civil status law was amended to include a third positive gender option, *divers*. We regard this legal change as an extralinguistic event that could impact the use of gender-inclusive language, particularly with respect to non-binary forms. From 2015 to 2018, the binary capital *I* was the most common form, but has been steadily decreasing since. Parentheses remain infrequent throughout the years, and slashes

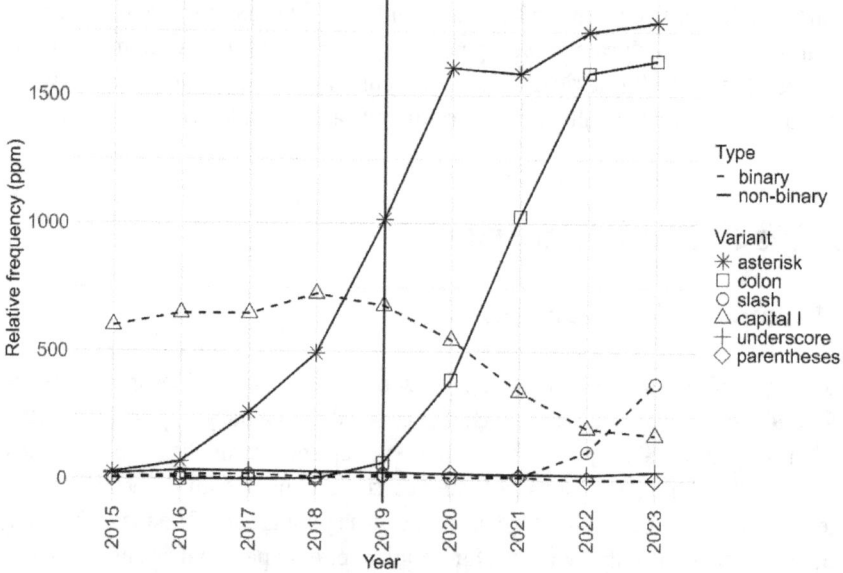

Fig. 1: Relative frequencies of gender-inclusive orthographies per year.

were rare before experiencing an increase after 2022, which we explain in the following discussion. Currently, the non-binary asterisk is dominant and continues to rise, although a flattening of the curve is observable in 2023. In 2022 and 2023, the colon nearly matches the asterisk, but still remains less frequent. This finding contrasts with Link's (2024: 10–11) corpus data, in which the colon is already more frequent than the asterisk, highlighting how the choice of textual basis can lead to different interpretations of the same phenomenon. The third non-binary option, the underscore, plays almost no role in our corpus.

To investigate whether the use of gender-inclusive orthographies differs significantly before and after the change in the civil status law, the data was split into two groups: one before 2019 and one from 2019 onward. A linear regression model was fitted to predict the relative frequency based on the interaction between the variables VARIANT and TIME GROUP. Since the relative frequency is not normally distributed, it was logarithmically transformed for the model. The asterisk was chosen as the reference level. The model shows a strong fit, with an R-squared value of 0.8503, meaning it explains approximately 85% of the variance in the data. The overall model is highly significant, as indicated by the F-statistic (19.63) and its p-value ($p < 0.001$).

The main effects of the different variants, which represent their impact before 2019 relative to the reference level (asterisk), are significant for all forms, except for

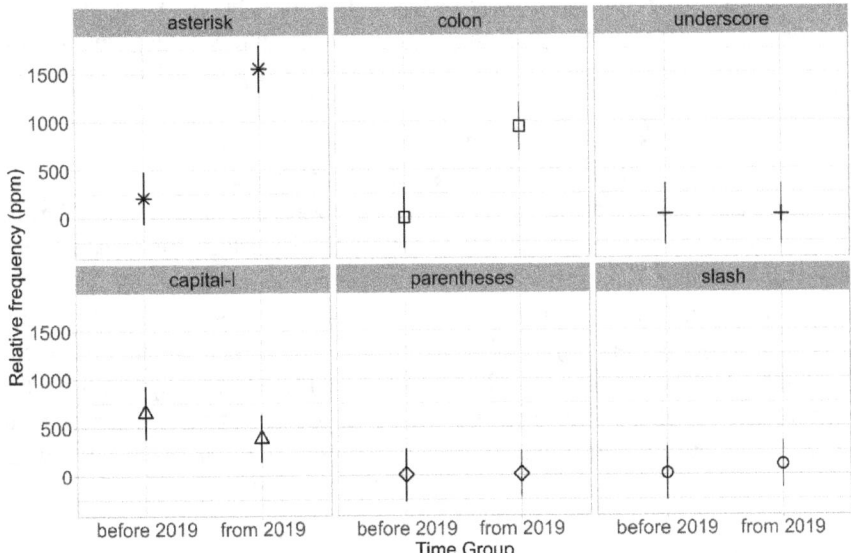

Fig. 2: Interaction plot for the linear regression model of relative frequency (per million words) predicted by the interaction of time group and variant. The top row shows the non-binary variants, while the bottom row displays the binary variants.

the underscore. The negative coefficients for colon (−4.8652), parentheses (−3.1387), and slash (−2.2517) indicate that they were significantly less frequent ($p < 0.01$) compared to the asterisk before 2019, while the capital *I* (1.6494) was significantly more common ($p < 0.05$). The main effect for TIME GROUP is also highly significant ($p < 0.001$), meaning that the reference value asterisk is approximately 12 times more frequent after 2019 than before.

The interaction terms illustrate how the influence of the variants shifted after 2019. The coefficient for the colon (3.9154) reflects a significant increase ($p < 0.001$) in frequency after 2019 relative to the asterisk. In contrast, the capital *I* experienced a substantial decrease in frequency ($p < 0.01$) after 2019, with its relative frequency dropping by approximately 96%, as indicated by the negative coefficient of −3.1474. The underscore and parentheses also exhibited a significant decline in frequency after 2019 ($p < 0.05$), whereas the slash remained largely unchanged ($p = 0.13$). Figure 2 visualizes these effects.

This analysis confirms that the non-binary variants asterisk and colon increased significantly after the change in the civil status law, underscoring the role of linguistic practices in reflecting societal change. In contrast, the underscore has remained largely irrelevant for representing non-binarity in our corpus, both before and after 2019. Similarly, parentheses and slash, which could theoretically function as binary markers, play no significant role in either time group. Before 2019, the binary capital *I* was the most common form, but its usage declined sharply afterward.

This shift suggests that non-binary neographies fulfil a linguistic need that binary forms cannot address. Binary forms lack the same socio-indexical significance (Kotthoff 2023: 209) and, at least theoretically, can always be replaced by pair forms. Waldendorf's data (2023: 8, Figure 2) confirm that fully-fledged binary pair forms (e.g., *Autorinnen und Autoren*) were the most frequent strategy in 2021. This indicates that binary strategies have not disappeared, but have predominantly shifted to pair forms rather than relying on word-internal strategies. Non-binary representations, by contrast, are currently limited to word-internal neographies. This distinction may signal an emerging division between binary strategies realized at the noun-phrase level and non-binary strategies confined to word-internal constructions.

4.1.2 Source-wise distribution

Next, we examine the use of gender symbols at the source level. Figure 3 shows the distribution of binary and non-binary variants across the 15 sources, sorted by their maximum frequency on the y-axis. The sources are arranged from top left to bottom right, starting with *taz* (y.max = 2,041 ppm) in the top left corner and ending with *Börsen-Zeitung* (y.max = 2.99 ppm) in the bottom right corner. From this, it is clear that the sources arrange on a spectrum, with *taz* being the most prominent driver of non-binary neographies. *Taz* is an alternative-left daily newspaper critical of societal structures (taz 2025). It contributes 94.38% of all tokens with non-binary neographies, aligning with research suggesting that the use of gender-inclusive language is often linked to political positioning (Bast et al. 2024; Jäckle 2022; Kotthoff 2017). Notably, *taz* was also the first newspaper to adopt the colon in 2016, with other sources following only in 2020. It can thus be considered a 'pioneer' in the use of non-binary gender-inclusive forms and serves as a reference point for what is maximally possible in terms of the frequency of gender symbols in journalistic texts.

However, the inclusion of *taz* raises important methodological considerations. Its exceptional contribution to non-binary neographies demonstrates its unique position, but excluding such a source could lead to a biased corpus selection. For instance, excluding sources based on the frequency of specific elements – whether high, as in *taz*, or low, as in *NZZ* or *Gala* – would raise significant questions about where to set thresholds for inclusion or exclusion. Would sources like *Brigitte* or

Couch, which also contribute a large number of non-binary tokens, then also need to be excluded? Such decisions risk introducing arbitrary biases into the corpus selection and make it challenging to define a generalizable middle.

The spectrum-like arrangement of sources underscores the need for separate analysis of individual sources to account for their unique contributions and contextual differences. For example, a comparison of the regression model presented in 4.1.1 with and without *taz* shows that while *taz* modulates certain effects – such as the prominence of non-binary neographies and the significance of interaction terms – significant changes remain observable across the remaining 14 sources for all variants in interaction with time. This indicates that *taz* is not the sole driver of linguistic variation within the corpus but rather a major contributor whose influence should be contextualized rather than overstated or dismissed. Link (2024: 4–13), for instance, deliberately excluded *taz* from her study comparing gender-inclusive language use in Germany, Austria, and Switzerland. Her rationale was that *taz* lacks equivalents in the other two countries and could distort her analysis of Germany. While this approach avoids over-representation, it also limits the conclusions she draws, such as her claim that political orientation has no significant influence on the use of gender-inclusive language (Link 2024: 1) – an assertion that might be questioned given that the most politically positioned source, *taz*, was not included. In summary, while *taz* undeniably shapes the upper bound of non-binary neographies, its inclusion highlights both its unique role as a driver of linguistic innovation and the methodological challenges in balancing representativeness and variability in corpus studies on gender-inclusive language.

The analysis also reveals that *taz* experiences a considerable decrease in binary forms over the years, indicating a substitution process for non-binary variants beginning after the change of the German civil status law. When only binary options were available, *taz* made extensive use of them. However, as soon as non-binary options became available and politically relevant, these began to be employed instead. As a result, *taz* stands out as the source with the strongest affinity for using word-internal strategies, regardless of whether they are binary or non-binary. This contrasts with *Brigitte*, Germany's most widely read women's magazine.[10] There, non-binary forms have increased significantly since 2019, while binary forms were not employed in meaningful numbers before non-binary options became available. *Brigitte* may therefore represent another key driver of change in the adoption of non-binary variants. Similarly, from 2020 onwards, the fashion and lifestyle magazine *Couch* also saw a noticeable rise in non-binary forms. This highlights how genre

---

10 https://www.ad-alliance.de/cms/portfolio/print/portfolio.html?p=/print/portfolio/brigitte, accessed: 27 January 2025.

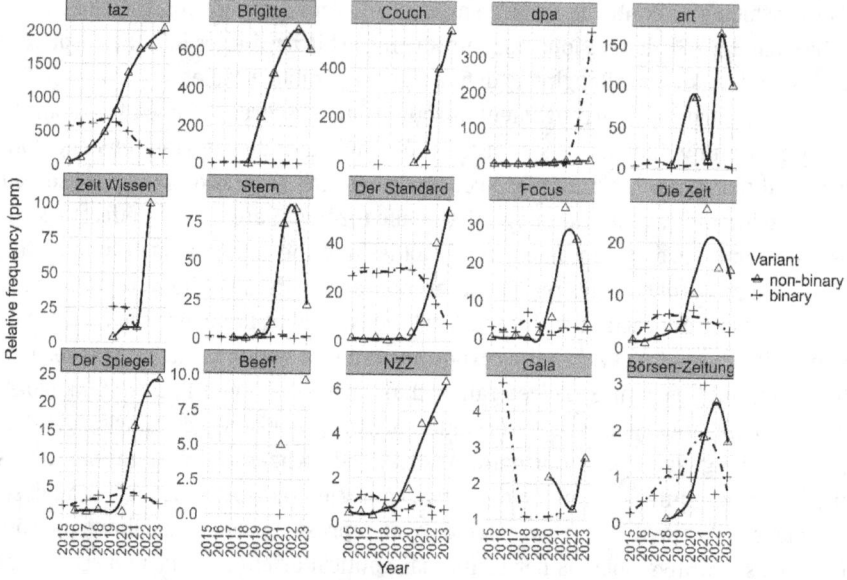

Fig. 3: Relative frequencies of binary and non-binary forms by source and year.

and audience – in this case, "young and modern women"[11] – might influence the use of gender-inclusive strategies. However, the status of *Couch* as a driver of change is questionable due to its significantly smaller audience and reach, especially when compared to *Brigitte* (0.19 million readers vs. 1.25 million readers).

Beyond that, only a few other sources show a clear upward trend in the use of non-binary forms over time, though at much lower frequencies (as indicated by the y-axis labels). These sources include the left-leaning Austrian daily *Der Standard*, the news magazine *Der Spiegel*, and the Swiss daily *Neue Zürcher Zeitung* (NZZ).[12] While NZZ has traditionally been viewed as liberal, it is increasingly criticized for its conservative or right-wing leanings (Eigenmann and Loser 2017). It frequently publishes critical articles on gender-inclusive language, making the increase in non-binary forms surprising. This shift may be explained by meta-linguistic usage, where gender-inclusive forms are used ironically or critically in articles discussing

---

[11] https://www.ad-alliance.de/cms/portfolio/print/portfolio.html?p=/print/portfolio/couch, accessed: 27 January 2025.

[12] Until 2022, the popular science magazine *ZEIT Wissen* also exhibited an increase in non-binary forms. However, in 2023, neither binary nor non-binary forms are attested in our subcorpus. This might be due to new editorial guidelines that we do not have access to, or mistakes in the DeReKo compilation.

gender issues: Waldendorf (2023: 16) highlights similar critical or mocking uses in the conservative German newspaper *Die Welt*.

For binary variants, most sources exhibit a generally decreasing or flattening trend. The only exception is *dpa*, the German Press Agency,[13] which shows a strong increase in the use of binary forms and remains the only source where binary variants outnumber non-binary ones. This increase can be attributed to the use of slashes, particularly in the forms *Autor/in* and *Autor/innen* ('author(s)'), which appeared 25,680 times in 2022 and 2023. In 2021, *dpa* committed to avoiding masculine generics and adopting gender-inclusive language.[14] Since authors' names are typically included in every press release, it is likely that masculine generics like *Autor* and *Autoren* were replaced with slash constructions following this policy change. Thus, *dpa* serves as an example of regulated change, where editorial decisions notably shape linguistic practices. Interestingly, despite the official acceptance of the slash as the only gender-inclusive form by the Council for German Orthography, its use remains rare outside of *dpa* (see Figures 1 and 2). This highlights the limited influence of normative regulations when it comes to conveying social meaning through language.

The distribution of gender symbols across text types has also been shown to vary in other corpora. For example, in the case of the city website of Hamburg, the majority of gender symbols are limited to specific subpages (Müller-Spitzer et al. 2024a). Therefore, claims about the frequency of gender symbols must always account for the textual basis and the inconsistent distribution across different text types. Ideally, the use of gender symbols should always be understood in the context of all personal nouns in a given text to accurately capture the relationships between them (Müller-Spitzer et al. 2024c). The following section addresses this by comparing the frequency of gender-inclusive orthographies with that of regular inflectional forms for a set of preselected nouns.

4.2 Lexicon-based approach

As outlined in the previous section, one of the challenges in researching personal nouns using corpus linguistic methods lies in the fact that the overall population of these forms remains unknown. Consequently, it is difficult to contextualize differ-

---

[13] The German Press Agency (*dpa*) is a news agency that provides current and neutral information to other media outlets, rather than publishing directly for end readers like newspapers or magazines do. It serves as a central source of news that editorial teams can process and publish individually.
[14] https://www.presseportal.de/pm/8218/4947122, accessed: 25 March 2024.

ent realizations of the same personal noun or to comprehensively relate all person references within a given corpus (Sökefeld et al. 2023: 34). Another issue pertains to the dual interpretation of the masculine base form as either gender-specific or generic. This distinction depends on contextual cues, which can be analyzed manually in small-scale corpus data (Müller-Spitzer et al. 2024c; Waldendorf 2023) but pose significant challenges in large-scale corpora such as the one employed in our study.

The analysis that follows compares binary and non-binary gender-inclusive orthographic forms of a preselected set of 131 personal nouns with their masculine base forms – without differentiating between their gender-specific and generic usages – and with the feminine derivations formed by *-in*. Thus, the entire inflectional paradigm of each item is accounted for and can be extracted from the corpus, enabling more meaningful frequency comparisons. For instance, the paradigm for the noun AUTOR ('author') includes:

- masculine (generic and gender-specific): *Autor, Autors, Autoren*
- feminine: *Autorin, Autorinnen*
- binary: *Autor/-in, Autor/-innen* (including variants with capital *I* and parantheses)
- non-binary: *Autor*in, Autor*innen* (including variants with colon and underscore)

The search items were derived from a list of personal nouns provided by the *Duden* editorial team. This original list contains 10,000 personal nouns with systematic gender differentiation. From this, we selected the 145 nouns with the highest frequency scores in DeReKo. However, post-corpus analysis revealed the need to exclude 14 items. This exclusion applied to population nouns, which are predominantly used as attributive adjectives (e.g., *Stuttgarter Flughafen* 'Stuttgart Airport', *Frankfurter Bahnhof* 'Frankfurt Central Station') and only superficially resemble masculine personal nouns (e.g., *(der) Stuttgarter* '(the) man from Stuttgart'). Additionally, two lexemes (*Zähler* 'meter/counter' and *Wetter* 'weather') were excluded as they are primarily used with their other, non-human meaning, with rare exceptions where they refer to individuals (in the sense of 'someone who counts' and 'someone who bets'). The remaining 131 nouns, along with their inflectional forms and frequency data from DeReKo, are detailed in Table S4 of the Supplementary Material.

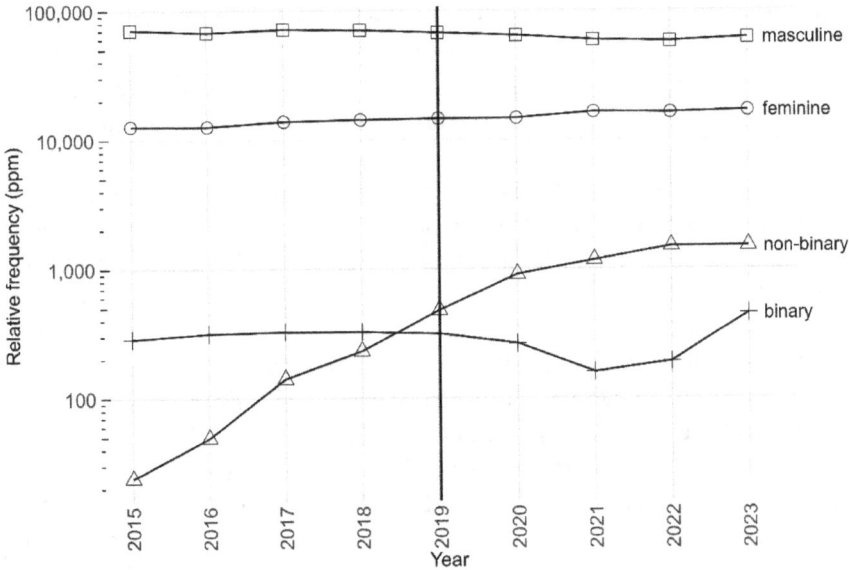

Fig. 4: Log-transformed relative frequencies of masculine, feminine, non-binary, and binary realizations for all 131 lexemes combined.

4.2.1 Development over time

Figure 4 illustrates the distribution of masculine, feminine, binary, and non-binary forms. The y-axis is log-transformed to prevent the curves for gender-inclusive variants from being obscured along the x-axis when raw frequencies are plotted.[15] Despite this transformation, the axis labels indicate raw frequencies, underscoring that masculine forms represent by far the most frequent and robust realization among the 131 lexemes. When aggregating all years, 84.85% of all tokens ($N = 9,787,168$) are masculine, 13.83% are feminine, 0.69% are non-binary, and 0.63% are binary.

As previously noted, the masculine forms may either refer to specific males or to mixed-gender groups – a distinction that can only be made through manual annotations and which is not represented in Figure 4. Feminine forms follow in sec-

---

[15] Figure S1 in the Supplementary Material presents raw frequency distributions, highlighting the relative rarity of gender-inclusive variants compared to feminine forms and, in particular, masculine forms, but obscuring trends for binary and non-binary forms due to their low frequency. A detailed view of individual gender-inclusive forms is provided in Figure S2, also using a log-transformed scale, for cases where granular trend analysis is required.

ond place, with an average of one tenth of the frequency of masculine forms. Non-binary forms exhibit a comparable exponential, though flattening, growth pattern, as observed in the corpus-driven analysis, surpassing binary forms in frequency between 2018 and 2019. From 2019 onwards, the frequency of the non-binary forms is constantly higher than that of the binary forms.

Similar to the analysis in Section 4.1.1, we applied a linear regression model to examine changes in forms before and after 2019, focusing on their relationship to the masculine base form after the amendment of Germany's civil status law. To address the non-normal distribution of relative frequencies, the data were log-transformed prior to analysis. The model demonstrates a strong fit, with an R-squared value of 0.9786, indicating that approximately 98% of the variance in the data is explained. Furthermore, the overall model is highly significant, as evidenced by the F-statistic (183) and its p-value ($p < 0.001$).

The main effects for the feminine, non-binary, and binary variants are all highly significant ($p < 0.001$), with negative coefficients confirming that these forms were used less frequently than the masculine base form prior to 2019. The main effect of the time group (before vs. after 2019) is not significant, indicating that the frequency of the masculine base form remained stable over time.

The interaction terms reveal how the use of gender-inclusive forms shifted after 2019. The feminine and binary variants show no significant change compared to the masculine base form, suggesting their relative stability over time. In contrast, the non-binary forms exhibit a significant increase ($p < 0.001$) in relation to the masculine base form after 2019. While non-binary variants remain a rare phenomenon overall, this substantial relative growth highlights their emerging relevance in the linguistic landscape.

Interestingly, when excluding the newspaper *taz* from the model, the binary variant also shows a significant increase after 2019 ($p < 0.05$), whereas it is not significant in the model that includes *taz*. The increase of non-binary variants remains highly significant, also without *taz*. This again suggests that while *taz* modulates certain patterns, linguistic variation persists across the remaining sources. Therefore, the observed changes in gender-inclusive forms are not solely driven by *taz* but are distributed more broadly within the corpus.

These findings underscore the importance of comparing different realizations of personal nouns and accounting for cross-source variation. This allows us to distinguish between absolute surface frequencies and relative developments in relation to base forms as well as source-specific effects, providing deeper insights into patterns of gender-inclusive language use.

4.2.2 Lexical variance

Next, we use the data from the lexicon-based approach for detailed analyses on the lexical level. This enables an examination of the distribution of masculine, feminine, binary, and non-binary realizations for each of the 131 items. In the following discussion, items are presented as lemmas in small capitals.

Masculine realizations are overwhelmingly dominant for the majority of lexemes: 126 out of 131 items (96.18%) appear as masculine in at least 50% of cases. Figure 5 illustrates proportions for the 20 most frequent items in our corpus, while Table 1 gives an overview of the top ten items in each category. Only four items exhibit a majority (i.e., more than 50%) of feminine forms. Two of these are political terms: KANZLER ('chancellor', 63.27% feminine) and BUNDESKANZLER ('federal chancellor', 51.21% feminine) – a pattern explained by Angela Merkel's 16-year tenure as German chancellor (2005–2021). This period also influenced other linguistic phenomena, such as compound formation with feminine first elements (Ochs 2024). Additionally, two job titles traditionally associated with women, according to stereotype research (Misersky et al. 2014), show feminine forms in more than 50% of instances: KASSIERER ('cashier', 61.64%) and SEKRETÄR ('secretary', 60.19%).

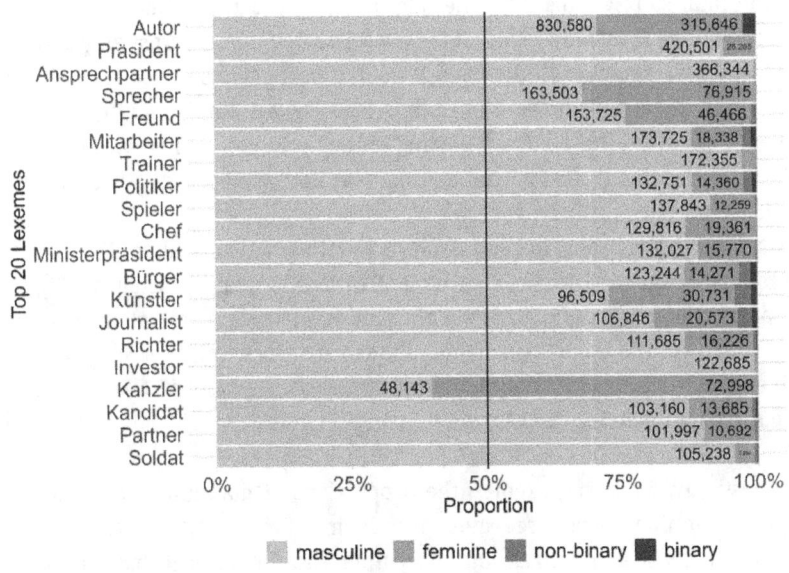

Fig. 5: Proportions of masculine, feminine, non-binary and binary realizations for the 20 most frequent items. Raw frequencies are indicated within the columns.

An exception to this trend is the lexeme ERZIEHER ('preschool teacher'), where neither feminine (41.01%) nor masculine (48.02%) realizations exceed 50%. This is not coincidental: ERZIEHER has the highest proportion of gender-inclusive realizations among all items, with 10.96% when binary and non-binary forms are summarized. The final column of Table 1 lists the remaining most frequent items based on the proportion of gender-inclusive forms. The data snippet highlights that gender-inclusive realizations remain a marginal phenomenon overall, with proportions almost universally below 10%. Notably, however, at least one gender-inclusive token (binary or non-binary) is attested for each of the 131 lexemes.

These distributions indicate that, in addition to considering the corpus base and sources when interpreting the frequency and patterns of gender-inclusive orthographies, it is essential to account for lexical differences as well (Müller-Spitzer et al. 2024c: 11). Analyzing only one single lexeme as a case study – for example, as done by Adler and Hansen (2020) or Krome (2021) – especially if, by chance, it represents an extreme case such as ERZIEHER, would not provide sufficient evidence to draw general conclusions about the broader use of gender-inclusive orthographies. It is therefore necessary to approach gender-inclusive orthographies from both aggregated perspectives, to understand overarching trends, and with detailed analyses, to capture the nuances of individual lexemes.

In the final step, we focus on the micro-diachronic development of a set of items, as so far we have only reported the overall distributions across all years. We selected the ten lexemes with the highest overall proportions of gender-inclusive forms to track their development over time (see Table 1, final column). Figure 6 displays the results of this analysis, starting in the upper left corner with ERZIEHER (10.96% gender-inclusive forms) and ending with TEILNEHMER in the bottom right corner (3.85% gender-inclusive forms).

For all items, the proportions in 2023 are as follows: 1) masculine, 2) feminine, 3) non-binary, 4) binary (with the exception of TÄNZER 'dancer', which has a slightly higher proportion of feminine forms). This pattern mirrors the overall distribution shown in Figure 4. The proportion of masculine forms is generally decreasing, while non-binary realizations are slowly gaining ground across this set of items. The most notable increase is seen with ERZIEHER, which reached 13.79% non-binary forms in 2023.

Interestingly, for some lexemes, the proportions of masculine and feminine forms are beginning to converge, most prominently for SCHÜLER, LESER and KÜNSTLER. For ERZIEHER and TÄNZER, the masculine and feminine forms are nearly equally frequent in 2023. We interpret this as an increase in the use of pair forms, which are captured as two separate tokens (one masculine, one feminine) in our search.

Tab. 1: Overview of the top ten items with the highest overall proportions of masculine, feminine, binary, and non-binary forms. For clarity, items are presented in their lemma form.

rank	masculine	feminine	binary	non-binary	binary + non-binary
1	HERSTELLER 99.75% 'producer'	KANZLER 63.26% 'chancellor'	ERZIEHER 6.74% 'preschool teacher'	MIETER 5.93% 'tenant'	ERZIEHER 10.96% 'preschool teacher'
2	COACH 99.66% 'coach'	KASSIERER 61.63% 'cashier'	ANWOHNER 3.55% 'resident'	ANWOHNER 4.83% 'resident'	MIETER 9.25% 'tenant'
3	ANSPRECHPARTNER 99.59% 'contact (person)'	SEKRETÄR 60.19% 'secretary'	MIETER 3.32% 'tenant'	ERZIEHER 4.23% 'preschool teacher'	ANWOHNER 8.38% 'resident'
4	ANBIETER 99.49% 'provider'	BUNDESKANZLER 51.21% 'federal chancellor'	BEWOHNER 2.38% 'inhabitant'	BEWOHNER 3.82% 'inhabitant'	BEWOHNER 6.19% 'inhabitant'
5	SPONSOR 99.42% 'sponsor'	SÄNGER 47.27% 'singer'	SCHÜLER 2.37% 'pupil'	SCHÜLER 3.61% 'pupil'	SCHÜLER 5.98% 'pupil'
6	INVESTOR 99.37% 'investor'	SOZIALMINISTER 42.48% 'social minister'	AUTOR 2.26% 'author'	LESER 3.46% 'reader'	LESER 5.28% 'reader'
7	ANLEGER 99.22% 'investor'	SCHAUSPIELER 41.42% 'actor'	RADFAHRER 1.97% 'cyclist'	TÄNZER 3.22% 'dancer'	TÄNZER 4.95% 'dancer'
8	HÄNDLER 98.57% 'retailer'	TÄNZER 41.05% 'dancer'	WÄHLER 1.93% 'voter'	KÜNSTLER 2.88% 'artist'	RADFAHRER 4.34% 'cyclist'
9	AUFSTEIGER 98.57% 'riser'	ERZIEHER 41.01% 'preschool teacher'	LESER 1.82% 'reader'	WISSENSCHAFTLER 2.78% 'scientist'	KÜNSTLER 3.93% 'artist'
10	ARBEITGEBER 97.96% 'employer'	SCHRIFTSTELLER 35.94% 'writer'	ZUHÖRER 1.73% 'listener'	RADFAHRER 2.37% 'cyclist'	TEILNEHMER 3.85% 'participant'

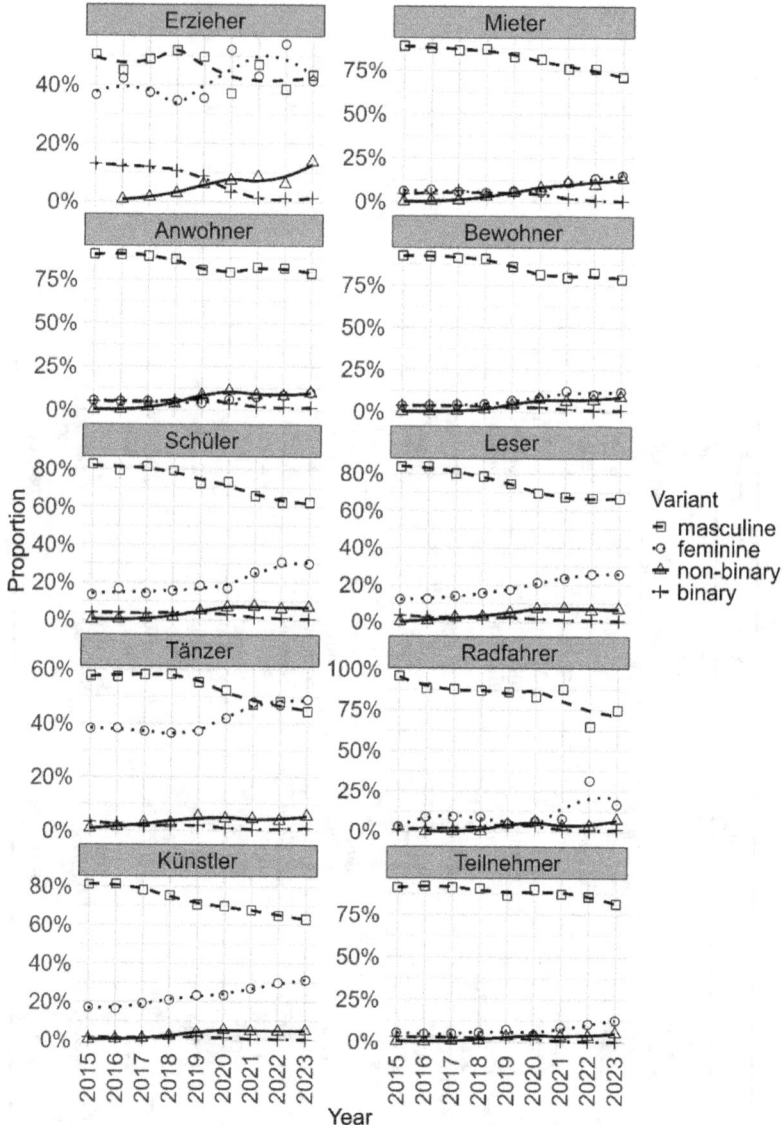

Fig. 6: Proportions of masculine, feminine, non-binary, and binary realizations for the ten lexemes with the highest overall share of gender-inclusive forms, with the trend reading from top-left to bottom-right.

It is also noteworthy that these ten items are primarily general or unspecific role nouns: MIETER, ANWOHNER, BEWOHNER, SCHÜLER, LESER, RADFAHRER and TEILNEHMER. A possible interpretation is that general personal nouns, which often refer to unspecific groups, are predominantly used in masculine generic forms. These can now be replaced by gender-inclusive variants or pair forms. In contrast, lexemes that are mostly used to refer to specific individuals – such as authors in news articles or political figures like KANZLER or PRÄSIDENT – are less likely to adopt gender-inclusive (or rather, gender-unspecific) variants. For KANZLER, only 0.06% of all tokens are gender-inclusive (binary or non-binary), for BUNDESKANZLER, it is even less (0.04%); and for PRÄSIDENT, it is only 0.01%. Data like this help us understand the lexical domains in which gender-inclusive forms are being used. To date, there is little empirical data on these lexical distributions. Further investigations into the semantic classes of personal nouns could help clarify this trend.

The lexemes with the highest proportion of masculine forms (Table 1, second column) are also predominantly general role nouns.[16] However, they differ from those discussed before in that, while they can refer to humans, they are more likely to denote non-human agents. Examples include HERSTELLER, ANSPRECHPARTNER, ANBIETER, and SPONSOR, which are more frequently applied to entities such as companies or sports clubs rather than individual humans. However, our data does not allow us to disentangle the different uses of masculine forms, as we cannot distinguish between them solely based on their surface form. This issue affects not only the distinction between human and non-human references, but also between gender-specific and generic uses of masculine forms. Only by differentiating between these two uses can we determine whether generic masculine forms are being replaced by gender-inclusive alternatives, while specific masculines may remain stable over time.

Currently, automatic detection of masculine generics is not possible (Sökefeld et al. 2023: 38). To our knowledge, only one study has addressed this issue through manual annotations of German press texts, differentiating human and non-human as well as gender-specific and generic uses of the masculine (Müller-Spitzer et al. 2024c). Given the extensive nature of our dataset, manual annotations are not feasible. However, focused investigations on smaller text samples or specific lexemes could provide valuable insights into this phenomenon. For instance, Waldendorf (2023: 7) conducted a manual analysis of a small sample of her corpus, finding that masculine generics still dominate, although her case study does not take a

---

[16] COACH is an exception in this context, as it holds a special status as an English loanword and is rarely, if ever, used in its feminine derivation, Coachin (appearing in only in 0.33% of cases according to Kopf 2022: 89).

diachronic approach. Moreover, her analysis does not address masculine specifics, which would be necessary to contextualize the use of masculine generic forms. Sökefeld (forthcoming) analyzed a small sample of lexemes, showing that masculine generics are declining to varying degrees, with an accompanying rise in gender-inclusive forms. This suggests a similar trend may be occurring in our data. However, based on our dataset, we can only conclude that masculine and feminine forms are generally stable over time, while non-binary forms remain a rising but still marginal phenomenon – at least in the written press texts analyzed here. Certain lexical items show a stronger tendency towards gender-inclusive usage, while others, particularly those ambiguous between human and non-human references, remain largely unaffected by these new variants.

5 Conclusion and outlook

Generating linguistic visibility and representing gender diversity is a key goal in both feminist and queer linguistic endeavors. While feminist approaches have established binary linguistic forms, the recognition of gender identities beyond the binary calls for new modes of linguistic representation. Our corpus-driven diachronic analysis of German press texts demonstrates that, at present, this is predominantly achieved through the use of word-internal gender symbols. The asterisk (*Schüler*innen*) and the colon (*Schüler:innen*) are by far dominant, while the underscore (*Schüler_innen*) plays a negligible role in our corpus. Binary word-internal forms, such as the capital *I* (*SchülerInnen*), are generally on the decline, especially since the amendment of the German civil status law in 2019. In contrast, other studies have found fully-fledged binary pair forms (*Schülerinnen und Schüler*) to be rising at a rate comparable to that of the non-binary asterisk and colon (Waldendorf 2023: 8). This suggests a domain-specific differentiation: Binary gender representations appear at the noun phrase level, while non-binary identities are conveyed word-internally.

Our lexicon-based approach further supplements these findings by providing insights into the frequency of gender-inclusive forms relative to conventional inflectional forms. We observe that masculine forms remain the dominant realization across lexemes and years, followed by feminine forms, with both binary and non-binary variants being relatively rare. Statistical analyses, however, showed that non-binary forms experience a significant increase in relation to the masculine base form after 2019, highlighting the importance of distinguishing between absolute surface frequencies and changes relative to base forms. Besides that, lexical choices are crucial when examining gender-inclusive orthographies. Our data indicate that the realization of gender-inclusive forms is highly dependent on individual lexemes and their semantic domains.

The influence of specific sources on the development of gender-inclusive language also warrants further investigation. For non-binary forms, the alternative-left newspaper *taz* is the primary contributor, followed by the women's magazine *Brigitte* and the lifestyle magazine *Couch*. Besides that, only a few sources show a clear upward trend in the use of non-binary forms. However, fitting the linear regression models without *taz* revealed that all changes in the use of gender-inclusive orthographies remained significant for the remaining 14 sources after 2019. Therefore, while *taz* modulates certain effects and may be a leading innovator, neographies spread more widely across the corpus. It remains to be seen whether this spread continues, whether trends begin to decrease again, or whether neographies become niche phenomena in certain media.

With this study, we provide quantitative baselines to the growing body of research on gender inclusive German. Understanding the development, frequency, and distribution of new orthographical forms is essential for fostering more productive discussions on the topic, both in public discourse and academic fields. Furthermore, our findings can serve as an empirical foundation for developing usage-oriented guidelines on gender-inclusive language, such as those used in universities and state institutions. Further analyses of additional press sources (e.g., queer magazines) and other text types (particularly social media) will help illuminate the contexts and domains in which gender-inclusive forms are most commonly used.

References

Acke, Hanna. 2019. Sprachwandel durch feministische Sprachkritik. *Zeitschrift für Literaturwissenschaft und Linguistik* 49(2). 303–320. https://doi.org/10.1007/s41244-019-00135-1.

Acke, Hanna. 2023. Excessiveness in a German social media debate on gender-fair language. *Neuphilologische Mitteilungen* 124(1). 46–77. https://doi.org/10.51814/nm.122738.

Adler, Astrid and Karolina Hansen. 2020. Studenten, Studentinnen, Studierende? Aktuelle Verwendungspräferenzen bei Personenbezeichnungen. *Muttersprache* 130(1). 47–63.

Adler, Astrid and Albrecht Plewnia. 2019. Die Macht der großen Zahlen. Aktuelle Spracheinstellungen in Deutschland. In Ludwig M. Eichinger and Albrecht Plewnia (eds.), *Neues vom heutigen Deutsch. Empirisch—Methodisch—Theoretisch*, 141–162. Berlin, Boston: De Gruyter. https://doi.org/10.1515/9783110622591-008.

AG Feministisch Sprachhandeln. 2014. Anregungen zum antidiskriminierenden Sprachhandeln. https://feministisch-sprachhandeln.org/wp-content/uploads/2015/04/sprachleitfaden_zweite_auflage.pdf. Accessed: 2 February 2025.

Bailey, April H., Marianne LaFrance and John F. Dovidio. 2019. Is man the measure of all things? A social cognitive account of androcentrism. *Personality and Social Psychology Review* 23(4). 307–331. https://doi.org/10.1177/1088868318782848.

Bast, Jennifer, Jürgen Maier, Georg Albert and Jan Georg Schneider. 2024. Gendered debates? The use of gender-sensitive language in German televised debates, 1997–2022. *European Journal of Politics and Gender* 1–25. https://doi.org/10.1332/25151088Y2024D000000023.

Blake, Christopher and Christoph Klimmt. 2010. Geschlechtergerechte Formulierungen in Nachrichtentexten. *Publizistik* 55. 289–304. https://doi.org/10.1007/s11616-010-0093-2.

Braun, Friederike, Susanne Oelkers, Karin Rogalski, Janine Bosak and Sabine Sczesny. 2007. "Aus Gründen der Verständlichkeit …": Der Einfluss generisch maskuliner und alternativer Personenbezeichnungen auf die kognitive Verarbeitung von Texten. *Psychologische Rundschau* 58(3). 183–189. https://doi.org/10.1026/0033-3042.58.3.183.

Burnett, Heather and Céline Pozniak. 2021. Political dimensions of gender inclusive writing in Parisian universities. *Journal of Sociolinguistics* 25(5). 808–831. https://doi.org/10.1111/josl.12489.

Butler, Judith. 1988. Performative acts and gender constitution: An essay in phenomenology and feminist theory. *Theatre Journal* 40(4). 519–531. https://doi.org/10.2307/3207893.

Diewald, Gabriele. 2018. Zur Diskussion: Geschlechtergerechte Sprache als Thema der germanistischen Linguistik – exemplarisch exerziert am Streit um das sogenannte generische Maskulinum. *Zeitschrift für germanistische Linguistik* 46. 283–299. https://doi.org/10.1515/zgl-2018-0016.

Diewald, Gabriele and Anja Steinhauer. 2020. *Handbuch geschlechtergerechte Sprache. Wie Sie angemessen und verständlich gendern*. Dudenverlag.

Doleschal, Ursula. 1992. *Movierung im Deutschen: Eine Darstellung der Bildung und Verwendung weiblicher Personenbezeichnungen*. München: Lincom Europa.

Eigenmann, David and Philipp Loser. 2017. Nach Deutschland, nach rechts. *Tages-Anzeiger* https://www.tagesanzeiger.ch/nach-deutschland-nach-rechts-957458637553. Accessed: 2 February 2025.

Eisenberg, Peter. 2020. Zur Vermeidung sprachlicher Diskriminierung im Deutschen. *Muttersprache* 130(1). 3–16.

Eisenberg, Peter. 2022. Weder geschlechtergerecht noch gendersensibel. *APuZ Aus Politik und Zeitgeschichte* 5–7. https://www.bpb.de/shop/zeitschriften/apuz/geschlechtergerechte-sprache-2022/346091/weder-geschlechtergerecht-noch-gendersensibel. Accessed: 2 February 2025.

Fleischer, Wolfgang and Irmhild Barz. 2012. *Wortbildung der deutschen Gegenwartssprache*. Berlin, Boston: De Gruyter. https://doi.org/10.1515/9783110256659.

Friedrich, Martin C. G., Vanessa Drößler, Nicole Oberlehberg and Elena Heise. 2021. The influence of the gender asterisk ("Gendersternchen") on comprehensibility and interest. *Frontiers in Psychology* 12. 1–11. https://doi.org/10.3389/fpsyg.2021.760062.

Friedrich, Martin C. G., Sebastian Gajewski, Katharina Hagenberg, Claudia Wenz and Elena Heise. 2024. Does the gender asterisk ("Gendersternchen") as a special form of gender-fair language impair comprehensibility? *Discourse Processes* 61(9). 439–461. https://doi.org/10.1080/0163853X.2024.2362027.

Genderleicht. 2024. Genderstern, Doppelpunkt und Binnen-I kurz und knapp erklärt. https://www.genderleicht.de/genderzeichen. Accessed: 2 February 2025.

Glim, Stefanie, Anna Körner, Holden Härtl and Ralf Rummer. 2023. Early ERP indices of gender-biased processing elicited by generic masculine role nouns and the feminine–masculine pair form. *Brain and Language* 242. 1–7. https://doi.org/10.1016/j.bandl.2023.105290.

Gygax, Pascal, Ute Gabriel, Oriane Sarrasin, Jane Oakhill and Alan Garnham. 2008. Generically intended, but specifically interpreted: When beauticians, musicians, and mechanics are all men. *Language and Cognitive Processes* 23(3). 464–485. https://doi.org/10.1080/01690960701702035.

Hellinger, Marlis and Hadumod Bußmann (eds.). 2001. *Gender across languages: The linguistic representation of women and men, volume 1*. Amsterdam, Philadelphia: John Benjamins.

Hellinger, Marlis and Hadumod Bußmann. 2003. Engendering female visibility in German. In Marlis Hellinger and Hadumod Bußmann (eds.), *Gender across languages: The linguistic representation of women and men. Volume 3*, 141–174. Amsterdam, Philadelphia: John Benjamins Publishing Co.

Jourian, T. J. 2015. Queering constructs: Proposing a dynamic gender and sexuality model. *The Educational Forum* 79(4). 459–474. https://doi.org/10.1080/00131725.2015.1068900.

Jäckle, Sebastian. 2022. Per aspera ad astra – Eine politikwissenschaftliche Analyse der Akzeptanz des Gendersterns in der deutschen Bevölkerung auf Basis einer Online-Umfrage. *Politische Vierteljahresschrift* 63(3). 469–497. https://doi.org/10.1007/s11615-022-00380-z.

Keith, Nina, Kristine Hartwig and Tobias Richter. 2022. Ladies first or ladies last: Do masculine generics evoke a reduced and later retrieval of female exemplars? *Collabra: Psychology* 8. https://doi.org/10.1525/collabra.32964.

Kopf, Kristin. 2022. Ist Sharon Manager? Anglizismen und das generische Maskulinum. In Gabriele Diewald and Damaris Nübling (eds.), *Genus – Sexus – Gender*, 65–104. Berlin, Boston: De Gruyter. https://doi.org/10.1515/9783110746396-003.

Kotthoff, Helga. 2017. Von Syrx, Sternchen, großem I und bedeutungsschweren Strichen. Über geschlechtergerechte Personenbezeichnungen in Texten und die Kreation eines schrägen Registers. In *Sprache Und Geschlecht. Band 1: Sprachpolitiken Und Grammatik*, 91–115. Duisburg: Universitätsverlag Rhein-Ruhr.

Kotthoff, Helga. 2023. Gendern unter soziolinguistischer Perspektive. *Deutsche Sprache* 3. 181–220. https://doi.org/10.37307/j.1868-775X.2023.03.02.

Kotthoff, Helga and Damaris Nübling. 2018. *Genderlinguistik: Eine einführung in Sprache, Gespräch und Geschlecht*. 1st edn. Tübingen: Narr.

Kotthoff, Helga and Damaris Nübling. 2024. *Genderlinguistik: Eine Einführung in Sprache, Gespräch und Geschlecht*. 2nd edn. Tübingen: Narr.

Krome, Sabine. 2020. Zwischen gesellschaftlichem Diskurs und Rechtschreibnormierung: Geschlechtergerechte Sprache als Herausforderung für gelungene Textrealisation. *Muttersprache* 130(1). 64–78.

Krome, Sabine. 2021. Gendern zwischen Sprachpolitik, orthografischer Norm, Sprach-und Schreibgebrauch. Bestandsaufnahme und orthografische Perspektiven zu einem umstrittenen Thema. *Sprachreport* 37. 22–29. https://doi.org/10.14618/SR-2-2021-KROM.

Kupietz, Marc, Cyril Belica, Holger Keibel and Andreas Witt. 2010. The German reference corpus DeReKo: A primordial sample for linguistic research. In *Proceedings of the seventh international conference on language resources and evaluation (LREC 2010)*, 1848–1854.

Kupietz, Marc, Harald Lüngen, Pawel Kamocki and Andreas Witt. 2018. The German reference corpus DeReKo: New developments – new opportunities. In *Proceedings of the 11th international conference on language resources and evaluation (LREC 2018)*, 4353–4360.

Kupisch, Tanja, Miriam Geiß, Natalia Mitrofanova and Marit Westergaard. 2022. Structural and phonological cues for gender assignment in monolingual and bilingual children acquiring German. Experiments with real and nonce words. *Glossa: A Journal of General Linguistics* 7(1). 1–37. https://doi.org/10.16995/glossa.5696.

Kurfer, Tobias. 2024. Schlecht informiert: Gendersprache in den Medien. In Ewa Trutkowski and André Meinunger (eds.), *Gendern – auf Teufel*in komm raus?*, 235–264. Kulturverlag Kadmos.

Kurz, Pia and Hannah De Mulder. 2023. A star is born? The German gender star and its effects on mental representation. *Psychology of Language and Communication* 27(1). 384–404. https://doi.org/10.58734/PLC-2023-0018.

Körner, Anita, Bleen Abraham, Ralf Rummer and Fritz Strack. 2022. Gender representations elicited by the gender star form. *Journal of Language and Social Psychology* 41. 553–571. https://doi.org/10.1177/0261927X221080181.

Lev, Arlene Istar. 2004. *Transgender emergence: Therapeutic guidelines for working with gender-variant people and their families*. Binghamton: Haworth Clinical Practice Press.

Link, Sabrina. 2024. The use of gender-fair language in Austria, Germany, and Switzerland: A contrastive, corpus-based study. *Lingua* 308. 103787. https://doi.org/10.1016/j.lingua.2024.103787.

Löhr, Ronja A. 2021. Gendergerechte Personenbezeichnungen 2.0. Wie nichtbinäre Personen den Genderstern und andere Bezeichnungsvarianten beurteilen. *Muttersprache* 131(2). 172–182. https://doi.org/10.53371/60206.

Löhr, Ronja A. 2022. "Ich denke, es ist sehr wichtig, dass sich so viele Menschen wie möglich repräsentiert fühlen". In Gabriele Diewald and Damaris Nübling (eds.), *Genus – Sexus – Gender*, 349–380. Berlin, Boston: De Gruyter. https://doi.org/10.1515/9783110746396-012.

Lüngen, Harald and C. Michael Sperberg-McQueen. 2012. A TEI P5 document grammar for the IDS text model. *Journal of the Text Encoding Initiative* 3. 1–18. https://doi.org/10.4000/jtei.508.

Meineke, Eckhard. 2023. *Studien zum genderneutralen Maskulinum*. Heidelberg: Universitätsverlag Winter.

Meuleneers, Paul. 2024. On the "invention" of the Gendersprache in German media discourse. In Falco Pfalzgraf (ed.), *Public attitudes towards gender-inclusive language: A multilingual perspective*, 159–182. Berlin, Boston: De Gruyter. https://doi.org/10.1515/9783111202280-007.

Misersky, Julia, Pascal M. Gygax, Paolo Canal, Ute Gabriel, Alan Garnham, Friederike Braun, Tania Chiarini, Kjellrun Englund, Adriana Hanulikova, Anton Öttl, Jana Valdrova, Lisa Von Stockhausen and Sabine Sczesny. 2014. Norms on the gender perception of role nouns in Czech, English, French, German, Italian, Norwegian, and Slovak. *Behavior Research Methods* 46(3). 841–871. https://doi.org/10.3758/s13428-013-0409-z.

Motschenbacher, Heiko. 2013. Gentlemen before ladies? A corpus-based study of conjunct order in personal binomials. *Journal of English Linguistics* 41(3). 212–242. https://doi.org/10.1177/0075424213489993.

Müller-Spitzer, Carolin. 2022. Der Kampf ums Gendern. *Kursbuch* 209. 28–45.

Müller-Spitzer, Carolin and Samira Ochs. 2023. Geschlechtergerechte Sprache auf den Webseiten deutscher, österreichischer, schweizerischer und Südtiroler Städte. *Sprachreport* 39(2). 1–5. https://doi.org/10.14618/sr-2-2023_mue.

Müller-Spitzer, Carolin, Samira Ochs and Jan Oliver Rüdiger. 2024a. Auf der Suche nach Genderzeichen: Die Hamburger Volksinitiative "Schluss mit Gendersprache in Verwaltung und Bildung" und die Verwendung von Genderzeichen auf der Webseite der Stadt Hamburg. https://lingdrafts.hypotheses.org/2671. Accessed: 26 July 2024.

Müller-Spitzer, Carolin, Samira Ochs, Jan Oliver Rüdiger and Sascha Wolfer. 2024b. Die Herausbildung neuer Routinen der Personenreferenz am Beispiel der deutschen Weihnachts- und Neujahrsansprachen. In Paul Meuleneers, Lisa Zacharski, Evelyn Ferstl and Damaris Nübling (eds.), *Genderbezogene Personenreferenzen: Routinen und Innovationen*, 213–236. Helmut Buske Verlag.

Müller-Spitzer, Carolin, Samira Ochs, Jan Oliver Rüdiger and Sascha Wolfer. 2024c. Less than one percent of words would be affected by gender-inclusive language in German press texts. *Humanities and Social Sciences Communications* 11(1). 1–13. https://doi.org/10.1057/s41599-024-03769-w.

Müller-Spitzer, Carolin, Jan Oliver Rüdiger and Sascha Wolfer. 2022. Olaf Scholz gendert. Eine Analyse von Personenbezeichnungen in Weihnachts- und Neujahrsansprachen. Billet. https://lingdrafts.hypotheses.org/2370.

Ochs, Samira. 2024. Komposita mit den relationalen Zweitgliedern Gatte und Gattin – eine korpusbasierte Studie aus genderlinguistischer Perspektive. *Zeitschrift für Wortbildung / Journal of Word Formation* 8(1). 1–40. https://doi.org/10.21248/zwjw.2024.1.104.

Pabst, Laura Mathilde and Marlene Kollmayer. 2023. How to make a difference: The impact of gender-fair language on text comprehensibility amongst adults with and without an academic background. *Frontiers in Psychology, Section: Gender, Sex and Sexualities* 14. 1–9. https://doi.org/10.3389/fpsyg.2023.1234860.

Pfalzgraf, Falco. 2024. Attitudes of the purist association Verein Deutsche Sprache (VDS) towards gender-inclusive use of German. A conceptual expansion of the term linguistic purism. In Falco Pfalzgraf (ed.), *Public attitudes towards gender-inclusive language*, 183–208. Berlin, Boston: De Gruyter. https://doi.org/10.1515/9783111202280-008.

Pusch, Luise F. 1979. Der Mensch ist ein Gewohnheitstier, doch weiter kommt man ohne ihr—Eine Antwort auf Kalverkämpers Kritik an Trömel-Plötz' Artikel über 'Linguistik und Frauensprache'. *Linguistische Berichte* 63(79). 84–102.

Pusch, Luise F. 1984. *Das Deutsche als Männersprache: Aufsätze und Glossen zur feministischen Linguistik*. Berlin: Suhrkamp.

Rosar, Anne. 2022. Mann und Frau, Damen und Herren, Mütter und Väter – Zur (Ir-)Reversibilität der Geschlechterordnung in Binomialen. In Gabriele Diewald and Damaris Nübling (eds.), *Genus – Sexus – Gender*, 267–292. De Gruyter. https://doi.org/10.1515/9783110746396-009.

Rüdiger, Jan Oliver. 2023. Corpusexplorer. Computer software. http://corpusexplorer.de.

Schmitz, Dominic. 2024. Instances of bias: The gendered semantics of generic masculines in German revealed by instance vectors. *Zeitschrift für Sprachwissenschaft* 43(2). 295–325. https://doi.org/10.1515/zfs-2024-2010.

Schmitz, Dominic, Viktoria Schneider and Janina Esser. 2023. No generiaddress in sight: An exploration of the semantics of masculine generics in German. *Glossa Psycholinguistics* 2. https://doi.org/10.5070/G6011192.

Siegenthaler, Aline. 2024. *Deutsch- und französischsprachige Leitfäden für gendersensible Sprache: Normierung und Variation in Hochschulen und Behörden*. Geneva: Université de Genève dissertation.

Simon, Horst J. 2022. Sprache Macht Emotion. *APuZ Aus Politik und Zeitgeschichte* 5–7. https://www.bpb.de/shop/zeitschriften/apuz/geschlechtergerechte-sprache-2022/346087/sprache-macht-emotionen. Accessed: 2 February 2025.

Stefanowitsch, Anatol and Kirsten Middeke. 2023. Gender-marking -ess: The suffix that failed. *Zeitschrift für Anglistik Und Amerikanistik* 71(3). 293–319. https://doi.org/10.1515/zaa-2023-2029.

Sökefeld, Carla. 2021. Gender(un)gerechte Personenbezeichnungen: Derzeitiger Sprachgebrauch, Einflussfaktoren auf die Sprachwahl und diachrone Entwicklung. *Sprachwissenschaft* 46(1). 111–141.

Sökefeld, Carla. forthcoming. Student*innen, Student/innen oder Student:innen? Kurzformen der graphisch markierten Movierung quantitativ und diachron. In Alexander Werth (ed.), *Die Movierung. Formen, Funktionen, Bewertungen.*, Berlin, Boston: De Gruyter.

Sökefeld, Carla, Melanie Andresen, Johanna Binnewitt and Heike Zinsmeister. 2023. Personal noun detection for German. In Harry Bunt (ed.), *Proceedings of the 19th joint acl - iso workshop on interoperable semantic annotation (isa-19)*, Nancy. https://sigsem.uvt.nl/isa19/ISA-19-proceedings.pdf.

taz. 2025. Zahlen, Fakten, Sensationen. Alles über uns, unsere Geschichte und was es sonst über das "linke Tageszeitungsprojekt" zu wissen gibt. https://taz.de/Zahlen-Fakten-Sensationen/!v=b33ef2ce-205d-4e54-abfd-a8a63bb236da. Accessed: 2 February 2025.

Thorne, Nat, Andrew Kam-Tuck Yip, Walter Pierre Bouman, Ellen Marshall and Jon Arcelus. 2019. The terminology of identities between, outside and beyond the gender binary – a systematic review. *International Journal of Transgenderism* 20(2–3). 138–154. https://doi.org/10.1080/15532739.2019.1640654.

Tross, J. 2023. *Divers versus verständlich?: Gendergerechte Formulierungen in Texten der Leichten Sprache*. Berlin: Frank & Timme GmbH. https://doi.org/10.57088/978-3-7329-8945-4.

Truan, N. 2019. The discursive construction of the people in European political discourse: Semantics and pragmatics of a contested concept in German, French, and British parliamentary debates. In Jan Zienkowski and Ruth Breeze (eds.), *Imagining the Peoples of Europe: Populist discourses across the political spectrum*, vol. 83, 201–228. John Benjamins Publishing Company. https://doi.org/10.1075/dapsac.83.09tru.

Trutkowski, Ewa and Helmut Weiß. 2023. Zeugen gesucht! Zur Geschichte des generischen Maskulinums im Deutschen. *Linguistische Berichte* 273. https://doi.org/10.46771/9783967692792_2.

Trömel-Plötz, Senta. 1978. Linguistik und Frauensprache. *Linguistische Berichte* 57(78). 49–68.

Völkening, Lena. 2022. Ist Gendern mit Glottisverschlusslaut ungrammatisch? Ein Analysevorschlag für das Suffix [ʔɪn] als phonologisches Wort. *Zeitschrift für Wortbildung / Journal of Word Formation* 6(1). 58–80. https://doi.org/10.3726/zwjw.2022.01.02.

Waldendorf, Anica. 2023. Words of change: The increase of gender-inclusive language in German media. *European Sociological Review* 40(2). 1–18. https://doi.org/10.1093/esr/jcad044.

WDR. 2023. WDR-Studie: So gendern die Deutschen. https://www1.wdr.de/nachrichten/gender-umfrage-infratest-dimap-100.html. Accessed: 2 February 2025.

Zacharski, Lisa. 2024. Using pair forms, criticizing the gender star – attitudes towards binary and non-binary gender-inclusive language in German. In F. Pfalzgraf (ed.), *Public attitudes towards gender-inclusive language: A multilingual perspective*, 209–242. Berlin, Boston: De Gruyter. https://doi.org/10.1515/9783111202280-009.

Zacharski, Lisa and Evelyn Ferstl. 2023. Gendered representations of person referents activated by the nonbinary gender star in German: A word-picture matching task. *Discourse Processes* 60(4–5). 294–319. https://doi.org/10.1080/0163853X.2023.2199531.

Zifonun, Gisela. 2021. Eine Linguistin denkt nach über den Genderstern. *Sprachreport* 37(2). 46–51. https://doi.org/10.14618/sr-2-2021-zifo.

Jens Fleischhauer and Dila Turus
Women are sexy and men provoke – Gender stereotypes and the interpretation of the German adjective *aufreizend*

Abstract: In this paper, we explore the use of the German adjective *aufreizend* based on corpus data. *Aufreizend* has two basic uses that can be translated into English as (i) 'arousing' (in the sense of 'sexually appealing/attractive') and (ii) 'provocative'. Our analysis reveals that although multiple factors are responsible for determining *aufreizend*'s interpretation in combination with human referents, the main factor that determines the interpretation is the referent's sex. The arousing interpretation predominantly applies to female referents, while the provocative interpretation primarily occurs with male referents. We relate this difference to gender stereotypes existing in the minds of language speakers.

Keywords: adjectives, corpus linguistics, Gender stereotypes, German, synonymy

1 Introduction: Gender stereotypes in language

Up to the 1980s, German TV commercials portrayed women predominantly either as simple housewives or as young sex objects (Kotelmann and Mikos 1981). The gender stereotypes represented in German TV commercials have not changed much in later years (e.g., Mikos 1988; Knoll et al. 2011). However, the number of distinct role models has increased (Vennemann and Holtz-Bacha 2008). Gender stereotypes not only affect the portrayal of women in TV commercials but also influence societal perceptions of the academic abilities of girls and boys, particularly in mathematics and languages (e.g., Steffens and Jelenec 2011).

We use the term *stereotype* in its sense used in social psychology[1] (e.g., Wright and Taylor 2003: 433), which refers to "the beliefs, shared by members of one group,

---

[1] The term *stereotype* is used in various disciplines, and its usage is inconsistent both between and within the disciplines; see, for example, Fábián et al. (2022) and Ziem (2022).

Jens Fleischhauer, Institute of Linguistics, Heinrich-Heine-University Düsseldorf, e-mail: fleischhauer@phil.uni-duesseldorf.de
Dila Turus, Institute of Linguistics, Heinrich-Heine-University Düsseldorf, e-mail: dila.turus@uni-duesseldorf.de

about the shared characteristics of another group".[2] In the context of the present paper, we are particularly interested in gender stereotypes, which are "the psychological characteristics believed to be differentially associated with women and men in a particular cultural group" (Williams et al. 1999: 513). However, we do not limit the notion to "psychological characteristics"; instead, we extend it to include non-psychological aspects such as physical appearance.

Stereotypes form a set of propositions represented as beliefs. From a linguistic perspective, stereotypes – or better: (some of the) propositions forming a stereotype – can be associated with lexical items.[3] As Kilian (2005) argues, the propositions forming a stereotype do not constitute part of a lexeme's lexical meaning; rather, they are merely associated with it. Thus, they do not necessarily appear in each context of use and can be canceled or overridden. In a pancultural study, Williams et al. (1999) investigated whether particular adjectives are frequently associated with male or female referents (for details of the study, we refer to the original paper and the references cited therein). The adjectives associated with male and female stereotypes are listed in Table 1. Looking at the list, it is striking that males are mainly associated with adjectives specifying their behavior (in a broad sense), such as *aggressive*, *courageous*, and *rude*. In contrast, only two adjectives relate to their physical constitution (*robust*, *strong*). The adjectives associated with women also mainly belong to the psychological domain. However, two adjectives are related to physical appearance, i.e., *attractive* and *sexy*.[4]

Tab. 1: List of adjectives stereotypically associated with men and women (Williams et al. 1999: 519).

Sex	Stereotypical adjectives
men	active, adventurous, aggressive, ambitious, autocratic, coarse, courageous, cruel, daring, dominant, energetic, enterprising, forceful, independent, inventive, logical, masculine, progressive, robust, rude, self-confident, stern, strong, tough, unemotional
women	affected, affectionate, anxious, attractive, charming, complaining, curious, dependent, dreamy, emotional, fearful, feminine, fussy, meek, mild, sensitive, sexy, shy, soft-hearted, submissive, superstitious, talkative, timid, weak, whiny

---

2 The distinction often made in the research literature between auto- and heterostereotypes (e.g., Fábián et al. 2022), that is, regarding one's group or a foreign group, is not relevant to our analysis, as this distinction cannot be traced in relation to the corpus data.
3 Stereotypes do not have to be tied to lexemes but can also be connected at the phrasal level as well as other levels of grammar. See, for instance, Feilke (1989); Fiedler and Schmid (2001); Pümpel-Mader (2010) and Ziem (2022).
4 See in particular Hausen (1976) for a historical discussion of German gender stereotypes in the 18th and 19th centuries.

Also, this study shows that adjectives like *sexy* are more frequently associated with women than with men. We find linguistic reflexes of these stereotypes in actual language use. Women, for example, are more often characterized in terms of their physical appearance than men (Moon 2014: 10). This has also been demonstrated, for instance, with respect to German fairy tales by Robinson (2010). Based on a detailed analysis of the Brothers Grimm's fairy tales, Robinson finds that physical appearance is the most important semantic category for characterizing girls. 58.5% of the adjective tokens used with nouns denoting girls refer to physical appearance; the adjective *schön* 'pretty' is particularly frequent. With nouns denoting boys, adjectives denoting physical appearance make up just 14% of all adjective tokens. The two categories mental skills (e.g., *klug* 'smart', *dumm* 'dumb') and size (e.g., *groß* 'tall', *klein* 'small') occur more frequently with nouns denoting boys than with nouns denoting girls (cf. Table 2).

Tab. 2: Token frequency and absolute token numbers of three semantic adjectival categories combined with nouns denoting girls and boys in the Brothers Grimm fairy tales (Robinson 2010: 103).

	'girls'	'boys'
physical appearance	140 (58.5%)	19 (14%)
mental skills	7 (3%)	25 (18.75%)
size	2 (1%)	18 (13.5%)
total numbers	242	134

Robinson shows that the frequency with which modifiers of different categories are used depends on the speaker's gender. Simplified, the picture that emerges is that girls are beautiful or ugly, while boys are clever, stupid, tall, or short. These results fit well with what we said above about gender stereotypes, which can be seen in the assignment of adjectives to male or female referents. In this paper, we take up this topic but show that the interpretation of a specific adjective – *aufreizend* – depends on whether the referent is male or female. The idea we put forward is that the interpretation of *aufreizend* varies between 'arousing' and 'provocative' depending on stereotypes associated with the speaker's gender. As we will show below, the first use predominantly shows up with female referents, whereas the second is more often found with male referents. Women are reduced to their outward appearance and are characterized by *aufreizend* as (sexually) attractive or as behaving – or dressing – in a sexually arousing way. With regard to men, *aufreizend* refers primarily to their behavior, which is interpreted as provocative. The appearance of the men or their clothing does not play a primary role but rather how they behave. As this is in line with the gender stereotypes outlined above, it shows that these do indeed have an influence on interpretation and therefore – as we conclude from this data – have linguistic reality.

That stereotypes associated with characteristics of human individuals can have an influence on the interpretation of adjectives has been shown, for example, by Moon (2014: 31). This paper deals specifically with age stereotypes and shows that, for instance, *confused* has a different meaning when used as a modifier for a noun describing a young person ('misguided views' or 'emotional turmoil') than when it serves as a modifier for a noun to describe an old person ('dementia'). Our study thus connects well with earlier work, although we adopt a different methodological approach and have a slightly different focus.

In Section 2, we discuss the different uses and interpretations of *aufreizend* in detail before formulating precise hypotheses regarding the factors that influence *aufreizend*'s interpretation in Section 3. Section 4, finally, presents the results of a corpus study validating the proposed hypotheses.

2 The adjective *aufreizend*

A search query in the digital version of the German dictionary *Duden* reveals one entry for the adjective *aufreizend*.[5] Its meaning is paraphrased as *lasziv, verführerisch, erregend*, which corresponds to 'lascivious/sexy, seductive, arousing, enticing' in English. The dictionary presents the two examples in (1) to illustrate the adjective's use:

(1) a. *aufreizende Posen*
    'arousing/sexy poses'
   b. *sie hat einen aufreizenden Gang*
    'she has an arousing/sexy walk'

The example in (1-a) characterizes someone's poses as being arousing, whereas in (1-b) a female's manner of walking is specified as arousing (the pronoun *sie* 'she' indicates that the referent is female).[6]

In (2), the adjective is used in combination with a male referent. It modifies the noun *Freundlichkeit* 'friendliness', which characterizes the behavior of the male referent. The interpretation of the example is not that the male referent is behaving arousingly but provocatively. The example comes from the German reference cor-

---

5 https://www.duden.de/rechtschreibung/aufreizend, accessed: 12 January 2024.
6 For an analysis of the perpetuation of gender stereotypes on linguistic examples, cf. Kotek et al. (2021) and the literature cited therein.

pus DeReKo (Leibniz-Institut für Deutsche Sprache 2021), which we also used for our corpus analysis described in Section 4.

(2) *In fast aufreizender Freundlichkeit widmet er sich dann den Grünen.*
'In almost provocative friendliness, he then devotes himself to the Green Party.'
(U21/SEP.05311 Süddeutsche Zeitung, 28/09/2021, p. 6; In geübter Gegnerschaft)

The two uses represented by the examples in (1) and (2) are paraphrased differently. *Aufreizend*'s use in (1), which we term the 'arousing interpretation', is paraphrased by expressions such as *erregend* 'arousing', *verführerisch* 'seductive' as well as *lasziv/sexy* 'sexy'. The use in (2) is paraphrased by, for instance, *provokant* 'provocative', *forsch* 'bold', and *frech* 'cheeky'. We refer to the second use as the 'provocative interpretation' of *aufreizend*.

Aufreizend is a relative adjective (e.g., Trost 2006 but also Fleischhauer 2016 for a comparison of different semantic analyses of relative adjectives), it is gradable, i.e., it can, for instance, form morphological comparative and superlative forms. Irrespective of its concrete use, *aufreizend* is a subjective adjective (e.g., Lasersohn 2005; Kaiser and Wang 2021). Speakers can disagree on whether a particular referent is arousing or not without contradiction. Thus, speaker A can say *Dieses Kleid ist aufreizend* 'This dress is arousing' and speaker B can disagree by saying *Nein, das ist nicht aufreizend* 'No, the dress is not arousing' without either A or B being wrong, i.e., faultless disagreement in terms of Kölbel (2003). This is different for objective adjectives like *rund* 'round': Something is either round or not, and disagreement between two speakers necessarily results in a contradiction. Furthermore, *aufreizend* is a multidimensional adjective as – unlike, for instance, *groß* 'tall' and *alt* 'age' – it does not assign its referent a value on a unique dimension such as 'size' or 'age' (cf. Sassoon 2013 for the issue of multidimensionality). Rather, the different uses of *aufreizend* already reveal that it can be evaluated with respect to different, varying dimensions.

Like other German adjectives, *aufreizend* occurs in four different syntactic uses. In (1) and (2), it is used as an attributive modifier that directly modifies a noun. The example in (3) illustrates the predicative use of the adjective. It forms the sentence predicate together with the inflected copula *sein* 'to be'. *Aufreizend* can also be used adverbially and then, as in (4), modifies a verb. The adjective is used to express that the swinging of the hips – but not necessarily the hips themselves – has been arousing. Finally, *aufreizend* is also used as an adadjectival modifier in the example in (5). It is not just the subject referent's walking which is characterized as provocative in (5) but the slowness of walking.

(3) *Besonders aufreizend ist es zum Beispiel, wenn Lord King, der Vorsitzende von British Airways, eine Zunahme seines Salärs um 117 Prozent auf 385 791 Pfund (1,2 Millionen Mark) ausweist.*
'It is particularly provocative, for example, when Lord King, the chairman of British Airways, reports a 117 percent increase in his salary to 385,791 pounds (1.2 million marks).'
(Z89/JUL.00074) Die Zeit, 07/07/1989, p. 20; Sommer des Unfriedens)

(4) *Da wurden zu "Moulin Rouge" aufreizend die Hüften geschwungen, beim Ententanz in die Knie gegangen und dank ausgeklügelter Technik konnten die BFCler ihre Röckchen in die Höhe sausen lassen.*
'At "Moulin Rouge," hips were provocatively swayed, knees were bent during the duck dance, and thanks to sophisticated technology, the BFC members were able to make their skirts soar upwards.'
(M07/MAR.01195 Mannheimer Morgen, 05/03/2007; Kurz und heftig: Schwester Fastnacht feiert Comeback)

(5) *Nach meiner dritten Kippe meinte das Vieh vermutlich, dass auch mir nun klar sein müsse, wer der Boss sei, und trottete aufreizend langsam am Auto vorbei.*
'After my third cigarette, the animal probably thought it was now clear to me who the boss was and sauntered provocatively slowly past the car.'
(T10/FEB.00076 die tageszeitung, 01/02/2010, p. 20; STIER OHNE KIPPEN)

In the remainder of the paper, we exclude predicative uses of *aufreizend* and restrict ourselves to its three instances as a modifier.

3 Hypotheses on *aufreizend*'s interpretation

In the last section, we argued that *aufreizend* comes in two different uses, which we termed (i) arousing interpretation and (ii) provocative interpretation. So far, it is an open question whether we are dealing with two strictly distinct senses – thus with an instance of polysemy – or whether the adjective has a single sense but is interpreted differently depending on its context of use. We adhere to Grice's version of Ockham's razor that "senses are not multiplied beyond necessity" (Grice 1989: 47), and follow the suggestion by Fritz (1995: 80) that we should not postulate different senses as long as we can identify context variables that account for observed interpretational differences.

As Fritz (1995: 80) states, a first step might be looking for syntactic differences to explain the interpretational differences. With respect to *aufreizend*, we can hypothesize that the different interpretations depend on the syntactic context, i.e., its use as an attributive, adverbial, or adadjectival modifier. This can be formulated as hypothesis 1 (**H1**) regarding the interpretation of *aufreizend*:

H1 The interpretation of *aufreizend* depends on the syntactic context.

It is not immediately apparent whether and, if so, in what way the interpretation of *aufreizend* should depend on the syntactic context. However, Kaiser and Wang (2021) showed that the syntactic position of subjective adjectives in English affects their subjectivity ratings. Although this is not an instance of putative polysemy, it demonstrates that the syntactic context can affect an adjective's interpretation.

A second factor that might affect the interpretation of *aufreizend* is the semantic properties of the modified expression. As we are only interested in human referents, an obvious distinction concerns the referent's gender. We can express this as hypothesis **H2**:

H2 The interpretation of *aufreizend* depends on the referent's sex.

Hypothesis **H2** gains some initial plausibility, as we already know that gender stereotypes exist in the language and that women are more often qualified for their appearance than men. Given this background, we can formulate an even more specific hypothesis concerning the relationship between the referent's gender and *aufreizend*'s interpretation:

H3 The arousing interpretation of *aufreizend* preferentially occurs with female referents, whereas the provocative interpretation shows a preference for male referents.

After having formulated a number of specific hypotheses on possible factors that might affect *aufreizend*'s interpretation, we can proceed and test them based on actual corpus data. The results presented in the next section show that hypothesis **H1** can be confirmed to some degree and that hypotheses **H2** and **H3** can be fully confirmed.

4 Corpus study

4.1 Background: Corpus study

To evaluate the different hypotheses presented in the preceding section, we extracted corpus data from the German reference corpus DeReKo. The search was carried out using *Archiv W* which is the biggest archive consisting of 12,845,486,163 words; it contains literary texts, newspapers, articles from *Wikipedia* and other sources covering a period from the 18th century to the present day. Using the web-based tool Cosmas II (Leibniz-Institut für Deutsche Sprache 2020), we searched for all occurrences of inflected *aufreizend* within the archive using the search string '&aufreizend'. The search yielded 9,897 hits, which were automatically presented in a random order. The annotation procedure has been carried out by the two authors independently. In case of disagreement, consensus has been reached by consulting a third annotator.

The final statistical analysis was run on 500 examples identified in the first annotation step.

4.2 Data annotation

In the first annotation step, we annotated the category of the referent associated with *aufreizend*. We were interested in two features: First, is the nominal referent associated with *aufreizend* human or not? And second, if it is a human, does it refer to a male or a female? The aim was to identify 500 sentences in which *aufreizend* is either directly or indirectly associated with a human referent of definite sex. The adjective is directly associated with a human referent if it functions as an attributive modifier of a human-denoting noun, for instance, *Frau* 'woman' in (6-a). It is indirectly associated with a human referent, if, for instance, it modifies a noun that is in a possessive relationship with a human referent (6-b) or modifies an action carried out by a human agent (4).

(6)   a.   [...] *wenn auf einer Plakatwand eine aufreizende Frau mit tiefem Ausschnitt [...] abgebildet ist.*
'[...] if an enticing woman with a deep neckline is depicted on a billboard.'
(T17/SEP.02694 die tageszeitung, 28/09/2017, p. 21; Wodka mit Dekolleté)
    b.   *Junge Frauen am Straßenrand oder in Waldeinfahrten in aufreizender Kleidung [...].*
'Young women on the roadside or in forest entrances in provocative clothing [...].'
(RHZ15/JAN.16655 Rhein-Zeitung, 20/01/2015, p. 17; Lustmobile aus Koblenz tauchen im Westerwald auf)

The example in (5), for instance, has been excluded from further analysis as the agent of trudging is an animal rather than a human. We also excluded sentences in which the referent's gender was either unclear or the nominal expression associated with *aufreizend* referred to a group of mixed-gender people.

Within the data ultimately used, there is an imbalance in the gender distribution. Female referents occur significantly more frequently than male ones, as can be seen in Table 3.

Tab. 3: Results of the gender annotation.

female referent	male referent
310	190

As already mentioned above, *aufreizend* does not always modify a referent directly. In some cases, the adjective modifies the human referent's activity. Therefore, we annotated in the next step whether the adjective modifies an individual or an eventuality. We use the term 'eventuality' as a cover term for states and events (following Bach 1986). *Aufreizend* modifies an eventuality if it functions as a modifier of an eventuality-denoting predicate (7-a) or as an adadjectival modifier applying to an adverbially used adjective (7-b).

(7) a. *Für den Rest des Films sieht man Ophélie und andere leichtbekleidete Mädchenkörper immer wieder aufreizend tanzen* [...].
'For the rest of the film, you see Ophélie and other scantily clad girls' bodies dancing arousingly.'
(SOL17/SEP.00683 Spiegel-Online, 07/09/2017; Männer, die auf Mädchen starren)
b. *[...] beim Bügeln oder Spülen geht er aufreizend bedächtig zu Werke.*
'[...] When ironing or washing dishes, he works provocatively deliberately.'
(FOC08/FEB.00431 FOCUS, 25/02/2008, p. 128–129; PARTNERSCHAFT)

We interpret *aufreizend* as a modifier of an individual if it applies to a (non-eventive) noun (6) or a modifier of a (non-eventive) noun (8).[7]

---

7 Cf. Fleischhauer (2023: 388–389) for a recent discussion of criteria distinguishing eventive from non-eventive nouns.

(8) […] *der in Oxford studiert hat und als aufreizend wohlhabender Gangster in Südamerika lebt* […].
'[…] who studied in Oxford and now lives as a provocatively wealthy gangster in South America.'
(Z58/SEP.00012 Die Zeit, 04/09/1958, p. 5; Der neue T.S. Eliot)

The results of the second annotation step are summarized in Table 4. The data shows a higher number of event-related uses of *aufreizend* than of individual-related ones. However, the two uses are unevenly distributed over the two sexes. With male referents, *aufreizend* is used in only 15.9% of all cases as an individual-related modifier, whereas it makes up 62.4% of all uses in relation to female referents.

Tab. 4: Results of the second annotation step.

	Individual	Event
male	31	159
female	193	117
total	224	276

In a third annotation step, we tested for a suitable paraphrase of *aufreizend*. If the adjective can be paraphrased by one of the modifiers associated with the arousing interpretation (e.g., *verführerisch* 'arousing'), we annotate its interpretation as 'arousing'. On the other hand, if a paraphrase with one of the modifiers associated with the provocative interpretation (e.g., *provokant* 'provocative') is suitable, we annotate its interpretation as 'provocative'. In some cases, a clear paraphrase was not possible, as in (9). Even the wider context did not allow us to decide which of the two paraphrases – or possibly some third paraphrase – fits better. In such cases, we have annotated the example as 'unclear'.

(9) *Die niederländische Hauptdarstellerin Elsie de Brauw, bekannt aus den Inszenierungen ihres Mannes Johan Simons, unterspielt ihre Rolle so aufreizend, dass man sich nicht für sie interessieren mag.*
'The Dutch lead actress Elsie de Brauw, known for her husband Johan Simons' productions, underplays her role so provocatively that one may not be interested in her.'
(FLT10/AUG.00078 Falter, 04/08/2010, p. 23; Schau nicht zurück)

Table 5 shows the results of the third annotation step. The data already indicate a clear gender dependence of the two interpretations. The arousing interpretation predominately occurs with female referents (96.6%), whereas the provocative interpretation occurs with such referents in only 13.8% of all cases.

Tab. 5: Results of the third annotation step.

	arousing	provocative	unclear
female ∧ event	76	24	11
female ∧ individual	179	0	20
male ∧ event	0	150	9
male ∧ individual	9	14	8
total	264	188	48

The arousing interpretation, on the other hand, rarely occurs with male referents and only appears in individual-related uses of the adjective (10). This interpretation does not occur at all within the data sample with the event-related uses.

(10)   [...] *beides schmeichelte seinem aufreizenden Nabel ungemein, und er* [...]
       '[...] both flattered his provocative navel immensely, and he [...]'
       (PRF06/JUL.00408 profil, 24/07/2006, p. 110; Das Traumschiff)

Female referents, on the other hand, are rarely characterized as being provocative. However, if the provocative interpretation applies to female referents, it is only in event-related uses of the adjective (11).

(11)   *Als sich etwa Pechstein neulich bei einem Rennen vor laufender Kamera zwar wortlos, aber allzu aufreizend über einen verkorksten Lauf der Kollegin Friesinger freute* [...].
       'When Pechstein recently silently, yet all too provocatively, rejoiced over a botched run by her colleague Friesinger during a race in front of the camera[...]'
       (S04/MAR.00192 Der Spiegel, 08/03/2004, p. 144; Attacken der Primadonnen)

Although there is a preference for the two uses to occur with referents of a specific sex, there also seems to be a preference for the 'provocative interpretation' to occur in event-related uses, as the data in Table 6 show. Thus, we can add hypothesis **H4** concerning the factors influencing *aufreizend*'s interpretation (11).

H4   The interpretation of *aufreizend* depends on whether it modifies an individual or an eventuality.

Tab. 6: Results of the classification of *aufreizend*'s use and its interpretation.

	arousing	provocative
Event	76	174
Individual	188	14

Finally, we annotated the syntactic context in which the adjective occurs. The values we used are 'attributive', 'adverbial', and 'adadjectival', corresponding to the different syntactic uses discussed above. The results for the annotation of the syntactic context are summarized in Tables 7 and 8. We present the results separately for the parameters 'interpretation' and 'category'. In both tables, numbers are split between female and male referents (f / m).

Tab. 7: Results of the cross-classification of the two parameters 'syntactic context' and 'interpretation'.

	attributive	adverbial	adadjectival
arousing	172 / 3	55 / 3	28 / 3
provocative	7 / 59	2 / 17	15 / 88
unclear	11 / 6	8 / 5	12 / 6

Tab. 8: Results of the cross-classification of the two parameters 'syntactic context' and 'category'.

	attributive	adverbial	adadjectival
event	54 / 56	36 / 20	29 / 81
individual	137 / 11	29 / 5	27 / 15

4.3 Results

In Section 3, we formulated three hypotheses concerning possible factors affecting *aufreizend*'s interpretation. **H1** states that the syntactic context determines the interpretation, whereas **H2** – or its more precise reformulation **H3** – proposes a dependency between the referent's gender and *aufreizend*'s interpretation. In the annotation procedure, we identified a further variable that could be relevant in determining the adjective's use, namely whether it functions as an individual-related or an event-related modifier (**H4**).

To test whether one or even a combination of these parameters is relevant for determining *aufreizend*'s use, we used a binomial Generalized Linear Model (GLM); this is a linear regression model in which the dependent variable – INTERPRETATION in our case – is binary ('arousing' vs 'provocative'). All cases of unclear interpretation have been removed from the analysis. The variables CATEGORY (values: 'event' vs 'individual'), GENDER (values: 'female' vs 'male') and SYNTACTIC CONTEXT (values: 'attributive', 'adverbial', 'adadjectival') function as the predictors. We run the statistical analysis using the R statistical software (R Core Team 2021), in particular by using the lme4 package (Bates et al. 2015).

The GLM was first used to test the interaction of the variables. In a second step, it was tested whether there were any additive effects associated with the variables. This was done to see if the relationship between the predictors and the dependent variable is nonlinear or if the effects of the predictors are interdependent. The GLM generated no results, neither for the tested interaction between the variables nor for additive effects. This is most likely because the correlation values of the predictors (computed using the 'cor.test()' function) were too high.

As regression models can be problematic for highly correlated variables, we also used the decision tree model (also called conditional inference tree) to model the data (cf. Tagliamonte and Baayen 2012). This is a regression model that classifies data by binary recursive partitioning. Levshina (2015: 291) describes the rationale of this model as follows: It first tests whether any predictor is associated with the dependent variable and chooses the one with the strongest association. Second, it makes a binary split and divides the data into two subsets. This process is repeated for each subset "until there are no variables that are associated with the outcome at the pre-defined level of statistical significance" (Levshina 2015: 291). The outcome of this process can be visualized as a decision tree.

We ran the decision tree model on our data using the package rpart (Therneau et al. 2013). The algorithm of this model automatically reduces complexity and prevents overfitting. As a consequence, branches that split between features of low importance are not taken into account. Within the algorithm, the function 'set.seed()' was used for the ten-fold cross-validation to calculate the classification accuracy value of the decision tree model. The accuracy value indicates how well a classification model makes correct predictions compared to all predictions. The range of the accuracy value was between 0.88 as the lowest value and 0.96 as its highest. In other words, these values indicate that the model can predict with a very high accuracy of 88% to 96% which interpretation of the adjective *aufreizend* will occur in a specific context.

The visualization of the resulting decision tree is presented in Figure 1. This tree shows the best fit for the data. Thus, it provides a correct result for the highest number of cases. Each node in the tree represents a binary partitioning of the data.

The strongest association is with GENDER. 'Female' is branching to the left, and the branching to the right represents 'male'. There is no further variable associated with the interpretation in the 'male' subset. Thus, the value 'male' is a very strong predictor of the interpretation of 'provocative'. A more complex pattern is found within the 'female' subset. For females, the next step in the decision is whether *aufreizend* is used as an individual-related modifier or not. If it is individual-related, the interpretation is 'arousing'. The interesting case arises when the modifier is event-related: Here, SYNTACTIC CONTEXT comes into play as an additional predictor. The interpretation is 'arousing' again if the adjective is used either as an adverbial or an attributive modifier. However, it tends towards the 'provocative' interpretation if it functions as an adadjectival modifier.

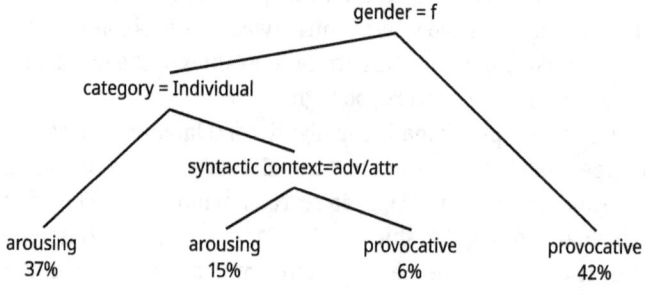

Fig. 1: Graphically presented results of the Decision Tree Model. The split is 'yes' to the left and 'no' to the right.

Finally, we compiled a confusion matrix for the evaluation of the classification model (Table 9). In contrast to the accuracy value, the confusion matrix allows for a more detailed analysis of the model's performance by providing detailed information about different types of errors, while the accuracy value indicates the percentage of correct predictions. The columns in the confusion matrix correspond to the annotated classes and the rows correspond to the predicted classes. According to the confusion matrix, our model correctly predicted the interpretation 'arousing' for 63 instances and incorrectly predicted this interpretation for only one instance. Furthermore, it correctly predicted the second interpretation ('provocative') for 24 instances and incorrectly predicted it for three. The results show that the rate of incorrect predictions is low and that errors mostly occur in the incorrect prediction of the 'arousing' interpretation.

The decision tree has a high degree of accuracy and results in a fewer number of incorrect decisions. The model has not generated any other tree that better fits

Tab. 9: Confusion matrix: true classification presented in the columns, predicted classification presented in the rows.

	arousing	provocative
arousing	63	1
provocative	3	24

the data. Most importantly, it demonstrated that the interpretation is determined by multiple factors but neither by GENDER nor SYNTACTIC CONTEXT alone. Thus, we can confirm all four hypotheses: **H1, H2, H3,** and **H4**. Nonetheless, GENDER turns out to be the strongest predictor and therefore most important in determining *aufreizend*'s interpretation. In the next section, we will look more closely at the feature combination 'female', 'event-related', 'adadjectival', which tends towards the second (i.e., provocative) interpretation, since this is the context in which category and syntactic context are most relevant.

4.4 When women are provocative: Female, event, and adadjectival modification

The previous section revealed that the main factor determining the interpretation of *aufreizend* is the referent's sex. If the referent is male, the interpretation is very likely to be 'provocative'. It is more complex with female referents, as in this case the parameters CATEGORY and SYNTACTIC CONTEXT come into play. Therefore, we like asking why the combination of the three features 'female', 'event', and 'adadjectival' is very likely to lead to the provocative interpretation of *aufreizend*. A representative example of this feature combination is shown in (12). *Aufreizend* modifies the adjective *gelassen* 'calm', which itself functions as an attributive modifier of the noun *CDU-Vorsitzende* 'CDU chairwoman'.

(12)   *Eine geradezu aufreizend gelassene CDU-Vorsitzende kritisiert die Schwesterpartei fast gar nicht* [...].
      'An almost provocatively calm CDU chairwoman criticizes the sister party hardly at all [...]'
      (U02/JAN.01665 Süddeutsche Zeitung, 11/01/2002, p. 3; Angela Merkel nach der Provokation von Kreuth und vor der Magdeburger Klausurtagung: Aber Nerven hat die Frau)

We think that the modifier's target, i.e., the adjective occurring in this specific feature combination, plays a central role in determining *aufreizend*'s interpretation.

The provocative interpretation predominantly arises with adjectives to characterize the manner of the female referent's behavior. In (12), for instance, the referent behaves calmly. The different adjectives occurring in this context are listed in (13).

(13) *lang* 'long', *langsam* 'slowly', *nüchtern* 'sober/plain', *lässig* 'casual', *kühl* 'cool(ly)', *forsch* 'bold', *frech* 'cheeky', *gelangweilt* 'bored', *gelassen* 'calm', *kämpferisch* 'aggressive', *naiv* 'naive'

An exception to the generalization that the adjectives characterize the referent's manner is *lang* 'long', which is used in the sense of 'a long time' in (14). In this example, the time that the two female tennis players went to the toilet – during the game – is described as being provocatively (i.e., too) long.

(14) *[...] als sie beide gemeinsam die Toilette aufsuchten und aufreizend lange nicht mehr auf den Platz zurückkehrten.*
'[...] when they both went to the toilet together and took a provocatively long time to return to their seats.'
(A16/AUG.05082 St. Galler Tagblatt, 12/08/2016; Kein stereotypes Doppel)

The arousing interpretation arises with adjectives – often participles – that refer to a state or activity (e.g., *posierend* 'posing', *lächelnd* 'smiling') or to adjectives that already carry an arousing meaning, such as *sinnlich* 'sexual, sensual' or *lasziv* 'sexy'. The complete list of adjectives occurring in this context within our sample is given in (15).

(15) *inszeniert* 'staged', *lächelnd* 'smiling', *posierend* 'posing', *wackelnd* 'shaking', *konturiert* 'contoured', *betrachtet* 'looked at, examined', *stöckeln* 'stagger' (walking on high-heels), *lasziv* 'sexy', *sinnlich* 'sexual, sensual', *anziehend* 'attractive'

Particularly interesting are the participles occurring in (15). They either refer to the presentation of a female body (e.g., *inszeniert* 'staged', *posierend* 'posing') or to an activity executed with the body (e.g., *lächelnd* 'smiling', *wackelnd* 'shaking'). An instructive example is shown in (16).

(16) *[...] die aufreizend wackelnden Hintern der Mädchen [...]*
'the arousingly wiggling bottoms of the girls [...]'
(P03/APR.03003 Die Presse, 26/04/2003, p. 2; muss, mich keiner sieht und ich niemanden erkenne, und würde mich...)

There is no overlap between the adjectives in the two lists, which is not surprising given that the respective adjectives belong to different semantic domains. Thus, we conclude that syntactic context and category are less relevant than the modifier target and the two parameters, and the two parameters appear to be relevant only in this specific parameter combination where different modifier targets arise. For some reason, the targets evoking the provocative interpretation outnumber those provoking the arousing interpretation. Therefore, syntactic context and category are epiphenomena caused by the modifier targets used in that context.

5 Conclusion

In the paper, we explored the factors determining the interpretation of *aufreizend* in combination with human referents. Based on a corpus study, we showed that multiple factors are responsible for its concrete interpretation. The referent's gender turned out to be the main factor: With female referents, *aufreizend* is predominantly interpreted as arousing, whereas the provocative interpretation predominates with male referents. However, it turned out that the feature combination 'female, event, adadjectival' presents a deviation from the general pattern. This combination has a high likelihood of causing the provocative interpretation. In Section 4.4, we related this deviation to the concrete expressions targeted by *aufreizend*. We have shown that the provocative interpretation results from manner expressions, whereas the arousing interpretation arises with eventive predicates expressing body movement or those that already have some arousing feature in their meaning. We concluded that neither the syntactic context nor the category but the modifier targets determine the interpretation.

The results of our study connect well to the general findings on gender stereotypes presented in Section 1. Women are more often characterized with respect to their physical appearance than men; stereotypical adjectives associated with women come from the domain of physical appearance (e.g., *schön* 'pretty' in the fairy tales of the Brothers Grimm, and *attractive* as well as *sexy* in the study of Williams et al. 1999). Given the prevailing gender stereotypes in the German-speaking community, the results of our study are not surprising but fit well into this pattern. We conclude that *aufreizend*'s interpretation arises contextually due to the syntactic context and the type of the referent. We attribute the dichotomy in interpretation to the presence of gender stereotypes in German, which lead to women being evaluated primarily on the basis of their physical appearance, while men are evaluated on the basis of other characteristics. Thus, the difference in interpretation proves to be a consequence of the presence of these gender stereotypes. One implication of this assertion is that this interpretative difference is also linked to the very existence of these specific gender stereotypes and would not come about without them or in the context of other gender stereotypes. This assertion can be verified on the basis of historical data on the change in gender stereotypes and thus allows the connection between social stereotypes and linguistic interpretations to be examined more closely.

In Section 3, finally, we raised the question of whether *aufreizend* is polysemous or not. Adopting a parsimonious approach along the lines of Grice (1989: 47), we reject an analysis in terms of polysemy as we can point to context factors (gender, reference type, syntactic context, modifier targets) that determine the exact interpretation. Thus, we opt for an analysis in which the arousing interpretation and the provocative interpretation result from a single, unified sense. In order to determine this unified sense, it would be relevant to include other uses – such as predicative use or the combination with non-human referents – in the analysis.

Finally, we wonder whether further adjectives exist – in German or other languages – that depend (at least in specific uses such as *aufreizend*) on their interpretation of the referent's gender. Thus, we leave it to future studies to determine whether and, if so, in which semantic domains the interpretation of modifiers is influenced by the referent's gender.

6 Acknowledgements

We would like to thank the participants of the Linguistic intersections of language and gender conference 2023 for their valuable comments on our paper, as well as two anonymous reviewers. In particular, we would like to thank Dominic Schmitz for his extensive help with the statistics.

References

Bach, Emmon. 1986. The algebra of events. *Linguistics and Philosophy* 9. 5–16. https://doi.org/10.1007/BF00627432.
Bates, Douglas, Martin Mächler, Ben Bolker and Steve Walker. 2015. Fitting linear mixed-effects models using lme4. *Journal of statistical software* 67(1). 1–48. https://doi.org/10.18637/jss.v067.i01.
Feilke, Helmuth. 1989. Funktionen verbaler Stereotype für die alltagssprachliche Wissensorganisation. In Clemens Knobloch (ed.), *Kognition und Kommunikation: Beiträge zur Psychologie der Zeichenverwendung*, 137–155. Münster: Nodus.
Fiedler, Klaus and Jeannette Schmid. 2001. How language contributes to persistence of stereotypes as well as other, more general, intergroup issues. In Rupert Brown and Samuel L. Gaertner (eds.), *Blackwell Handbook of Social Psychology: Intergroup processes*, 261–280. Malden: Blackwell.

Fleischhauer, Jens. 2016. *Degree gradation of verbs*. Berlin, Boston: düsseldorf university press. https://doi.org/10.1515/9783110720273.
Fleischhauer, Jens. 2023. Prospective aspect and current relevance: A case study of the German prospective stehen vor NP light verb construction. *Journal of Germanic Linguistics* 35(4). 371–408. https://doi.org/10.1017/S1470542722000198.
Fritz, Gerd. 1995. Metonymische Muster und Metaphernfamilien. Bemerkungen zur Struktur und Geschichte der Verwendungsweisen von *scharf*. In Götz Hindelang, Eckard Rolf and Werner Zillig (eds.), *Der Gebrauch der Sprache*, 77–107. Münster: Lit Verlag.
Fábián, Annamária, Armin Owzar and Igor Trost. 2022. Auto- und Heterostereotypie im Europa des 19. Jahrhunderts. In Annamária Fábián, Armin Owzar and Igor Trost (eds.), *Auto- und Heterostereotypie im Europa des 19. Jahrhunderts: Linguistische, literaturwissenschaftliche, historische und politikwissenschaftliche Perspektiven*, 1–14. Berlin: J.B. Metzler. https://doi.org/10.1007/978-3-662-65287-9_1.
Grice, Paul. 1989. *Studies in the way of words*. Cambridge: Harvard University Press.
Hausen, Karin. 1976. Die Polarisierung der "Geschlechtscharaktere" – Eine Spiegelung der Dissoziation von Erwerbs- und Familienleben. In Werner Conze (ed.), *Sozialgeschichte der Familie in der Neuzeit Europas*, 363–393. Stuttgart: Klett.
Kaiser, Elsi and Catherine Wang. 2021. Packaging information as fact versus opinion: Consequences of the (information-) structural position of subjective adjectives. *Discourse Processes* 58(7). 617–641. https://doi.org/10.1080/0163853X.2020.1838196.
Kilian, Jörg. 2005. Assoziative Stereotype. Sprachtheoretische, sprachkritische und sprachdidaktische Anmerkungen zum lexikalisch verknüpften Mythos, Aberglauben, Vorurteil. In Dietrich Busse, Thomas Niehr and Martin Wengeler (eds.), *Brisante Semantik: Neuere Konzepte und Forschungsergebnisse einer kulturwissenschaftlichen Linguistik*, Tübingen: Niemeyer. https://doi.org/10.1515/9783110918328.117.
Knoll, Silke, Martin Eisend and Josefine Steinhagen. 2011. Gender roles in advertising. *International Journal of Advertising* 30(5). 867–888. https://doi.org/10.2501/IJA-30-5-867-888.
Kotek, Hadas, Rikker Dockum, Sarah Babinski and Christopher Geissler. 2021. Gender bias and stereotypes in linguistic example sentences. *Language* 97(4). 653–677. https://doi.org/10.1353/lan.2021.0060.
Kotelmann, Joachim and Lothar Mikos. 1981. *Frühjahrsputz und Südseezauber. Die Darstellung der Frau in der Fernsehwerbung und das Bewusstsein von Zuschauerinnen*. Baden-Baden: E. Baur Verlag.
Kölbel, Max. 2003. Faultless Disagreement. *Proceedings of the Aristotelian Society* 104. 53–73. https://doi.org/10.1111/j.0066-7373.2004.00081.x.
Lasersohn, Peter. 2005. Context dependence, disagreement, and predicates of personal taste. *Linguistics and Philosophy* 28. 643–686. https://doi.org/10.1007/s10988-005-0596-x.
Leibniz-Institut für Deutsche Sprache. 2020. *COSMAS II (Corpus Search, Management and Analysis System)*. Mannheim: Leibniz-Institut für Deutsche Sprache. https://www2.ids-mannheim.de/cosmas2.
Leibniz-Institut für Deutsche Sprache. 2021. *Deutsches Referenzkorpus / Archiv der Korpora geschriebener Gegenwartssprache 2021-I (Release vom 02.02.2021)*. Mannheim: Leibniz-Institut für Deutsche Sprache. https://cosmas2.ids-mannheim.de/cosmas2-web. Accessed: 9 March 2025.
Levshina, Natalia. 2015. *How to do linguistics with R: Data exploration and statistical analysis*. Amsterdam, Philadelphia: John Benjamins.
Mikos, Lothar. 1988. Frühjahrsputz revisited. Das Frauenbild in der Fernsehwerbung hat sich kaum verändert. *medium* 18(4). 54–56.

Moon, Rosamund. 2014. From *gorgeous* to *grumpy*: Adjectives, age and gender. *Gender and Language* 8(1). 5–41. https://doi.org/10.1558/genl.v8i1.5.

Pümpel-Mader, Maria. 2010. *Personenstereotype. Eine linguistische Untersuchung zu Form und Funktion von Stereotypen*. Heidelberg: Winter.

R Core Team. 2021. *R: A language and environment for statistical computing*. R Foundation for Statistical Computing Vienna, Austria. https://www.R-project.org. Accessed: 9 March 2025.

Robinson, Orrin. 2010. *Grimm Language*. Amsterdam, Philadelphia: John Benjamins.

Sassoon, Galit. 2013. A typology of multidimensional adjectives. *Journal of Semantics* 30. 335–380. https://doi.org/10.1093/jos/ffs012.

Steffens, Melanie and Petra Jelenec. 2011. Separating implicit gender stereotypes regarding math and language: Implicit ability stereotypes are self-serving for boys and men, but not for girls and women. *Sex Roles* 64. 324–335. https://doi.org/10.1007/s11199-010-9924-x.

Tagliamonte, Sali and Harald Baayen. 2012. Models, forests, and trees of York English: Was/were variation as a case study for statistical practice. *Language Variation and Change* 24(2). 135–178. https://doi.org/10.1017/S0954394512000129.

Therneau, Terry, Beth Atkinson and Brian Ripley. 2013. *Rpart: Recursive partitioning*. R package version 4.1–3. http://CRAN.R-project.org/package=rpart. Accessed: 9 March 2025.

Trost, Igor. 2006. *Das deutsche Adjektiv. Untersuchungen zur Semantik, Komparation, Wortbildung und Syntax*. Hamburg: Buske. https://doi.org/10.37307/j.2198-2430.2008.02.12.

Vennemann, Angela and Christina Holtz-Bacha. 2008. Mehr als Frühjahrsputz und Südseezauber? Frauenbilder in der Fernsehwerbung und ihre Rezeption. In Christina Holtz-Bacha (ed.), *Stereotype? Frauen und Männer in der Werbung*, 76–106. Wiesbaden: VS Verlag für Sozialwissenschaften. https://doi.org/10.1007/978-3-531-93358-0_5.

Williams, John, Robert Satterwhite and Deborah Best. 1999. Pancultural gender stereotypes revisited: The five factor model. *Sex Roles* 40. 513–525. https://doi.org/10.1023/A:1018831928829.

Wright, Stephen and Donald Taylor. 2003. The Social Psychology of Cultural Diversity: Social Stereotyping, Prejudice, and Discrimination. In Michael Hogg and Joel Cooper (eds.), *The SAGE Handbook of Social Psychology*, 432–457. London: Sage. https://doi.org/10.4135/9781848608221.n16.

Ziem, Alexander. 2022. Die Vierdimensionalität von Stereotypen als linguistische Herausforderung. In Annamária Fábián, Armin Owzar and Igor Trost (eds.), *Auto- und Heterostereotypie im Europa des 19. Jahrhunderts Linguistische, literaturwissenschaftliche, historische und politikwissenschaftliche Perspektiven*, 33–52. Berlin: J.B. Metzler. https://doi.org/10.1007/978-3-662-65287-9_3.

Sol Tovar

Understanding (mis)gender(ing) and pronouns from a politeness theory standpoint

Abstract: Certain linguistic forms have a "wounding potential". The most recognizable forms of "linguistic wounding" are direct insults. However, gendered forms – i.e., words that openly signal someone's gender, such as pronouns, gendered morphemes or lexemes – also carry this potential. Based on the links shown by Motschenbacher (2010) between gender and Brown and Levinson's (1987) and Watts' (2003) work on politeness theory, this study aims to lay out a method for the analysis of (mis)gendering as an (im)politeness strategy. This method involves the analysis of interactions and the use of gendered forms as "face-work" considering Motschenbacher's conceptualisation of "gender face", Culpeper's categorisation of impoliteness strategies and Watts' views on (im)politeness as politic behavior within a theory of social practice. In this contribution, an in-depth case analysis of a piece of impolite discourse is carried out, bringing together helpful categories of analysis from the existing literature and laying down the groundwork for future work on gendering and politeness.

Keywords: impoliteness linguistic wounding, misgendering politeness theory, politic behavior, political discourse

1 Introduction

It is "often difficult to untangle [the] link between the folk understanding of politeness and the theoretical concept" (Dimitrova-Galaczi 2002: 1–2). As a theoretical construct, linguistic (im)politeness goes beyond the widespread, traditional "social-norm" idea that politeness arises when actions align with societal norms and impoliteness occurs when actions contradict these norms (Fraser 1990: 220). Linguistic impoliteness encompasses at the same time linguistic behaviors which would commonly not be considered simply impolite but deliberately hurtful, rude, and even discriminatory. Therefore, I wish to emphasize that analyzing misgendering as an impoliteness strategy does not imply a reduction of this process as something as inconsequential as, for instance, not saying "please" or "thank you".[1]

To fully understand the underlying motivations behind the use of certain gendered forms to refer to transgender, non-binary and gender-nonconforming individuals, a politeness theory-based approach to the analysis of gender, gendering, and misgendering built upon the concept of "gender face" (Motschenbacher 2010: 171–172) is needed. In this contribution, an in-depth case analysis will be carried out to illustrate how misgendering operates as a form of linguistic wounding, impacting individuals' gender face. In addition, since "[w]hat is 'polite' or 'impolite' language can only be assessed as such by analyzing the context of real social practice" (Watts 2003: 141), it is imperative to analyze how context affects the interpretation of these forms. By examining real-world instances of misgendering as an impoliteness strategy, I aim to lay out the groundwork for a comprehensive analysis of (im)politeness strategies in discourses around and about gender. To that end, I will first introduce the relevant theoretical concepts before applying them in my analysis.

2 On politeness theory and linguistic wounding

Motschenbacher (2010: 170) builds upon Butler's (1997) discussion of hate speech and the wounding potential of words by defining two types of "linguistic wounding": first-order and second-order. First-order linguistic wounding is connected to the illocutionary and perlocutionary force of the speech act (i.e., the intention of the speaker to harm and the hearer's/referent's perception of the speech act as injurious). Second-order linguistic wounding is linked to the wounding potential of certain linguistic categories (e.g., the use of words that have a gender marking, like 3rd person pronouns in the case of English, or certain nouns with a human referent, e.g., *Bundeskanzler* 'federal chancellor.MASC' and *Bundeskanzlerin* 'federal chancellor.FEM', in the case of German). Consequently, second-order linguistic wounding is unavoidable, since the use of these forms is needed in communication, though it is worth pointing out that "[i]t is not the categories as such that cause harm, but the normativity they have acquired throughout their discursive history" (Motschenbacher 2010: 173).

It is this wounding potential that makes these forms ostensibly impolite, as their use can be connected to politeness and impoliteness strategies employed as part of the facework (Goffman 1967: 5) done by members of different communities of prac-

---

[1] I would like to thank an anonymous reviewer for noting how framing misgendering as impoliteness could lead to an unintended trivialization of discrimination.

tice (Eckert and McConnell-Ginet 1992). As a result, misgendering could be implemented as a Face Threatening Act (FTA; Brown and Levinson 1987) to the addressee's "gender face" (Motschenbacher 2010: 171–172), which is deeply connected to what Culpeper (2011: 200) calls "social identity face". In terms of face needs, a person's positive gender face would involve their "need to be accepted with respect to their desired gender identities", whereas their negative gender face would involve their "need not to be restricted in terms of their desired gender practices" (Motschenbacher 2010: 172).

2.1 A brief overview of impoliteness strategies

In the present study, impoliteness is analyzed based on Culpeper's (1996) categorization of impoliteness strategies (which was later expanded in Culpeper 2005, 2011; Culpeper et al. 2003). Culpeper's framework for categorizing impoliteness superstrategies mirrors that of Brown and Levinson (1987) for politeness strategies and is reproduced here (cf. Culpeper et al. 2003: 1554–1555):

1. *Bald on record impoliteness.* [...] [B]ald on record impoliteness is typically deployed where there is much face at stake, and where there is an intention on the part of the speaker to attack the face of the hearer.
2. *Positive impoliteness.* The use of strategies designed to damage the addressee's positive face wants ('ignore, snub the other', 'exclude the other from the activity', 'disassociate from the other', 'be disinterested, unconcerned, unsympathetic', 'use inappropriate identity markers', 'use obscure or secretive language', 'seek disagreement', 'make the other feel uncomfortable[...]', 'use taboo words', 'call the other names', etc.).
3. *Negative impoliteness.* The use of strategies designed to damage the addressee's negative face wants ('frighten', 'condescend, scorn, or ridicule', 'invade the other's space', 'explicitly associate the other with a negative aspect', 'put the other's indebtedness on record', 'hinder or block the other—physically or linguistically', etc.).
4. *Sarcasm or mock politeness.* The use of politeness strategies that are obviously insincere, and thus remain surface realizations. Sarcasm (mock politeness for social disharmony) is clearly the opposite of banter (mock impoliteness for social harmony).
5. *Withhold politeness.* Keep silent or fail to act where politeness work is expected.

If we were to see these superstrategies as a decision tree (see Figure 1), the first choice would be whether to be impolite or to withhold politeness. If one chooses to

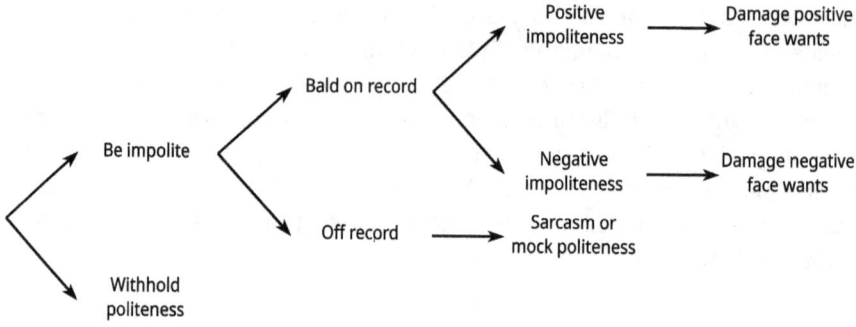

Fig. 1: Decision tree for the use of impoliteness superstrategies.

be impolite, this can be done bald on record or off record (through an implicature, as with sarcasm or mock politeness); and if done bald on record, one can damage positive face wants or negative face wants through positive or negative impoliteness strategies.

Considering these superstrategies, I argue that deadnaming and misgendering are a form of bald on-record impoliteness, in particular a positive impoliteness strategy, as they would correspond to Culpeper et al.'s (2003: 1555) "use of inappropriate identity markers". Bald on-record impoliteness serves as "a means of controlling others as well as maintaining dominant groups in society at the expense of others" (Culpeper 2011: 200). It relies heavily on first-order linguistic wounding – that is, the deliberate use of words that have a strong wounding potential – and can threaten both the positive and the negative face of the other.

2.2 Impoliteness and politic behavior

In his discussion of linguistic politeness, Watts (2003) notes the distinction between politic and non-politic behavior within a theory of social practice. Politic behavior is then defined as "linguistic behavior which is perceived to be appropriate to the social constraints of the ongoing interaction" (Watts 2003: 19). Considering the non-saliency aspect of politic behavior is of particular interest in this case analysis, as it has been pointed out that impoliteness is "the normal and expectable communicative behavior [...] in political conflicts between political leaders, parties and their followers, especially during election campaigns or during periods of hostile relationships between government and opposition" (Kienpointner 2008: 244).

The theory of social practice rests on the premise that the way individuals engage in social interactions is influenced by their past experiences and backgrounds (Watts 2003: 256). Therefore, since impoliteness is expected in the discourse of politicians, certain instances of impoliteness could be seen as politic behavior (i.e., "aggressive facework"; Watts 2003: 259) whereas others as non-politic behavior. To determine that the linguistic behavior is politic, it should be considered canonical and adhere to the established norms and power dynamics within a social group (in this case, members of the *Bundestag*).

3 Study background and methods

To provide a comprehensive analysis, it is essential to first establish the contextual backdrop behind this piece of discourse. Two contrasting members of parliament are involved: Beatrix von Storch, a cisgender woman from the right-wing populist party Alternative für Deutschland (AfD), and Tessa Ganserer, a transgender woman from the left-wing green party Bündnis 90/Die Grünen. Alternative für Deutschland is "a right-wing nationalist party" (Johnson and Barbe 2022: 76), which is critical of the European Union and has been described as having "an overtly nationalist, anti-immigrant, anti-Islam agenda" (Goldenberg 2021). Bündnis 90/Die Grünen is "a coalition of the West German Green Party and the East German protest movement Bündnis 90 (...) comprised of environmental, peace, and human rights activists" (Johnson and Barbe 2022: 75).

The piece of discourse analyzed in this study is AfD representative Beatrix von Storch's intervention during a session of parliament in which women's rights were being discussed in anticipation of International Women's Day. It starts with a reference to J. K. Rowling's (2020) article on German magazine *Emma* entitled *Frauen werden abgeschafft!* ('Women are being abolished!'), which triggers her discussion of the topic of gender. The focus of the analysis lies on the impoliteness strategies used by von Storch when referring to Green representative Tessa Ganserer.

Said piece of discourse was sourced from a publicly available recording (Deutscher Bundestag 2022a) as well as the official stenographic records (Deutscher Bundestag 2022b) of the 17th session of the German *Bundestag* (federal parliament) held on February 17, 2022. The coded transcript (as found in Section 6) corresponds to a segment of the video recording of the session (Deutscher Bundestag 2022a) spanning from minute 50:23 to 53:31, comprising von Storch's full intervention. For the sake of clarity, interruptions and reactions which were recorded in the stenographic records (Deutscher Bundestag 2022b) were removed.

QualCoder 3.2 (Curtain 2023), an open source Computer-Assisted Qualitative Data Analysis Software, was employed to analyze the piece of discourse. The data were systematically coded using a top-down approach to identify gendered forms and linguistic wounds, distinguishing between bald on-record and off-record impoliteness strategies. In the case of bald-on record impoliteness, instances of misgendering and deadnaming were coded separately, and off-record strategies were divided into mock politeness and indirect FTAs.

Speakers' intentions are known to be hard to determine objectively, yet it has been argued that speakers "manifest their intentions (...) through facework" (Lim 1994: 228). Following this line of argumentation, these instances of linguistic impoliteness were considered alongside the context and co-text to carry out an analysis of Beatrix von Storch's facework. This analysis will in turn allow us to draw conclusions about her intent.

Consequently, the following questions will guide the case analysis:
1. What impoliteness strategies were used by Beatrix von Storch?
2. How is the use of gendered linguistic forms linked to the face-work done by Beatrix von Storch?
    (a) Which gendered linguistic forms have been used in reference to Tessa Ganserer?
    (b) What is the intention or wounding potential behind those forms?

4 Case analysis

Beatrix von Storch employs a variety of impoliteness strategies; each one of them has different purposes, which will be discussed and exemplified here. It is worth noting, that von Storch uses impoliteness strategies not just in addressing and referring to Ganserer, but also when addressing other members of parliament as a group. This can be seen very early in her discourse in Example (1):

(1) *Sie fast alle hier sind Frauenabschaffer, weil Sie fast alle hier der Genderideologie anhängen.*
    'Almost all of you here are women abolitionists because almost all of you here adhere to gender ideology.'

Beatrix von Storch accuses members of parliament of being *Frauenabschaffer* (literally 'women abolitionists', 'misogynists') because of their adherence to what she calls "gender ideology". In this bald on-record display of impoliteness, she uses both positive and negative impoliteness strategies (Culpeper et al. 2003: 1555). Positive strategies attack the positive face of the other and include disassociating from the other ("almost all of you" are misogynists, but "we", the AfD, are not) and seeking disagreement (she claims that those who oppose her "adhere to gender ideology", which implies a divisive stance). Negative strategies attack the negative face of the other and include overtly associating a person or group with a negative attribute or characteristic (calling the members of the other party *Frauenabschaffer*).

She also uses indirect impoliteness strategies, as seen in Example (2), where she does not attack other members of parliament directly but calls parliament a *Theater* 'theater', implying that the discussion of the *Selbstbestimmungsgesetz* is not serious or is a joke. She combines this with mock politeness when she adds "wir warten schon mit Freude darauf", since she is not genuinely happy about the discussion of the law.

(2) *Das Selbstbestimmungsgesetz kommt demnächst auch in diesem Theater; wir warten schon mit Freude darauf.*
'The Self-Determination Act [a law on self-determination regarding gender registration] is coming soon to this theater as well; we are already waiting for it with joy.'

As we have seen, impoliteness strategies are often used in combination with one another and not only in isolation. When von Storch refers to Ganserer, she threatens Ganserer's positive gender-face in order to maintain her position of power, gaining status within her own reference group (AfD politicians and voters). She does this by constantly using inappropriate identity markers to refer to Ganserer, misgendering and deadnaming her. There are multiple examples in her discourse, such as (3), (4), (5), (6) and (7) in which other strategies are also used.

(3) *Wenn der Kollege Markus Ganserer Rock, Lippenstift, Hackenschuhe trägt, dann ist das völlig in Ordnung; es ist aber seine Privatsache.*
'If the.MASC colleague.MASC Markus Ganserer wears a skirt, lipstick and heels, that's perfectly fine, but it's his private matter.'

Another way von Storch can exercise her power is through indirect FTAs by saying something seemingly neutral that the addressee will interpret as face-threatening (Watts 2003: 215). For instance, in Example (4), Storch says that Ganserer is biologically and legally male, which is in principle a neutral statement since Ganserer was assigned male at birth and had indeed chosen not to legally alter her name and gender as a gesture symbolizing her protest against the German Transsexual Law, which does not allow self-determination. However, von Storch brings up this fact to threaten Ganserer's positive gender-face.

(4) *Biologisch und juristisch ist und bleibt er ein Mann.*
'Biologically and legally, he is and remains a man.'

(5) *Und wenn er als solcher über die grüne Frauenquote in den Bundestag einzieht und hier als Frau geführt wird, dann ist das schlicht rechtswidrig.*
'And if he enters the Bundestag as such [a man] because of the women's quota of the Green party and is listed here as a woman, then that is simply unlawful.'

Mock politeness is also used by von Storch as a way to perform a FTA "with the use of politeness strategies that are obviously insincere, and thus remain surface realization" (Culpeper 2005: 42). In Example (6), von Storch claims to be "grateful" to Ganserer while deadnaming her and in Example (7) von Storch uses the honorific *Herr* ('Mr'), misgendering her in doing so.

(6) *Ich bin Markus Ganserer aber für zwei Dinge dankbar: erstens, weil sein Beispiel uns so schön vor Augen führt, dass es einen Unterschied macht, ob man sich als Frau verkleidet oder ob man eine Frau ist, und zweitens, weil er die Frauenquote final ad absurdum geführt hat.*
'I am grateful to Markus Ganserer for two things: firstly, because his example shows us so beautifully that it makes a difference whether you dress up as a woman or whether you are a woman, and secondly, because he has finally demonstrated the absurdity of the women's quota.'

(7) *Der Queer-Beauftragte der Bundesregierung, Sven Lehmann, meint, jeder, der Herrn Ganserer nicht als Frau akzeptiere, sei transphob. Transphob ist offensichtlich ein anderes Wort für "nicht blöd".*
'The Queer Commissioner of the Federal Government, Sven Lehmann, says that anyone who does not accept Mr Ganserer as a woman is transphobic. Transphobic is obviously another word for "not stupid".'

Examples (6) and (7) also demonstrate how von Storch makes claims that indirectly threaten the face of others. For instance, when she thanks Ganserer in Example (6) for demonstrating the "absurdity" of the *Frauenquote*, she is in turn scorning all members of parliament who agree with the implementation of said quota (a negative impoliteness strategy). Likewise, she indirectly calls those who respect Ganserer's pronouns "stupid" in Example (7) when she claims that if not treating Ganserer as a woman is transphobic, then being transphobic is "not being stupid", threatening both their positive and negative face by calling them names and being condescending.

Departing from the observations made in Section 2.2 and considering a theory of social practice (Watts 2003), Example (2) would represent a case of politic behavior, since it is expected that a party which is against passing a certain law would undertake aggressive facework (criticizing the *Bundestag* in general) to express their positioning. However, it becomes clear that when personal attacks come into play, as when von Storch misgenders or deadnames Ganserer or calls members of parliament who support Ganserer stupid, the linguistic behavior can only be classified as impolite, as long as we are considering Ganserer and all members of parliament the "hearer".

This impolite behavior could be considered political behavior as well if we interpret that the intended "hearer" of von Storch's discourse is her own social field (people who align with the AfD). Considering that political organizations are social marketplaces (Watts 2003: 149), by linguistically wounding Ganserer, von Storch is gaining social capital. By being impolite to Ganserer, von Storch is "giving something to the addressee [i.e., her social field] on the justified assumption that the addressee will give something back [e.g., political support, votes][...]thus creating and sharing a common understanding" (Watts 2003: 153). This would therefore be expected, canonical behavior between members of the same political party.

5 Summing up and looking forward

The analysis of the parliamentary discourse of Beatrix von Storch revealed a complex interplay of impoliteness strategies. Employing both bald on-record and indirect impoliteness, von Storch asserted her power, threatening the face of her political opponents. Through the tactic of using inappropriate identity markers (gendered linguistic forms and names), she threatened Ganserer's positive gender-face by using the masculine forms of pronouns, nouns, articles, and adjectives, as well as her "legal" name, while maintaining her own status within her reference group and gaining social capital. It also showed that by analyzing the facework done by Beatrix von Storch, it was possible to shed light on the intentions behind her use of said words, which were to maintain power and gain status (social capital) in her own community. The wounding potential of gendered words was also confirmed, since they were used to carry out FTAs that threatened the positive gender-face of Tessa Ganserer.

Future research could explore in more depth politeness strategies surrounding discourses about transgender, non-binary and gender-nonconforming individuals. In addition, a cross-cultural comparison of politeness and impoliteness strategies around gender would shed light on how different cultures and languages address the topic. Finally, it would be key to explore cases in which the perlocutionary and illocutionary force of the speech acts do not align and linguistic behaviors around gender(ing) which are intended as polite as seen as impolite and vice versa.

6 Appendix

Codes:
- Bald on record impoliteness
  - Use of inappropriate identity markers
    - Deadnaming
    - Misgendering
- Off-record impoliteness
  - Indirect FTA
  - Mock politeness

Sehr geehrte Frau Präsidentin! Meine Damen und Herren! "Frauen werden abgeschafft!", das ist der Titel eines Beitrags in der "EMMA" von der Harry-Potter-Erfinderin J. K. Rowling, und das genau betreiben Sie fast alle hier. Sie fast alle hier sind Frauenabschaffer, weil Sie fast alle hier der Genderideologie anhängen.

Sie behaupten, das Geschlecht habe mit Biologie nichts zu tun und jeder könne sein Geschlecht irgendwie selbst bestimmen. Das Selbstbestimmungsgesetz kommt demnächst auch in diesem Theater; wir warten schon mit Freude darauf.

Rowling hat es begriffen. Die Genderideologie gefährdet vor allem Frauen und Mädchen: Männer brechen Rekorde im Frauenschwimmen, Männer in der Damenumkleide, Sexualverbrecher im Frauengefängnis, weil sie sich gerade als Frauen fühlen. Rowling lehnt diesen Quatsch ab und wird deswegen mit obsessivem Hass verfolgt.

Die Transideologie ist totalitär, und sie ist zwangsläufig totalitär. Wer so offenkundig die Natur, die Wahrheit leugnet, der muss die Wahrheit selbst zum Verbrechen erklären und jeden, der die Wahrheit ausspricht, zum Verbrecher.

Der Bundestag liefert ein gutes Beispiel. Wenn der Kollege Markus Ganserer Rock, Lippenstift, Hackenschuhe trägt, dann ist das völlig in Ordnung; es ist aber seine Privatsache. Biologisch und juristisch ist und bleibt er ein Mann. Und wenn er als solcher über die grüne Frauenquote in den Bundestag einzieht und hier als Frau geführt wird, dann ist das schlicht rechtswidrig.

Ich bin Markus Ganserer aber für zwei Dinge dankbar: erstens, weil sein Beispiel uns so schön vor Augen führt, dass es einen Unterschied macht, ob man sich als Frau verkleidet oder ob man eine Frau ist, und zweitens, weil er die Frauenquote final ad absurdum geführt hat.

Hätte sich Robert Habeck im richtigen Moment als Roberta bezeichnet, dann wäre Roberta vermutlich jetzt Bundeskanzlerin.

Der Queer-Beauftragte der Bundesregierung, Sven Lehmann, meint, jeder, der Herrn Ganserer nicht als Frau akzeptiere, sei transphob.

Transphob ist offensichtlich ein anderes Wort für "nicht blöd". Nicht blöd sind auch die Initiatoren von "Geschlecht zählt". Das sind ausdrücklich Feministinnen und Grüne, die gegen Ganserers Mandat nun klagen. Sie verstehen, dass es ohne Biologie keine Frauen gibt und ohne Frauen auch keine Frauenrechte.

Der Weltfrauentag ist ein guter Moment, um festzustellen: Ein Fisch ist kein Fahrrad, ein Mann ist keine Frau, und Gender ist gaga. Jede Wahrheit braucht einen Mutigen, der sie ausspricht, und in diesem Parlament ist das die AfD.

Vielen Dank. (Deutscher Bundestag 2022b: 1143)

References

Brown, Penelope and Stephen C. Levinson. 1987. *Politeness: Some universals in language usage*, vol. 4. Cambridge: Cambridge University Press.
Butler, Judith. 1997. *Excitable speech: A politics of the performative*. New York: Routledge.
Culpeper, Jonathan. 1996. Towards an anatomy of impoliteness. *Journal of Pragmatics* 25(3). 349–367. https://doi.org/10.1016/0378-2166(95)00014-3.
Culpeper, Jonathan. 2005. Impoliteness and entertainment in the television quiz show: The weakest link. *Journal of Politeness Research. Language, Behaviour, Culture* 1(1). https://doi.org/10.1515/jplr.2005.1.1.35.
Culpeper, Jonathan. 2011. *Impoliteness: Using language to cause offence*. Cambridge: Cambridge University Press.
Culpeper, Jonathan, Derek Bousfield and Anne Wichmann. 2003. Impoliteness revisited: With special reference to dynamic and prosodic aspects. *Journal of Pragmatics* 35(10–11). 1545–1579. https://doi.org/10.1016/S0378-2166(02)00118-2.
Curtain, Colin. 2023. *Qualcoder*. https://qualcoder.wordpress.com. Accessed: 9 March 2025.
Deutscher Bundestag. 2022a. 17. Sitzung vom 17.02.2022, TOP 8 Vereinbarte Debatte - Internationaler Frauentag. https://dbtg.tv/cvid/7533697. Accessed: 27 November 2023.
Deutscher Bundestag. 2022b. Plenarprotokoll 20/17: Stenografischer Bericht. 17. Sitzung. https://dserver.bundestag.de/btp/20/20017.pdf. Accessed: 27 November 2023.
Dimitrova-Galaczi, Evelina. 2002. Issues in the definition and conceptualization of politeness. *Studies in Applied Linguistics and TESOL* 2(1). https://doi.org/10.7916/salt.v2i1.1650.
Eckert, Penelope and Sally McConnell-Ginet. 1992. Communities of practice: Where language, gender and power all live. In Kira Hall, Mary Bucholtz and Birch Moonwomon (eds.), *Locating power, proceedings of the 1992 berkeley women and language conference*, 89–99. Berkeley: Berkeley Women and Language Group.
Fraser, Bruce. 1990. Perspectives on politeness. *Journal of Pragmatics* 14(2). 219–236.
Goffman, Erving. 1967. *Interaction ritual: Essays on face-to-face interaction*. Chicago: Aldine.
Goldenberg, Rina. 2021. A guide to Germany's political parties. https://www.dw.com/en/spd-green-party-fdp-cdu-left-party-afd/a-38085900. Accessed: 15 December 2024.
Johnson, Wendell G. and Katharina Barbe. 2022. *Modern Germany*. Santa Barbara: Bloomsbury.
Kienpointner, Manfred. 2008. Impoliteness and emotional arguments. *Journal of Politeness Research. Language, Behaviour, Culture* 4(2). 243–265.

Lim, Tae-Seop. 1994. Facework and interpersonal relationships. In Stella Ting-Toomey (ed.), *The challenge of facework: Cross-cultural and interpersonal issues* SUNY series in Human Communication, 209–229. Albany: State University of New York Press.
Motschenbacher, Heiko. 2010. *Language, gender and sexual identity*. Amsterdam, Philadelphia: John Benjamins. https://doi.org/10.1075/impact.29.
Rowling, J. K. 2020. Frauen werden abgeschafft! https://www.emma.de/artikel/jk-rowling-frauen-werden-abgeschafft-338023. Accessed: 3 November 2023.
Watts, Richard J. 2003. *Politeness*. Cambridge: Cambridge University Press.

Dominic Schmitz
Pronoun comprehension from a discriminative perspective: A proof of concept

Abstract: The English pronoun system is not as straightforward as often stated by grammarians. The third-person singular pronouns *he* and *she* are not only used to refer to male and female individuals, but are also used to refer to individuals of any gender. Similarly, the pronoun *they*, commonly found as a third-person plural pronoun, is increasingly often used in its generic sense to refer to single individuals of any gender. Yet, there is little research available on the semantics and the comprehension of such specific and generic pronouns. Making use of naive discriminative learning, instance vectors, and linear discriminative learning, the present paper proposes a novel computational approach to the study of pronoun semantics and comprehension. As an exemplary case, the comprehension of generic *they* is compared to the comprehension of specific *he*, specific *she*, and plural *they*. Measures extracted from the comprehension process deliver meaningful insights into the comprehension of the given pronouns, rendering the proposed methodology a promising one for future research.

Keywords: discriminative learning, distributional semantics, pronoun comprehension, pronoun semantics

1 Introduction: Third-person pronouns in contemporary English

In contemporary English, "[g]ender classes can be differentiated only on the basis of relations with pronouns" (Huddleston and Pullum 2002: 485). Pronouns are functional elements of a language which are used to replace or serve the function of noun phrases. In their most common use, pronouns refer directly to entities in the world and are, with that, assumed to adopt the meaning of the entities they refer to (Conrod 2020).

The pronominal gender system of English traditionally differentiates three grammatical genders: masculine (*he*), feminine (*she*), and neuter (*it*). The three

---

Dominic Schmitz, Department of English Language and Linguistics, Heinrich Heine University Düsseldorf, e-mail: dominic.schmitz@uni-duesseldorf.de

grammatical genders are distinguished semantically, based on the two features of humanness and the biological sex of the relevant referent (Siemund 2008), making the gender system a covert one in which morphophonological information cannot be used to determine a noun's gender (Corbett 1991). Following the semantic basis, male antecedents are referred to by masculine pronouns (e.g., *the man and **his** dog*), female antecedents are referred to by feminine pronouns (e.g., *the woman and **her** dog*), and all other antecedents are referred to by neuter pronouns (e.g., *the house and **its** roof*).

However, while the gender system predominantly functions on the basis of humanness and biological sex, there is a considerable grey area (Siemund 2008; Audring 2009; McConnell-Ginet 2015; Conrod 2019). For example, within groups of homosexual men, the use of *she* instead of *he* to refer to other group members has been observed to express positive as well as negative character traits (Rudes and Healy 1979). Mathiot (1979) reports on the use of *he* instead of *she* for women, most likely used to highlight their competence, hinting at the assumed superiority of men. Both examples cast doubt on the absolute nature of biological sex as the definitive feature of gender in English. There are also cases which question the definitive nature of humanness as basis of gender assignment; several of them are mentioned by Siemund (2008). Usage of *he* and *she* instead of *it* is frequently found for animals, especially for higher domestic animals and for animals for which the outer appearance clearly identifies biological sex (e.g., lions). In some cases, the usage of *he* and *she* has become highly conventionalized, ignoring the actual biological sex of the pertinent animal: Dogs are referred to by *he* and cats by *she*, respectively. A case of reversed nature is the use of *it* to refer to babies, toddlers, and children. Finally, the pronouns *he* and *she* may even be used to refer to antecedents which are neither human nor show biological sex, be they of supernatural nature (e.g., gods, apparitions; Poutsma 1914) or inanimate. An example of the latter case are ships and countries, for which speakers regularly use *she* instead of *it*. While the exact nature of this kind of pronoun use is still unclear, one idea is that the use of *he* and *she* personifies referents, i.e., it shows their importance, while the use of *it* for humans underlyingly shows the importance of biological sex within society (Siemund 2008). In sum, humanness and biological sex apparently do neither straightforwardly nor exhaustively capture the variation of usage within the English pronominal gender system.

A further case in which the typically associated gender of a pronoun and the biological sex of referents do not coincide is the use of epicene pronouns.[1] Epicenes

---

[1] Yet another case is the use of neopronouns. However, this case is beyond the scope of the present study.

are understood as pronouns that can refer to all individuals regardless of gender, as epicenes supposedly give no information or notional content on the referent's biological sex (e.g. Baron 1981; Newman 1997; Baranowski 2002). When used as epicenes, *he* and *she* are typically called 'generic *he*' and 'generic *she*', with the generic use of *she* being far less frequent than that of *he* (Hekanaho 2020; Conrod 2020). Examples for generic *he* and *she* are given in Examples (1) and (2).

(1) They voted for whoever looked like **he** would finally fix the plumbing. (OED 2023: s.v. <he>)

(2) When someone works for less than **she** can live on..then **she** has made a great sacrifice for you. (OED 2023: s.v. <she>)

Traditionally, grammarians have declared the masculine pronoun, i.e., *he*, to be the default unmarked gender of English for more than two centuries (Corbett 1991). However, regardless of its stipulated gender-neutral nature, the use of *he* as default epicene does not come without a long history of debate about its appropriateness (Conrod 2020). McConnell-Ginet (2015) argues that the use of generic *he* cannot be considered to be gender-neutral, as gender assumptions or associations connected to non-epicene *he* inhibit true gender-neutrality. Indeed, for the generic usage of *he* (and also for that of *she*) a number of studies have shown that utterances intended to be gender-neutral were comprehended as not gender-neutral. Instead, both pronouns biased participants' associations towards the masculine (*he*) or feminine (*she*) interpretation, respectively (Martyna 1978; MacKay and Fulkerson 1979; Miller and James 2009). Thus, the generic usage of *he* (and *she*) apparently is not perceived as gender-neutral.

Several alternatives to generic *he* have been devised in English over the last decades, however, not with much success (Baron 1981; Livia 2001). Some of the more known alternatives are phrases like *he or she*, contractions like *s/he*, and singular *they* (Adami 2009). Singular *they* used to refer to single antecedents has been part of the English language at least since the 15th century. However, grammarians commonly disapprove of its usage (Conrod 2020). Nonetheless, several different types of singular *they* developed within English (Conrod 2019). Two of them are considered to be generic, the difference between them being whether they refer to an indefinite or definite antecedent, see Examples (3) and (4).

(3) Someone ran out of the classroom, but **they** forgot **their** backpack. (Conrod 2019: 81)

(4) The ideal student completes the homework, but not if **they** have an emergency. (Conrod 2019: 81)

While research on singular *they* has increased during the last decades, most studies are concerned with singular *they* from a sociolinguistic or syntactic perspective, asking which types of singular *they* there are (e.g. Bjorkman 2017; Conrod 2019, 2020), to which degree they are accepted among speakers (e.g. Bradley 2020), and how singular *they* can be accounted for in terms of syntactic agreement (e.g. Conrod 2019, 2022).

To summarize, English pronoun gender is assumed to rely on semantics. In any of the aforementioned cases, the usage of a pertinent pronoun can be retraced to certain semantic features of its antecedent. However, the classification of potential antecedents for pertinent pronouns appears to be not as straightforward as often stated. Several pronouns, i.e., *he*, *she*, and *they*, are used for very different types of antecedents, i.e., human and non-human, animate and inanimate, singular and plural, non-generic and generic, as well as male, female, and neuter antecedents. With one pronoun referring to semantically different antecedents, the question arises whether the comprehension of pronouns themselves is different depending on their antecedents. For instance, does generic *they* bear semantics similar to those of plural *they*? That is, are generic *they* and plural *they* treated similarly in the comprehension process? There are only very few studies available that investigated related questions or pronoun semantics and their comprehension to begin with. Notably, Sanford and Filik (2007) conducted an eye-tracking study, in which the authors found that generic *they* preserved portions of the plural semantics of plural *they*.

The aim of the present study is the proposition of a novel approach to the analysis of pronoun comprehension by means of computational methods. These methods constitute a framework novel to the research on pronouns and will allow future studies to investigate similarities and dissimilarities in comprehension between different pronouns but also between specific usages of a pertinent pronoun form. As an exemplary case, the comprehension of generic *they* will be compared to the comprehension of specific *he*, specific *she*, and plural *they*.

2 Method

The methodological approach proposed consists of five main parts. First, a text corpus containing attestations of the pronouns under investigation is required. Second, based on this corpus, vector representations of the semantics of words within the corpus are created. Third, individual semantic vectors for each occurrence of the pronouns under investigation are computed. Fourth, using the semantic vectors of the respective pronouns and further words, a mental lexicon and the comprehension processes therein are modeled. Fifth, from this simulated lexicon, measures are extracted to analyze the comprehension of the respective pronouns. The corpus, data, and scripts are available at the OSF: https://osf.io/bvxu5 (accessed: 21 January 2024).

2.1 A corpus of third-person pronouns

To work on the comprehension of third-person pronouns using the approach proposed in this paper, one first requires a corpus of the usage of third-person pronouns. The corpus used for the present study is based on newspaper articles contained in the Contemporary Corpus of American English (Davies 2008). For non-generic *he*, *she*, and *they*, attestations are easily found. For generic *they*, however, finding attestations is somewhat more difficult. This is mainly due to two reasons. First, plural *they* is far more frequent than generic *they*. Second, corpora are commonly not tagged in a way that reflects whether a token of *they* is plural or generic.

For this reason, instead of searching directly for attestations of *they*, the following search queries were used: *one must, anybody, anyone, someone, somebody*, and *person*. While the indefinite pronouns frequently co-occur with the use of generic *they* (cf. Example (3) above), the noun *person* invites general observations, which in turn may call for the use of an epicene expression.

For each pronoun under investigation, i.e., *he*, *she*, generic *they*, and plural *they*, the aim was to collect at least 50 attestations. In the created corpus, there are 100 attestations of *he*, 52 attestations of *she*, 139 attestations of plural *they*, and 81 attestations of generic *they*. To enrich the corpus with linguistic material beyond pronouns, randomly selected sentences from COCA without attestations of the pronouns under investigation were added to arrive at a total number of 1000 sentences.

As a prerequisite for the next steps, the corpus was automatically tagged using the RNNTagger software (Schmid 1999). The software identifies the lemma of each word; these lemmas, instead of inflected forms, were then used in the following step.

2.2 Capturing semantics with vectors

Capturing the semantics of lexical units with vectors is an idea that originates in distributional semantics, which follows the distributional hypothesis: Differences in meaning are represented by differences in distribution (Harris 1954; Boleda 2020). If words occur in similar contexts, their semantics are expected to be similar. If words, however, frequently occur in different contexts, their semantics are expected to be different as well. Following this idea, semantics can be captured by mathematical vectors, which are computed based on the distribution of words in large amounts of text. There are several algorithms with which one may arrive at such semantic vectors, e.g., Word2Vec (Mikolov et al. 2013), GloVe (Pennington et al. 2014), fastText (Bojanowski et al. 2016), or naive discriminative learning (henceforth NDL; Baayen et al. 2011; Baayen and Ramscar 2015).

The latter, NDL, is grounded in psychological theory on cognitive mechanisms (Pearce and Bouton 2001; Rescorla 1988), which has been shown to successfully model important learning effects in humans and animals alike (Kamin 1969; Ramscar et al. 2010). Following the Rescorla-Wagner rules (Rescorla and Wagner 1972; Wagner and Rescorla 1972), learning is understood as a result of informative relations within events, which in turn consist of cues and outcomes. With each new event encountered, the associations between cues and outcomes are constantly recalibrated. The associations of a given outcome and all cues encountered thus far at a given point in time can be understood as the outcome's relation to the world around the learning individual. The recalibration of associations happens in such a way that weights of an association increase every time the involved cue and outcome co-occur, while association weights decrease if a pertinent cue occurs without a given outcome. Once the learning process is finished, i.e., once all available events have been encountered, the final associations represent the interrelations of a pertinent outcome with all cues encountered during the learning process. Transferring this concept onto language, cues and outcomes may, for example, be content and function words as well as inflectional and/or derivational functions (e.g., singular vs. plural; derivational suffixes like *-ee*, *-ation*, and *-ment*) found in a text corpus annotated according to the needs of the pertinent investigation. For the present study, NDL was used to compute semantic vectors for all lemmas of the corpus introduced in Section 2.1.

However, computing semantic vectors using NDL leads to one critical issue for the present investigation: For words with identical forms, their senses are conflated into one vector representation (Lapesa et al. 2018). That is, one vector for the form *they* will be computed, conflating the semantics of plural *they* and generic *they*. Facing a similar issue in a study on generic and non-generic masculine role nouns in German, Schmitz (2024) made use of instance vectors, following ideas by Lapesa et al. (2018). Instance vectors are "vector representations for individual instances of words, i.e., tokens, rather than lemmas, i.e., types" (Lapesa et al. 2018: 291f). Following Lapesa et al. (2018), for the computation of each instance vector, a window of n context words around a given target word is taken into account. The mean of the n preceding and following context words' vectors constitutes the given target word's instance vector. For the present investigation, a context word window of $n = 2$ was used, which, according to Lapesa et al. (2018), captures true semantic similarity. Following common practice in distributional semantics, function words were not counted as context words. That is, instance vectors were created on the basis of content words. The vectors of context words can be taken from any approach to distributional semantics. For the present investigation, instance vectors were computed for all target pronouns attestations based on the NDL vectors of their surroundings.

2.3 Modelling the lexicon with discriminative learning

To model comprehension – and thereby gain insight into the semantic features of the pronouns under investigation – the present study makes use of linear discriminative learning (henceforth LDL; Baayen et al. 2019). In an implementation of LDL, the mental lexicon is simulated by generating a system of form-meaning relations that discriminates between different forms and meanings. Such an implementation allows the detailed investigation of entries and their relationship to each other within the mental lexicon.

For the simulated mental lexicon, LDL implementations generally require two things: semantics and forms of lexical entries. Semantics are most commonly represented by semantic vectors, such as those introduced in Section 2.2. Forms are also represented as vectors, which most commonly contain binary-coded information on whether certain n-graphs or n-phones are part of a given word form. For each word form's individual form vector c, the presence of an n-graph/n-phone cue is marked with 1, while the absence of a given cue is marked with 0. The interested reader is referred to Heitmeier et al. (2021) for a detailed overview of different design choices in the implementation of LDL models.

The entirety of semantic vectors to be included constitutes the S matrix and the entirety of form vectors to be included constitutes the C matrix of the respective implementation. Thus, each entry of the lexicon is represented twice: Once by a semantic vectors, which contains its meaning, and once by a form vector, which describes its phonology or orthography.

With the S and the C matrix at hand, one can compute the comprehension and production processes of the mental lexicon via multivariate multiple regression. Comprehension is modelled by simple linear mappings from the form matrix C to the semantic matrix S and production is modelled by likewise mappings from the semantic matrix S to the form matrix C. These mappings specify how strongly input nodes are associated to output nodes. A comprehension weight matrix F is obtained solving

$$S = CF, \qquad (1)$$

while a production weight matrix G is obtained solving

$$C = SG. \qquad (2)$$

In full-sized implementations of LDL, CF and SG are approximations of the S and C matrix due to their high dimensionality and the workings of linear regression. That is,

$$\hat{S} = CF \qquad (3)$$

contains the predicted semantic vectors and

$$\hat{C} = SG \qquad (4)$$

contains the predicted form vectors. It is these predicted vectors in $\hat{S}$ that we are interested in, as they are the result of the simulated comprehension process. In other words, the result of mapping forms onto meanings is an approximation to the original input semantics. These approximated meanings are taken as the result of the comprehension process, i.e., the result of the interrelations of forms and meanings in the mental lexicon. From these predicted meanings, then, one may derive an array of semantic measures directly connected to the comprehension of the pertinent lexical entry.

While architecture of LDL, as it is illustrated in Figure 1, might appear simplistic to some readers, previous research has shown that such linear mappings result in overall high accuracies (e.g. Baayen et al. 2018, 2019) and that semantic as well as phonological measures derived from such an implementation can explain a variety of empirical measures, e.g., acoustic duration (e.g., Chuang et al. 2021; Schmitz et al. 2021; Stein and Plag 2021), but also real word and pseudoword semantics (e.g., Chuang et al. 2021; Schmitz et al. 2021), and the male comprehension bias in generic masculines (Schmitz et al. 2023).

2.4 Including pronouns in the discriminative lexicon

To model the comprehension of third-person pronouns in the mental lexicon, not one but multiple implementations of LDL were needed. That is, as explained in Section 2.2, the semantics of each target pronoun was not captured in one semantic vector but in as many vectors as there were corpus attestations of the respective pronoun. Including all of these vectors within the same semantic matrix S and, with that, the simulated mental lexicon would go against common assumptions of the latter, i.e., one would not assume a single pronoun to have multiple entries in the mental lexicon.

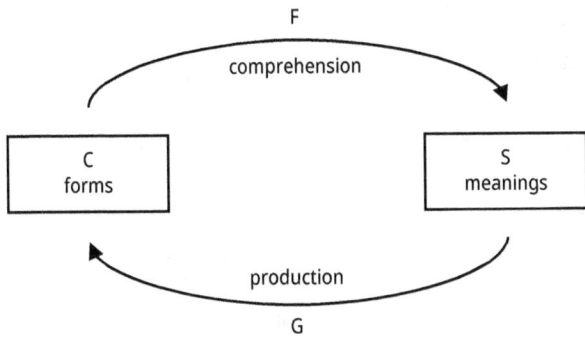

Fig. 1: Illustration of the comprehension and production mapping.

The LDL models were implemented in Julia using the JudiLing package (Luo et al. 2021) for the implementation itself and the JudiLingMeasures package (Heitmeier 2023) to compute measures based on the implementations. Besides the four pronoun vectors per LDL model, all other words of the corpus were included. In total, each implementation simulated a mental lexicon based on 3,524 entries. While the semantics of entries was represented by the NDL and instance vectors as explained above, form vectors were based on the orthography of entries and coded as trigraphs.

Measures extracted from each implementation of LDL were semantic CO-ACTIVATION, comprehension UNCERTAINTY, and semantic neighborhood DENSITY. These measures have been shown to successfully reflect the comprehended semantics of lexical entries and to model related experimental data (e.g., Schmitz et al. 2021; Stein and Plag 2021; Chuang et al. 2021; Heitmeier et al. 2023). CO-ACTIVATION is the Euclidean norm, that is the square root of the sum of the squared values, of a given predicted semantic vector. Higher values indicate higher degrees of co-activation. UNCERTAINTY represents the degree of dissimilarity between corresponding rows, with higher values indicating greater uncertainty. DENSITY is the mean cosine similarity of a target word's predicted vector with its ten most similar neighbors. Similarity is computed using cosine similarity.

3 Results

The distribution of the three comprehension measures across pronouns within the fifty LDL implementations is given in Figure 2. The measures were compared between pronouns using Bonferroni-corrected pairwise Wilcoxon tests. The results of these comparisons are given in Table 1.

Tab. 1: Results of Bonferroni-corrected pairwise Wilcoxon tests comparing the three comprehension measures across pronouns.

	CO-ACTIVATION			UNCERTAINTY			DENSITY		
	he	she	they$_g$	he	she	they$_g$	he	she	they$_g$
she	1.000			1.000			0.803		
they$_g$	0.234	0.329		0.314	1.000		0.001	0.038	
they$_p$	<0.001	<0.001	0.740	0.002	0.003	0.781	1.000	1.000	0.067

For CO-ACTIVATION, the values of *he* and *she* are significantly different from those of plural *they*, with plural *they* showing on average higher values, i.e., higher levels of semantic co-activation. As for generic *they*, it shows levels of co-activation in-between those of *he*/*she* and plural *they*, rendering it non-significantly different from the other pronouns.

For UNCERTAINTY, similar differences are found. The uncertainty values of plural *they* are significantly different from those of *he* and *she*, but not from those of generic *they*. Again, plural *they* comes with the highest mean value, followed by generic *they*, which in turn is followed by *he* and *she*. Hence, plural *they* shows the highest degree of uncertainty, while *he* and *she* show the lowest degree of uncertainty.

For DENSITY, differences pattern differently. Here, *he* and *she* are significantly different from generic *they*, while plural *they* is not significantly different from generic *they*. Overall, plural *they* comes with the densest semantic neighborhoods on average, followed by *he* and *she*, which in turn are followed by generic *they*. That is, *he*, *she*, and plural *they* come with the most semantically similar direct neighbors. For generic *they*, one finds a rather broad distribution of semantic neighborhood densities. Comparing interquartile ranges, this impression is confirmed: $IQR_{he} = 0.146$, $IQR_{she} = 0.201$, $IQR_{pluralthey} = 0.275$ vs. $IQR_{genericthey} = 0.319$.

4 Discussion

The present study set out to showcase an approach novel to the research on pronouns. Using computational methods – naive discriminative learning, instance vectors, and linear discriminative learning – the semantics of *he*, *she*, generic *they*, and

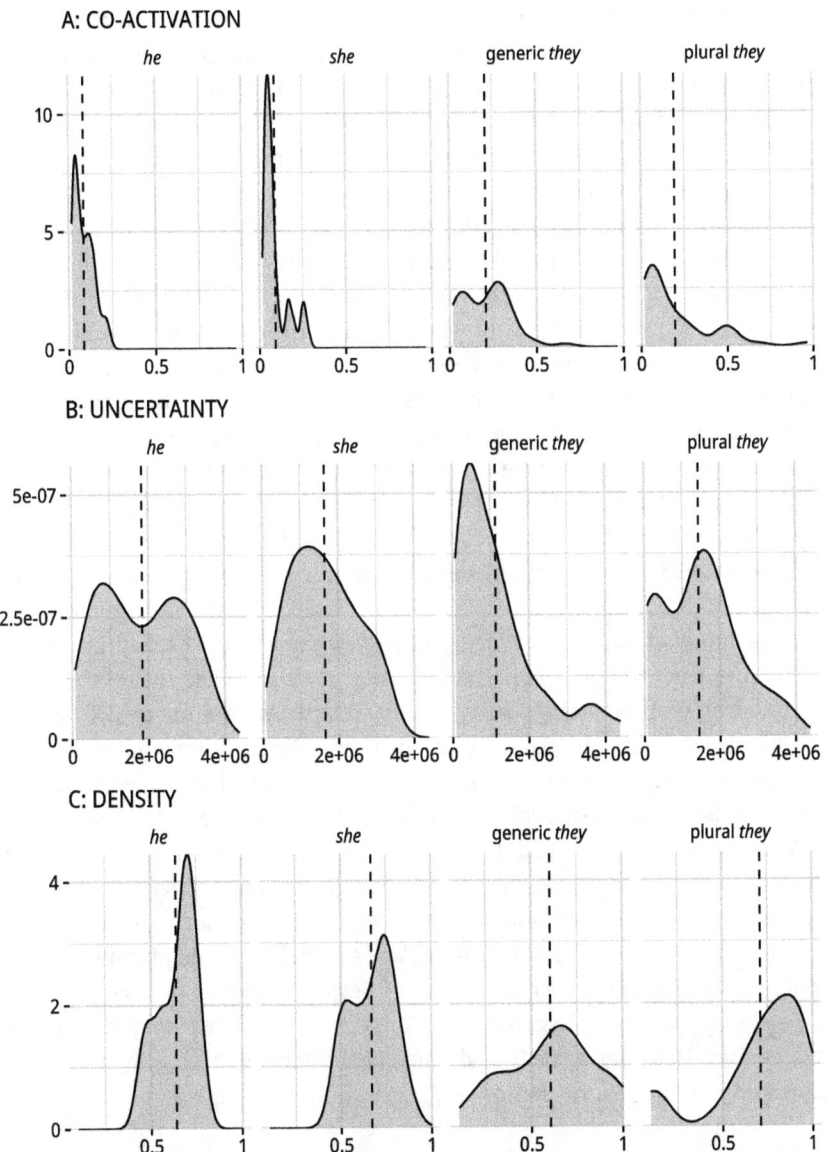

Fig. 2: Distribution of semantic CO-ACTIVATION (Panel A), comprehension UNCERTAINTY (Panel B), and semantic neighborhood DENSITY (Panel C) across pronouns within the fifty LDL implementations. Dashed lines indicate the pronoun-specific mean.

plural *they* were captured, and their comprehension was simulated. From fifty such simulations, measures on the comprehension of the pronouns under investigation were extracted and compared. But what do these measures tell us about the respective pronouns and their comprehension?

For semantic co-activation, it was found that plural *they* showed the highest degree of co-activation across the four pronouns under investigation. Hence, plural *they* co-activates the most entries in the lexicon when it is retrieved during the comprehension process. As plural *they* is the only third-person plural pronoun, all entries that have a plural form should be somewhat connected to plural *they*, as it is the pronoun used to refer to these plurals. For *he* and *she*, on the other hand, the degree of semantic co-activation was lowest. Taking into account that the set of referents for *he* and *she* is clearly more restricted than those of plural *they* (cf. Section 1), fewer co-activated lexical entries appear sensible. For generic *they*, a degree of semantic co-activation between that of plural *they* and that of *he* and *she* was found. One potential explanation for this finding is the set of potential referents: The set should at least contain all potential referents of *he* and *she* that fall into the categories of indefinite and definite non-specific antecedents, see Examples (3) and (4).

For comprehension uncertainty, plural *they* came with the highest values. Again, as the set of referents of plural *they* is clearly bigger than that of the singular pronouns, comprehending its semantics is relatively more uncertain, because there is a bigger set of potential referent semantics to chose from. Analogously, the comprehension uncertainty for *he* and *she* is lowest, while that of generic *they* is in-between the uncertainty levels of plural *they* and *he* and *she*.

For semantic neighborhood density, it was found that *he*, *she* and plural *they* come with denser semantic neighborhoods than generic *they*. That is, the ten nearest neighbors of *he*, *she* and plural *they* are significantly closer to their meaning than the ten nearest neighbors of generic *they*. As for *he*, *she*, and plural *they*, their sets of potential referents are rather clear (cf. Section 1). These potential referents, then, make up their near neighborhood. For generic *they*, however, the set of referents is much less clear or restricted. One might interpret this finding as a direct manifestation of the generic part of the generic *they*.

5 Conclusion

In sum, three main findings emerged from the present study. First, the bigger the set of potential referents, the higher the degree of semantic co-activation during the comprehension process. Second, the bigger the set of potential referents, the more uncertainty is found in the comprehension process. Third, the more restricted a set of referents, the denser the semantic neighborhood of a pronoun. These findings were obtained using computational methods novel to the research on pronouns. However, these findings should also be taken with a grain of salt due to the rather limited number of observations. Future studies will show whether the results of the present study are confirmed by studies making use of a more substantial amount of data, and how similar investigations play out for other pronouns. Additionally, the emergence of ready-to-use LLMs like GPT and BERT allows for the inclusion of context-dependent vectors for each pronoun token. Using such semantic representations may render the vectors used to simulate a mental lexicon via LDL somewhat more realistic. A step beyond replication and expansion will be the validation of the comprehension measures against behavioral data. That is, it will be shown whether such measures are able to explain, for example, differences between reaction times in studies on pronoun choice or pronoun fit. Overall, the methods proposed in the present study will allow future studies to investigate comprehension similarities and dissimilarities between different pronouns but also between specific usages of a pertinent pronoun form.

References

Adami, Elisabetta. 2009. "To each reader his, their or her pronoun". Prescribed, proscribed and disregarded uses of generic pronouns in English. In Antoinette Renouf and Andrew Kehoe (eds.), *Corpus linguistics*, vol. 69, 281–308. Amsterdam: Brill. https://doi.org/10.1163/9789042025981_016.
Audring, Jenny. 2009. *Reinventing pronoun gender*. Amsterdam: University of Amsterdam dissertation.
Baayen, R. Harald, Yu-Ying Chuang and James P. Blevins. 2018. Inflectional morphology with linear mappings. *The Mental Lexicon* 13. 230–268. https://doi.org/10.1075/ml.18010.baa.
Baayen, R. Harald, Yu-Ying Chuang, Elnaz Shafaei-Bajestan and James P. Blevins. 2019. The discriminative lexicon: A unified computational model for the lexicon and lexical processing in comprehension and production grounded not in (de)composition but in linear discriminative learning. *Complexity* 2019. 4895891. https://doi.org/10.1155/2019/4895891.
Baayen, R. Harald, Petar Milin, Dusica Filipović Đurđević, Peter Hendrix and Marco Marelli. 2011. An amorphous model for morphological processing in visual comprehension based on naive discriminative learning. *Psychological Review* 118. 438–481. https://doi.org/10.1037/a0023851.
Baayen, R. Harald and Michael Ramscar. 2015. Abstraction, storage and naive discriminative learning. In Ewa Dabrowska and Dagmar Divjak (eds.), *Handbook of cognitive linguistics*, 100–120. Berlin, München, Boston: De Gruyter. https://doi.org/10.1515/9783110292022-006.
Baranowski, Maciej. 2002. Current usage of the epicene pronoun in written English. *Journal of Sociolinguistics* 6. 378–397. https://doi.org/10.1111/1467-9481.00193.
Baron, Dennis E. 1981. The epicene pronoun: The word that failed. *American Speech* 56. 83. https://doi.org/10.2307/455007.

Bjorkman, Bronwyn M. 2017. Singular they and the syntactic representation of gender in English. *Glossa: a journal of general linguistics* 2. https://doi.org/10.5334/gjgl.374.

Bojanowski, Piotr, Edouard Grave, Armand Joulin and Tomas Mikolov. 2016. Enriching word vectors with subword information. *Transactions of the Association for Computational Linguistics* 5. 135–146. https://doi.org/10.48550/arxiv.1607.04606.

Boleda, Gemma. 2020. Distributional semantics and linguistic theory. *Annual Review of Linguistics* 6. 213–234. https://doi.org/10.1146/annurev-linguistics-011619-030303.

Bradley, Evan D. 2020. The influence of linguistic and social attitudes on grammaticality judgments of singular 'they'. *Language Sciences* 78. 101272. https://doi.org/10.1016/J.LANGSCI.2020.101272.

Chuang, Yu-Ying, Marie Lenka Vollmer, Elnaz Shafaei-Bajestan, Susanne Gahl, Peter Hendrix and R. Harald Baayen. 2021. The processing of pseudoword form and meaning in production and comprehension: A computational modeling approach using linear discriminative learning. *Behavior Research Methods* 53. 945–976. https://doi.org/10.3758/s13428-020-01356-w.

Conrod, Kirby. 2019. *Pronouns raising and emerging*. Seattle: University of Washington dissertation.

Conrod, Kirby. 2020. Pronouns and gender in language. In Kira Hall and Rusty Barrett (eds.), *The Oxford handbook of language and sexuality*, Oxford: Oxford University Press. https://doi.org/10.1093/oxfordhb/9780190212926.013.63.

Conrod, Kirby. 2022. Abolishing gender on D. *Canadian Journal of Linguistics/Revue canadienne de linguistique* 67. 216–241. https://doi.org/10.1017/cnj.2022.27.

Corbett, Greville G. 1991. *Gender*. Cambridge: Cambridge University Press. https://doi.org/10.1017/CBO9781139166119.

Davies, Mark. 2008. The corpus of contemporary American English (coca). https://www.english-corpora.org/coca. Accessed: 9 March 2025.

Harris, Zellig S. 1954. Distributional structure. *WORD* 10. 146–162. https://doi.org/10.1080/00437956.1954.11659520.

Heitmeier, Maria. 2023. Judilingmeasures: Calculate measures for LDL models developed with JudiLing. https://github.com/MariaHei/JudiLingMeasures.jl. Accessed: 9 March 2025.

Heitmeier, Maria, Yu Ying Chuang and R. Harald Baayen. 2021. Modeling morphology with linear discriminative learning: Considerations and design choices. *Frontiers in Psychology* 12. 4929. https://doi.org/10.3389/FPSYG.2021.720713.

Heitmeier, Maria, Yu-Ying Chuang and R. Harald Baayen. 2023. How trial-to-trial learning shapes mappings in the mental lexicon: Modelling lexical decision with linear discriminative learning. *Cognitive Psychology* 146. 101598. https://doi.org/10.1016/j.cogpsych.2023.101598.

Hekanaho, Laura. 2020. *Generic and nonbinary pronouns: Usage, acceptability and attitudes*. Helsinki: University of Helsinki dissertation.

Huddleston, Rodney and Geoffrey K. Pullum. 2002. *The Cambridge grammar of the English language*. Cambridge: Cambridge University Press. https://doi.org/10.1017/9781316423530.

Kamin, Leon J. 1969. Predictability, surprise, attention, and conditioning. In Byron A. Campbell and Russell M. Church (eds.), *Punishment and aversive behavior*, 279–296. New York: Appleton-Century-Crofts.

Lapesa, Gabriella, Lea Kawaletz, Ingo Plag, Marios Andreou, Max Kisselew and Sebastian Padó. 2018. Disambiguation of newly derived nominalizations in context: A distributional semantics approach. *Word Structure* 11. 277–312. https://doi.org/10.3366/WORD.2018.0131.

Livia, Anna. 2001. *Pronoun envy: Literary uses of linguistic gender*. New York, Oxford: Oxford University Press. https://doi.org/10.1093/oso/9780195138528.001.0001.

Luo, X., Yu-Ying Chuang and R. Harald Baayen. 2021. Judiling: An implementation in Julia of linear discriminative learning algorithms for language model. https://megamindhenry.github.io/JudiLing.jl/stable. Accessed: 9 March 2025.

MacKay, Donald G. and David C. Fulkerson. 1979. On the comprehension and production of pronouns. *Journal of Verbal Learning and Verbal Behavior* 18. 661–673. https://doi.org/10.1016/S0022-5371(79)90369-4.

Martyna, Wendy. 1978. What does 'he' mean? Use of the generic masculine. *Journal of Communication* 28. 131–138. https://doi.org/10.1111/J.1460-2466.1978.TB01576.X.

Mathiot, Madeleine. 1979. Sex roles as revealed through referential gender in American English. In Madeleine Mathiot (ed.), *Ethnolinguistics*, 1–48. Berlin, Boston: De Gruyter. https://doi.org/10.1515/9783110804157-002.

McConnell-Ginet, Sally. 2015. Gender and its relation to sex: The myth of 'natural' gender. In Greville G. Corbett (ed.), *The expression of gender*, 3–38. Berlin, Boston: De Gruyter.

Mikolov, Tomas, Kai Chen, Gregory S. Corrado and Jeffrey Dean. 2013. Efficient estimation of word representations in vector space. In *International conference on learning representations*, https://doi.org/10.48550/arxiv.1301.3781.

Miller, Megan M. and Lori E. James. 2009. Is the generic pronoun he still comprehended as excluding women? *The American Journal of Psychology* 122. 483–496. https://doi.org/10.2307/27784423.

Newman, Michael. 1997. *Epicene pronouns: The linguistics of a prescriptive problem*. New York: Garland.

OED. 2023. *Oxford English dictionary online*. Oxford: Oxford University Press.

Pearce, John M. and Mark E. Bouton. 2001. Theories of associative learning in animals. *Annual Review of Psychology* 52. 111–139. https://doi.org/10.1146/annurev.psych.52.1.111.

Pennington, Jeffrey, Richard Socher and Christopher Manning. 2014. GloVe: Global vectors for word representation. In Alessandro Moschitti, Bo Pang and Walter Daelemans (eds.), *Proceedings of the 2014 conference on empirical methods in natural language processing (EMNLP)*, 1532–1543. Doha, Qatar: Association for Computational Linguistics. https://doi.org/10.3115/v1/D14-1162.

Poutsma, Hendrik. 1914. *A grammar of Late Modern English*. Groningen: Noordhoff.

Ramscar, Michael, Daniel Yarlett, Melody Dye, Katie Denny and Kirsten Thorpe. 2010. The effects of feature-label-order and their implications for symbolic learning. *Cognitive Science* 34. 909–957. https://doi.org/10.1111/j.1551-6709.2009.01092.x.

Rescorla, Robert A. 1988. Pavlovian conditioning: It's not what you think it is. *American Psychologist* 43. 151–160. https://doi.org/10.1037/0003-066X.43.3.151.

Rescorla, Robert A. and Allan R. Wagner. 1972. A theory of Pavlovian conditioning: Variations in the effectiveness of reinforcement and nonreinforcement. In Abraham H. Black and William F. Prokasy (eds.), *Classical conditioning II: Current research and theory*, 64–99. New York: Appleton-Century-Crofts.

Rudes, Blair A. and Bernard Healy. 1979. Is she for real? The concepts of femaleness and maleness in the gay world. In Madeleine Mathiot (ed.), *Ethnolinguistics*, 49–62. Berlin, Boston: De Gruyter. https://doi.org/10.1515/9783110804157-003.

Sanford, Anthony J. and Ruth Filik. 2007. They as a gender-unspecified singular pronoun: Eye tracking reveals a processing cost. *Quarterly Journal of Experimental Psychology* 60. 171–178. https://doi.org/10.1080/17470210600973390.

Schmid, Helmut. 1999. Improvements in part-of-speech tagging with an application to German. In Susan Armstrong, Kenneth Church, Pierre Isabelle, Sandra Manzi, Evelyne Tzoukermann and David Yarowsky (eds.), *Natural language processing using very large corpora*, 13–25. Springer. https://doi.org/10.1007/978-94-017-2390-9_2.

Schmitz, Dominic. 2024. Instances of bias: The gendered semantics of generic masculines in German revealed by instance vectors. *Zeitschrift für Sprachwissenschaft* 43(2). 295–325. https://doi.org/10.1515/zfs-2024-2010.

Schmitz, Dominic, Ingo Plag, Dinah Baer-Henney and Simon David Stein. 2021. Durational differences of word-final /s/ emerge from the lexicon: Modelling morpho-phonetic effects in pseudowords with linear discriminative learning. *Frontiers in Psychology* 12. https://doi.org/10.3389/fpsyg.2021.680889.

Schmitz, Dominic, Viktoria Schneider and Janina Esser. 2023. No generiaddress in sight: An exploration of the semantics of masculine generics in German. *Glossa Psycholinguistics* 2. https://doi.org/10.5070/G6011192.

Siemund, Peter. 2008. *Pronominal gender in English: A study of English varieties from a cross-linguistic perspective*. London: Routledge.

Stein, Simon David and Ingo Plag. 2021. Morpho-phonetic effects in speech production: Modeling the acoustic duration of English derived words with linear discriminative learning. *Frontiers in Psychology* 12. https://doi.org/10.3389/fpsyg.2021.678712.

Wagner, Allan R. and Robert A. Rescorla. 1972. Inhibition in Pavlovian conditioning: Application of a theory. In Robert A. Boakes and M. S. Halliday (eds.), *Inhibition and learning*, 301–334. Academic Press Inc.

Simon David Stein and Viktoria Schneider

Effects of English generic singular *they* on the gender processing of L1 German speakers

Abstract: In both German and English, generic masculine pronouns, such as *his*, are often used to include people of all genders (e.g., *On his first day at school, a pupil is usually very nervous*). However, previous studies found that generic masculine forms have a clear male bias. English, as opposed to German, features an increasingly commonly used, supposedly gender-neutral alternative to generic masculine pronouns: singular *they* (e.g., *On their first day at school, a pupil is usually very nervous*). Given that there is no straightforward German alternative, how do German learners of English interpret English singular *they*? Are they aware of its supposed gender-neutrality? We conducted an experiment asking L1 German participants to write a short story about a pupil and provide the pupil's name (cf. Moulton et al. 1978). Each participant received one of two versions of the task, one group starting the story following a sentence with a generically used *his* and the other following a sentence with a generically used *their*. We find a significant (albeit weak) effect, consistent with previous findings, showing that the stimulus version with *they* leads to fewer male protagonists. German learners of English do indeed seem to perceive English singular *they* as more gender-neutral than generic *his*. The results have implications for English language learning of L1 German speakers, and more generally for gender bias in language.

Keywords: English, gender-neutral language, generic masculine, German, L2 transfer, male bias, pronoun interpretation, singular they

1 Introduction

In both German and English, generic masculine pronouns, such as *seinem* 'his' in (1) and *his* in (2), are often used to include people of all genders.

(1) *An seinem ersten Schultag ist ein Schüler für gewöhnlich sehr nervös.*

Simon David Stein, Department of English Language and Linguistics, Heinrich Heine University Düsseldorf, e-mail: simon.stein@uni-duesseldorf.de
Viktoria Schneider, Department of English Language and Linguistics, Heinrich Heine University Düsseldorf, e-mail: viktoria.schneider@uni-duesseldorf.de

Open Access. © 2025 the author(s), published by De Gruyter. [CC BY] This work is licensed under the Creative Commons Attribution 4.0 International License.
https://doi.org/10.1515/9783111388694-007

(2)   On his first day at school, a pupil is usually very nervous.

However, previous studies found that generic masculine forms, both pronouns and role nouns, have a clear male bias (e.g., Martyna 1978; Rothmund and Scheele 2004; Braun et al. 2005; Gabriel et al. 2008; Gygax et al. 2008, 2009; Miller and James 2009; McConnell-Ginet 2015; Schmitz et al. 2023; Schmitz 2024). English, as opposed to German, features an increasingly commonly used, supposedly gender-neutral alternative to generic masculine pronouns: singular *they* (Conrod 2020). This is exemplified with the possessive pronoun *their* in (3).

(3)   On their first day at school, a pupil is usually very nervous.

But how do German learners of English interpret English singular *they*? Gender biases in the L1 are often observed to be transferred to L2 (Cook 2018; Koster and Loerts 2020; Schoenmakers et al. 2022), but there is no straightforward one-to-one mapping of singular *they* onto a German neutral alternative.[1] Are German speakers aware of the supposed gender-neutrality of singular *they* in English?

Previous research on L1 to L2 transfer of gender found that the interpretation of the gender of a referent is highly dependent on the gender assignment in the L1 (e.g., Cook 2018; Sabourin et al. 2016; Koster and Loerts 2020; Schoenmakers et al. 2022; Sato et al. 2013). For example, Sabourin et al. (2016) found that native speakers of English perform worse in gender assignment in German and Romance languages, which have grammatical gender class systems, than native speakers which are already used to a grammatical class system. For L1 German L2 English speakers, one could hypothesize a transfer of the grammatical gender of generic masculine forms in German to English generics. Broadly speaking, in German, the male form of a role noun (e.g., *Arbeiter* 'worker') or of a pronoun (e.g., *seinem* 'his') can be used to refer to people regardless of referent gender (e.g., Gabriel et al. 2008; Gygax et al. 2008, 2009; Schmitz et al. 2023). In English, this is true for pronouns as well: It is possible to use the masculine pronoun *his* for generic reference (e.g., Baron 1981; Conrod 2020; Hekanaho 2020), as illustrated above in (2). This means that a form with a one-to-one mapping is available (*seinem* → *his*). This generic masculine form is commonly used in German, and English features a direct equivalent.

However, English has had a gender-neutral alternative to the generic masculine for several decades: generic singular *they* (Conrod 2020). Recent studies showed that singular *they* can be interpreted in different ways but can indeed also be interpreted

---

[1] There is a plural interpretation of *they* mapping onto German third-person plural *sie*. While we do not test for plural interpretation in the present study, and the stimulus sentence is unambiguously singular, we consider it an interesting avenue for future studies to investigate to what extent plurality affects gender interpretation.

as gender-neutral (Conrod 2020). Additionally, a computational study using a cognitively grounded learning algorithm indicates that singular *they* is semantically close to other gender-neutral forms, like, for example, *everyone, no one, anyone* (Schmitz, in this book). It is currently unclear to what extent German speakers are aware of this gender-neutral option.

In order to test the gender processing of singular *they* by L1 German speakers, we conducted an online experiment. In the experiment, German participants were asked to write a short story about a pupil and provide the pupil's name (cf. Moulton et al. 1978). Each participant received one of two versions of the writing task, one group starting the story following a sentence with a generically used *his* as in (2) and the other following a sentence with a generically used *their* as in (3). We expected the stimulus version with the generic masculine pronoun *his* to lead to more male pupils as protagonists and to allow for less variation of protagonist genders than generic *their*.

2 Transfer effects of gender biases

2.1 Language transfer

Some studies on the transfer of grammatical features from L1 to L2 have shown that their structure in the L1 influences their use in the L2 (e.g., Cook 2018; Sabourin et al. 2016; Koster and Loerts 2020; Schoenmakers et al. 2022; Sato et al. 2013). In other words, these studies found effects of language transfer from the L1 into the patterns of the L2.

Of particular interest for the present study is the L1 to L2 transfer of gender bias. It has been shown that, for example, L1 speakers of Russian (a language with grammatical gender) can have difficulties processing English gendered pronouns incongruent with the grammatical gender of the corresponding nouns in Russian (Cook 2018). However, this effect was only found for animate nouns, not for inanimate ones. Koster and Loerts (2020) showed that learners of German and Dutch as L2s (respectively) have difficulties with the assignment of gender classes for nouns due to differences in grammatical gender assignment in the two languages. One main finding of a study by Sabourin et al. (2016) was that L1 English speakers perform worse than native speakers in gender assignment in German and in Romance languages, which have grammatical gender class systems.

Sato et al. (2013) found that stereotypicality influence how English L1 speakers assign gender in L2 French. French learners of L2 English transfer a male-dominant bias based on the French gender system. Furthermore, the effect weakens with a higher proficiency in the L2. French, like German, has a male bias in its gender system. If an effect on gender assignment in L2 English is found for French L1 speakers, it is reasonable to suspect that a similar effect could arise with German L1 speakers.

As we can see, existing research suggests that transfer of gender bias between languages is, in general, possible. Despite this, it is an open question in how far a male bias in the German gender system could be specifically transferred to the interpretation of English generic singular *they*, a pronoun for which, as established above, no direct equivalent is available in German. To illustrate this in more detail, let us take a look at the gender assignment systems of German and English and their generic masculine forms.

2.2 The generic masculine

Before looking at the generic masculine, let us start with a brief overview of gender assignment in general. Grammatical gender is used for noun classes (Hockett 1958). The number of gender classes for nouns is language-dependent (Siemund 2008). The gender assignment of one noun is, in turn, reflected in, for example, articles, adjectives, pronouns, etc. (Corbett 1991). In order to assign a gender class to a noun, different systems are used. For example, the distinction between male and female gender can be related to the referent gender or referent sex (Corbett 1991). Further notional distinctions are, among others, animate and inanimate, human and non-human, and large and small. Gender assignment, as well as which system this assignment uses as basis, is language-dependent. Some languages use perceived real-world distinctions, others use morphological and phonological information, and other languages might use a mixture of both patterns or categorize nouns into gender classes in yet other ways (Corbett 2007). Thus, gender assignment in a language can rely on semantic criteria, syntactic criteria or a mixture of both. In a language that uses semantic criteria, a noun is categorized by a semantic feature, for example, gender, animacy, or humanity. In a syntactic gender assignment system, in contrast, morphological, phonological, and syntactic features determine the gender of a noun, often ignoring the actual gender of a referent (Corbett 2007).

In English, gender is generally semantically assigned, whereas in German, gender is generally morphosyntactically assigned. More precisely, English words like *man*, *woman*, and *hat* receive their gender class via semantic criteria. That is, a man is male, receives the male gender class, and is referred to by the pronoun *he*. A woman is female, receives the female gender class, and is referred to by the pronoun *she*. A hat is an object and is therefore assigned a neuter gender class and referred to by the pronoun *it* (Siemund 2008). In German, on the other hand, gender is (mostly) assigned by morphosyntactic features, and different morphosyntactic items (e.g., adjectives) have to agree. For example, the word *Lehrer* 'teacher' is masculine in German. If the referent is male, the referent gender and the gender class agree, as in Example (4).

However, the form *Lehrer* can also refer to teachers in general, no matter whether referents are male or of other genders, as in (5). As this is a generic usage, this particular masculine form is called "generic masculine". Importantly, this form is not only generic, but also gender-neutral, supposedly including referents of all genders (Doleschal 2002; Diewald 2018; Nübling and Kotthoff 2018).

(4) *Der Lehrer steht vor seiner Klasse.*
'The (male) teacher is standing in front of his class.'

(5) *Ein Lehrer sollte immer nett sein.*
'A teacher should always be nice.'

A second, famously cited, example where referent gender does not correlate with grammatical gender is the German word *Mädchen* 'girl'. The suffix *-chen* is a diminutive in German and always triggers the gender class neuter, irrespective of the fact that the referent gender is female (Corbett 1991: 227f.).

For pronouns, a similar male bias is observed in German. The examples in (6) and (7) show that masculine forms of pronouns (*seinem, seiner*) are used to refer to referents of any gender.

(6) *An seinem ersten Schultag ist ein Schüler für gewöhnlich sehr nervös.*
'On his first day at school, a pupil is usually very nervous.'

(7) *Ein Lehrer sollte immer nett zu seiner Klasse sein.*
'A teacher should always be nice to his class.'

Given these two different ways of gender assignment, the question arises how gender interpretation and potential gender biases manifest across systems. We know that generic masculine forms are often not interpreted as truly gender-neutral (e.g., Martyna 1978; Rothmund and Scheele 2004; Braun et al. 2005; Gabriel et al. 2008; Gygax et al. 2008, 2009; Miller and James 2009; McConnell-Ginet 2015; Schmitz et al. 2023; Schmitz 2024). It is reasonable to expect that the interpretation of English generic masculine forms (like generic *his*) by L1 German speakers is subject to the same male bias as German generic masculine forms (like generic *seinem*), or even that this bias in English will be enhanced by the corresponding bias in German in an effect of transfer. In other words, the bias in German may be directly carried over to English. However, it is less clear how L1 German speakers would interpret a supposedly more gender-neutral alternative like generic singular *their*, for which no direct equivalent exists in German. On the one hand, given the highly binarily gendered nature of German's morphosyntactically governed gender system, and given the lack of a German equivalent to generic singular *their*, it is possible to expect L1–L2 transfer effects which inhibit gender-neutral interpretations of singular *their* for L1 German speakers. In other words, L1 German speakers could show a male bias not only for generic *his* but also for generic *their*, because they associated generic forms with the masculine and are not aware of the intended gender-neutrality of *their* (e.g., Conrod 2020). On the other hand, it is possible to expect that *their* will be interpreted at least as more gender-neutral than generic *his*. This is because due to potential transfer effects, the interpretation of *his* will be strongly affected by the (male) interpretation of *seinem*, while the interpretation of *they* will not. We arrive at the following hypotheses:

H1: German learners of English will show a male bias for generic *his*.
H2: German learners of English will also show a male bias for generic *their*.
H3: The male bias for generic *their* will be weaker than for generic *his*.

As we can see, interestingly, both the expectation that *they* will feature a male bias for L1 German speakers and the opposite expectation that it will not feature a bias, or at least not feature as strong a bias as *his*, can be justified by transfer effects. Note that the design of the study does not hinge on which expectation we follow: We simply investigate whether L1 Germans speakers interpret the English generic pronoun *their* as more gender-neutral than the English generic masculine pronoun *his*.

3 Method

We conducted a type of experiment that we refer to as the *short story approach*. The short story approach is a tried and tested, highly controlled, and thoroughly disguised approach for eliciting gender bias in language and was pioneered as early as the seventies by Moulton et al. (1978). In a nutshell, this approach requires participants to write a short story following a stimulus sentence that contains a specific pronoun. The gender that participants choose for their protagonist then serves as a proxy to gauge the influence of this pronoun on participants' gender associations.

The online questionnaire was created using SoSci Survey and designed as follows. First, in order to conceal the true purpose of the study, participants were told that the aim of the study was to test how German as a first language affects creative writing in English. Participants were informed that they can only participate if they are adults with German as L1 who have learned English, that the collected data remain anonymous, that they can quit the study at any time without giving reasons and without any negative consequences. They then gave their informed consent to participate.

The participants received written instructions for the short story task in German. The task asked them to write a short story (about 10 sentences), fitting a specific theme, about a fictional character. The instructions emphasized that the character had to be fictional and that participants were not allowed to write about themselves. The theme was a stimulus sentence that either included the generic masculine pronoun *his* and read *On his first day at school, a pupil is usually very nervous*, or included generic singular *their* and thus read *On their first day at school, a pupil is usually very nervous*. The role noun *pupil* was chosen for two reasons. First, it is one of the rare role nouns that can be assumed to have an approximately equal distribution of male and female referents in most German- and English-speaking countries.[2] We thus hold constant potential gender associations based on real-world distributions or based on stereotypes connected to specific role nouns. Second, we opted for *pupil* because this word does not morphophonologically resemble typical German gendered role nouns, opposed to, for instance, *student*, which resembles the German word *Student* 'student' but also specifically 'male student'. We thus hold constant potential cross-linguistic gender biases introduced by word form.

Following an empty text field where participants typed their story, we asked participants to give their fictional character a name or, if they had already done so in the story itself, to re-type the name. This ensured that, together with the pronouns participants use in their stories, we have sufficient information to infer the intended gender of their protagonists. This question also re-emphasized that participants were not to write about themselves. The question was followed by a demographic section where we asked for participants' age, gender, additional L1s, additional L2s, onset of English acquisition, and time spent abroad in English-speaking countries. Finally, we asked what participants believed was the true purpose of the study. This was crucial because we were interested only in subconscious gender associations, rather than conscious decisions in the choice of protagonist gender that would potentially be subject to a social desirability bias.

We distributed the questionnaire online and randomly assigned participants either the stimulus with the generic masculine pronoun *his* or the stimulus with generic singular *their*. Including only questionnaires where participants reached the final page, our dataset comprised 53 L1 German speakers in total. Of these, we excluded four whose response to our question about the purpose of the study included any suspicion related to gender or pronouns. We excluded an additional participant

---

2 See, e.g., data by the Federal Statistical Office of Germany: https://www.destatis.de/DE/Presse/Pressemitteilungen/2024/03/PD24_101_211.html, accessed: 07 February 2025.

who did not answer the questions properly and was likely a bot, another one who did not provide a character name and informed us they had not understood the prompt, and another one whose protagonist gender could neither be reliably categorized based on the pronouns in their story nor based on the character name provided ("Maths"). The cleaned dataset comprised 46 participants (39 female, 7 male; age 18–60 with $\bar{x}$ = 27.49 and s_x = 8.94; with the onset of English learning at $\bar{x}$ = 8.37, s_x = 2.44 years), of which 27 drew the stimulus with the pronoun *his* and 19 drew the stimulus with the pronoun *their*.

We analyzed the data statistically, using binomial logistic regression in R (R Core Team 2023).[3] This choice of model was motivated by the type of response variable (a categorical binary outcome PROTAGONIST GENDER with the protagonist being male or female) and the fact that we wanted to simultaneously control for important covariates.

Let us briefly look at the variables used for the analysis. Our response variable is PROTAGONIST GENDER. After cleaning the data as described above, the coding for this variable turned out to be unambiguous for the remaining participants, as all remaining participants provided both character names and consistent female or male pronouns in their story. PROTAGONIST GENDER can thus take the values male or female in our dataset.[4] Our predictor of interest is PRONOUN USED IN STIMULUS, either his or their. As explained above, we expect the generic masculine pronoun *his* to show a male bias in protagonist genders, while generic singular *their* could also show a bias, but potentially a weaker one.

Moving on to the covariates, we include AGE OF PARTICIPANT. It is possible to expect a general male bias in protagonist gender to be weaker for younger participants due to an increased awareness of questions of representation. Next, we control for GENDER OF PARTICIPANT, which in our sample takes the values female or male. We can expect male participants to more frequently write about male protagonists than female participants, and female participants to more frequently write about female protagonists than male participants. This is due to a bias known as the "self-imagery hypothesis", which is the assumption that people tend to interpret generics to agree with their own gender (MacKay and Fulkerson 1979: 671). Finally, we have three covariates gauging different kinds of language proficiency. PARTICIPANT HAS ADDITIONAL L1, with either yes or no, specifies whether the participant has any L1s in addition to German. We pooled this variable rather than allowing one category for each individual L1, which, due to our diverse participants, could have caused overfitting

---

[3] The interested reader can view the data, including the short stories, and the scripts with all full models in the supplementary materials at https://osf.io/hbm3n, accessed: 16 July 2023.
[4] Note that none of the participants in this sample chose to give their protagonist another gender than male or female.

Tab. 1: Overview of variables used in the analysis of gender bias in the interpretation of generic *his* and generic singular *their*.

Variable name	Description
Response variable	
PROTAGONIST GENDER	Gender of the short story's protagonist
Predictor variables	
PRONOUN USED IN STIMULUS	Specifies whether participants saw a generic masculine *his* or generic singular *their*
AGE OF PARTICIPANT	The age of the participant in years
GENDER OF PARTICIPANT	The gender of the participant
PARTICIPANT HAS ADDITIONAL L1	Specifies whether the participant has another L1 (other than German)
ONSET OF ENGLISH ACQUISITION	The age at which the participant had started learning English in years
TIME IN ENGLISH-SPEAKING COUNTRIES	The total duration of a participant having lived in an English-speaking country in months

issues in the model. ONSET OF ENGLISH ACQUISITION specifies the age at which participants started learning English. TIME IN ENGLISH-SPEAKING COUNTRIES specifies the time in months that participants had spent abroad in one or more English-speaking countries. For these variables, we can expect that the more proficient participants are in terms of additional L1s or in terms of English, the more familiar they will be with gender-neutral pronouns cross-linguistically, or specifically with the intended gender-neutrality of singular *they* in English. This could further reduce the overall male bias in protagonist genders. Table 1 provides a summary of the variables included in the model.

4 Results

We first performed a reality check on the data from the generic masculine stimulus to see whether it produces the male bias known from the literature. Figure 1 plots the distribution of protagonist genders following the stimulus sentence with *his*. We can see that following this supposedly generic masculine pronoun, we find significantly more male protagonists than female protagonists (χ^2 = 10.704, df = 1, p = 0.001), replicating the known bias from English L1 speakers for our participant sample.

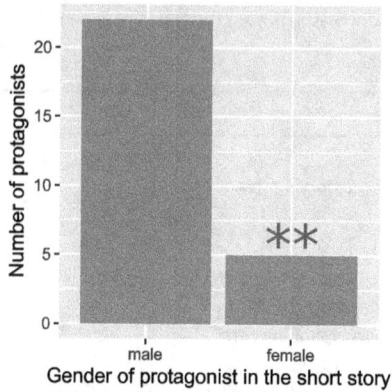
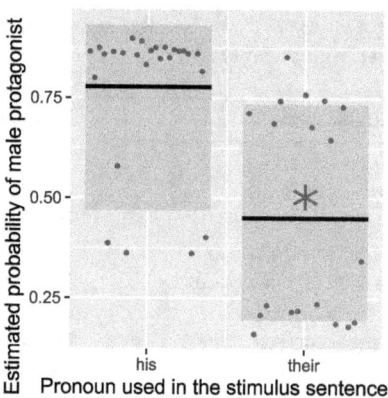

Fig. 1: Distribution of protagonist genders following the stimulus with generic *his*.

Fig. 2: Effect of generically used pronoun *his* or *their* on the probability of male protagonists.

Tab. 2: Binomial logistic regression model reporting effects on the probability of male PROTAGONIST GENDER.

	Estimate	SE	z	$P_{|z|}$
Intercept	2.7171	1.7737	1.53	0.1256
PRONOUN USED IN STIMULUS their	-1.4484	0.7256	-2.00	0.0459
AGE OF PARTICIPANT	-0.0610	0.0470	-1.30	0.1936
GENDER OF PARTICIPANT male	0.3394	1.0077	0.34	0.7362
PARTICIPANT HAS ADDITIONAL L1 yes	0.0697	0.9517	0.07	0.9417
ONSET OF ENGLISH ACQUISITION	0.0064	0.1650	0.04	0.9688
TIME IN ENGLISH-SPEAKING COUNTRIES	0.0530	0.0538	0.99	0.3244

We then modeled all data, including both generic *his* and generic *their*, using binomial logistic regression as described in Section 3. Table 2 reports the effects of all variables on the probability of a protagonist having male gender (rather than female gender). We can see that none of the covariates yields a significant effect, perhaps due to the relatively small sample size and thus, for some of the variables, relatively low amount of data points per category. All the more strikingly, we do find a significant negative effect of PRONOUN on PROTAGONIST GENDER. When the stimulus sentence features generic singular *their* instead of generic masculine *his*, the probability of the protagonist's gender being male is significantly lowered. Note that the p-value of .0459 is close to the conventional threshold for significance of .05. While this threshold is arbitrary, we think that conservatively-phrased conclusions are always well-advised. Moving away from p-values and quantifying the evidence from a Bayesian perspective, we could, for example, say that we do find evidence for our hypothesis, but only "weak" evidence. We use the Bayes Factor approximated by the difference in BIC values between our model in Table 2 and the same model without PRONOUN (Wagenmakers 2007). We find that the data is more likely under H_1 than under H_0 (BF_{01} = .79). Assuming that it is a priori equally plausible that PRONOUN affects and does not affect PROTAGONIST GENDER, the posterior probability of H_1 ($Pr_{H_1}|D$ = .55) is then labeled "weak" evidence, according to the Raftery (1995) classification scheme. We think that attempts at replication and falsification of this effect in the near future would be welcome to substantiate its stability.

To visualize the result, Figure 2 plots the effect of PRONOUN on the probability of male protagonists. The lower bar for *their* shows that the stimulus version with this pronoun leads to significantly fewer male protagonists than the stimulus version with the pronoun *his*. Following the stimulus sentence with *his*, we can see that the model estimates the probability of a protagonist being male at above 75 %, while following the stimulus sentence with *their*, this probability is estimated to be slightly below 50 %. In an ideal world, this nearly equal probability of female and male protagonists, plus a demographically reasonable probability of other gender identities, is what we would expect from a truly gender-neutral pronoun. In our non-ideal world, the data still offer two takeaways: First, that similarly to L1 English speakers, generic masculine *his* is not truly gender-neutral for L1 German speakers either, and second, that for these speakers generic *their* does a better job at being neutral than does generic *his*.

5 Discussion

We have investigated the following hypotheses about how L1 German speakers interpret English generic singular *their* with regard to gender neutrality:
H1: German learners of English will show a male bias for generic *his*.
H2: German learners of English will also show a male bias for generic *their*.
H3: The male bias for generic *their* will be weaker than for generic *his*.

Compared to generic masculine *his*, for which we were able to replicate the male bias found in previous research (H1), the results have shown that L1 German speakers interpret generic singular *they* as more neutral (H3). These results are encouraging in the context of English language learning of L1 German speakers, but they also have implications for gender bias in language more generally.

Let us first discuss our reality check (H1), i.e., the successful replication of the male bias associated with the generic masculine (in this case, the pronoun *his*). This finding is in line with other studies that found masculine generics (pronouns or role nouns) to be associated with male referents rather than referents of other genders (e.g., Martyna 1978; Rothmund and Scheele 2004; Braun et al. 2005; Gabriel et al. 2008; Gygax et al. 2008, 2009; Miller and James 2009; McConnell-Ginet 2015; Schmitz et al. 2023; Schmitz 2024). The fact that we find crosslinguistic support for this finding with L1 German speakers may hint at an L1–L2 gender bias transfer. Of course, it is hard to disentangle how much of this male bias results from the participants' knowledge of English, a language in which this bias exists, and how much of it results from their transferred knowledge of German, a language in which this bias also exists. For L1 German speakers, the bias in the latter may strengthen the bias in the former, but this remains an open empirical question. In this study, we did not find an effect of English proficiency on the probability of PROTAGONIST GENDER (as operationalized by ONSET OF ENGLISH ACQUISITION and TIME SPENT IN ENGLISH-SPEAKING COUNTRIES), which could have been indicative of the direction of this interplay between the two languages and their biases. Even so, future studies should attempt to test more systematically for proficiency effects. These studies could also try to replicate the effects with L1 English speakers as a control group.

One argument that is often raised against studies claiming to have found masculine generics to be male-biased is that this bias may not be associated with language, but with language-external factors. It may be the case that the masculine interpretation of English generics results from an across-the-board male bias in the thinking of language users that does not necessarily involve accessing linguistic knowledge. This is what Silveira (1980) calls a general "people = male" bias. Henley (1989: 72) adds that this might be an instance of a larger thought bias pattern, "the generic = specific" bias. Rothmund and Scheele (2004) suggest that this stereotypical view is a heuristic strategy. If no context information is available and gender-specific hints are lacking, people are likely to associate males because "the typical representative of the category HUMAN has the characteristic MALE" (Rothmund and Scheele 2004: 50, our translation). While the people = male bias may exist for our participants, the setup of our study allowed us to show that it alone cannot account for the associations of our participants, but that language must play a role here. This is because we directly compared the generic masculine pronoun that showed the male bias (*his*) to another pronoun that did not (*their*). Given that this pronoun was the only difference between the stimuli, we can confidently state that at least part of the male bias we found is directly related to language, rather than merely to a general bias unaffected by linguistic stimuli.

Moving on from the reality check and turning to the answer to our research question (H2 and H3), interestingly, the male bias decreases with the use of a gender-neutral pronoun *their* in English (i.e., we find support for H3). This suggests that generic *their* can truly be interpreted more neutral by L1 German speakers, similar to L1 English speakers. If this is correct, this would be good news for singular *they* as a candidate for reducing gender bias that even works crosslinguistically.

In terms of transfer effects, we discussed the possibility (see Section 2.1) that transfer can affect the strength of the bias of generic singular *their* compared to generic masculine *his* in both directions. On the one hand, L1 German speakers may associate generics in general with the masculine and, consequently, with male referents, making even generic singular *they* vulnerable to bias. On the other hand, due to the direct mapping of *seinem* to *his*, but the lack of a German equivalent for generic singular *they*, *his* may be biased more strongly than *their* for L1 German speakers. The latter assumption would be able to better explain at least partly the difference in gender-neutrality we found between *his* and *their*.

We can think of one additional explanation for this finding to consider, which is, similar to the case of *his* discussed above, the proficiency of the participants in our experiment (cf. Sato et al. 2013). A higher proficiency in the L2 weakens the effect of a transfer from a participant's L1 language. As explained above, in our case, since German features a male bias in the interpretation of its generic forms, L1 German speakers could be expected to feature a bias not only in the English generic masculine, but also for generic *their*. However, when these speakers are highly proficient in English, this bias could be blocked, as these speakers are more familiar with the intended neutrality of *their*. While we did not find an effect of the variation of English proficiency in our data, it may be that the overall level of proficiency of our participants was high enough to lead to a more gender-neutral interpretation of *their*.

On a general methodological note, despite the relative small sample size, we were able to find a significant effect of PRONOUN USED IN STIMULUS on PROTAGONIST GENDER. To investigate the stability of that effect, we hope that the present study can serve as a template for future studies. The short story approach can make it challenging to recruit a large number of participants since people are tasked to produce a piece of creative writing, requiring more effort than other types of questionnaire (e.g., the average multiple choice survey), which we speculate may have led to a lower return rate. However, we think that the short story approach is also a very elegant and underused paradigm. It offers a high degree of experimental control and a thorough disguise of the study's purpose, while still being able to access subconscious gender associations. In short, it is as implicit as one can get without using real-time methods (reaction times, brain imaging, etc.). In addition, the rich creative writing data we collected can be re-used for other types of study, for instance, in second-language learning contexts or literary and cultural studies.

6 Conclusion

With this study we have provided a template[5] to test for crosslinguistic biases in the gender interpretation of generics, reviving a time-tested, implicit but easy-to-implement method of eliciting gender bias (cf. Moulton et al. 1978). Using a short story writing task to test whether L1 German speakers interpret generic singular *they* as more gender-neutral than generic masculine *his*, we found a significant (but weak) effect in support of this hypothesis. Directly comparing a generic masculine form with a more gender-neutral alternative allowed us to attribute at least parts of the bias of the generic masculine to its linguistic form itself, rather than to a general, non-linguistic people = male bias. We have discussed different directions in which such an effect can be interpreted to be influenced by L1–L2 transfer effects, which for L1 German speakers may strengthen the male bias of generic masculine *his*, and either enhances or reduces the difference in bias strength of generic masculine *his* compared to generic singular *they*. We have also suggested that future studies should pay close attention to proficiency as an additional factor modulating the transfer of gender bias. Finally, we have argued in favor of the short story approach as a method that allows for implicit testing of linguistic gender bias in an elegant way and yields rich data that can also be used for other purposes. We hope to spark further research in this direction that tests more alternative forms in more languages with larger datasets, and we are excited to observe which journey generic singular *they* and similar alternatives (for example, neopronouns like *ze/hir, fae/faer*, or *ey/em*) will take.

References

Baron, Dennis E. 1981. The epicene pronoun: The word that failed. *American Speech* 56. 83. https://doi.org/10.2307/455007.

Braun, Friederike, Sabine Sczesny and Dagmar Stahlberg. 2005. Cognitive effects of masculine generics in German: An overview of empirical findings. *Communications* 30(1). 1–21. https://doi.org/10.1515/comm.2005.30.1.1.

Conrod, Kirby. 2020. Pronouns and gender in language. In Kira Hall and Rusty Barrett (eds.), *The Oxford handbook of language and sexuality*, Oxford: Oxford University Press. https://doi.org/10.1093/oxfordhb/9780190212926.013.63.

Cook, Svetlana V. 2018. Gender matters: From L1 grammar to L2 semantics. *Bilingualism: Language and Cognition* 21(1). 13–31. https://doi.org/10.1017/S1366728916000766.

---

[5] Also see again the supplementary materials at https://osf.io/hbm3n, accessed: 16 July 2023.

Corbett, Greville G. 1991. *Gender*. Cambridge: Cambridge University Press. https://doi.org/10.1017/CBO9781139166119.

Corbett, Greville G. 2007. Gender and noun classes. In Timothy Shopen (ed.), *Language typology and syntactic description*, 241–279. Cambridge University Press. https://doi.org/10.1017/CBO9780511618437.004.

Diewald, Gabriele. 2018. Zur Diskussion: Geschlechtergerechte Sprache als Thema der germanistischen Linguistik – exemplarisch exerziert am Streit um das sogenannte generische Maskulinum. *Zeitschrift für germanistische Linguistik* 46. 283–299. https://doi.org/10.1515/zgl-2018-0016.

Doleschal, Ursula. 2002. Das generische Maskulinum im Deutschen. Ein historischer Spaziergang durch die deutsche Grammatikschreibung von der Renaissance bis zur Postmoderne. *Linguistik Online* 11(2). 39–70. https://doi.org/10.13092/lo.11.915.

Gabriel, Ute, Pascal Mark Gygax, Oriane Sarrasin, Alan Gamham and Jane Oakhill. 2008. Au pairs are rarely male: Norms on the gender perception of role names across English, French, and German. *Behavior Research Methods* 40(1). 206–212. https://doi.org/10.3758/BRM.40.1.206.

Gygax, Pascal, Ute Gabriel, Oriane Sarrasin, Jane Oakhill and Alan Garnham. 2008. Generically intended, but specifically interpreted: When beauticians, musicians, and mechanics are all men. *Language and Cognitive Processes* 23(3). 464–485. https://doi.org/10.1080/01690960701702035.

Gygax, Pascal Mark, Ute Gabriel, Oriane Sarrasin, Jane Oakhill and Alan Garnham. 2009. Some grammatical rules are more difficult than others. *European Journal of Psychology of Education* 24. 235–246. https://doi.org/10.1007/BF03173014.

Hekanaho, Laura. 2020. *Generic and nonbinary pronouns: Usage, acceptability and attitudes*. Helsinki: University of Helsinki dissertation.

Henley, Nancy M. 1989. Molehill or mountain? What we know and don't know about sex bias in language. In Mary Crawford and Margaret Gentry (eds.), *Gender and thought: Psychological perspectives*, 59–78. New York: Springer. https://doi.org/10.1007/978-1-4612-3588-0_4.

Hockett, Charles F. 1958. *A course in modern linguistics*. New York: The Macmillan Company. https://doi.org/10.1111/j.1467-1770.1958.tb00870.x.

Koster, Dietha and Hanneke Loerts. 2020. Food for psycholinguistic thought on gender in Dutch and German: A literature review on L1 and L2 production and processing. In Gunther De Vogelaer, Dietha Koster and Torsten Leuschner (eds.), *German and Dutch in contrast: Synchronic, diachronic and psycholinguistic perspectives*, 329–356. Berlin, Boston: De Gruyter. https://doi.org/10.1515/9783110668476-012.

MacKay, Donald G. and David C. Fulkerson. 1979. On the comprehension and production of pronouns. *Journal of Verbal Learning and Verbal Behavior* 18. 661–673. https://doi.org/10.1016/S0022-5371(79)90369-4.

Martyna, Wendy. 1978. What does 'he' mean? Use of the generic masculine. *Journal of Communication* 28. 131–138. https://doi.org/10.1111/J.1460-2466.1978.TB01576.X.

McConnell-Ginet, Sally. 2015. Gender and its relation to sex: The myth of 'natural' gender. In Greville G. Corbett (ed.), *The expression of gender*, 3–38. Berlin, Boston: De Gruyter.

Miller, Megan M. and Lori E. James. 2009. Is the generic pronoun he still comprehended as excluding women? *The American Journal of Psychology* 122. 483–496. https://doi.org/10.2307/27784423.

Moulton, Janice, George M. Robinson and Cherin Elias. 1978. Sex bias in language use. *American Psychologist* 33. 1032–1036. https://doi.org/10.1037/0003-066X.33.11.1032.

Nübling, Damaris and Helga Kotthoff. 2018. *Genderlinguistik: Eine Einführung in Sprache, Gespräch und Geschlecht*. Tübingen: Narr Francke Attempto.

R Core Team. 2023. R: A language and environment for statistical computing. http://www.R-project.org. Accessed: 9 March 2025.

Raftery, Adrian E. 1995. Bayesian model selection in social research. *Sociological Methodology* 25. 111–163. https://doi.org/10.2307/271063.
Rothmund, Jutta and Brigitte Scheele. 2004. Personenbezeichnungsmodelle auf dem Prüfstand. *Zeitschrift für Psychologie / Journal of Psychology* 212. 40–54. https://doi.org/10.1026/0044-3409.212.1.40.
Sabourin, Laura, Laurie A. Stowe and Ger J. De Haan. 2016. Transfer effects in learning a second language grammatical gender system. *Second Language Research* 22(1). 1–29. https://doi.org/10.1191/0267658306SR259OA.
Sato, Sayaka, Pascal M. Gygax and Ute Gabriel. 2013. Gender inferences: Grammatical features and their impact on the representation of gender in bilinguals. *Bilingualism* 16(4). 792–807. https://doi.org/10.1017/S1366728912000739.
Schmitz, Dominic. 2024. Instances of bias: The gendered semantics of generic masculines in German revealed by instance vectors. *Zeitschrift für Sprachwissenschaft* 43(2). 295–325. https://doi.org/10.1515/zfs-2024-2010.
Schmitz, Dominic, Viktoria Schneider and Janina Esser. 2023. No generiaddress in sight: An exploration of the semantics of masculine generics in German. *Glossa Psycholinguistics* 2. https://doi.org/10.5070/G6011192.
Schoenmakers, Gert-Jan, Theresa Redl, Sebastian Collin, Rozanne Versendaal, Peter de Swart and Helen de Hoop. 2022. Processing mismatching gendered possessive pronouns in L1 Dutch and L2 French. *Dutch Journal of Applied Linguistics* 11. https://doi.org/10.51751/dujal9948.
Siemund, Peter. 2008. *Pronominal gender in English: A study of English varieties from a cross-linguistic perspective*. London: Routledge.
Silveira, Jeanette. 1980. Generic masculine words and thinking. *Women's Studies International Quarterly* 3(2–3). 165–178. https://doi.org/10.1016/S0148-0685(80)92113-2.
Wagenmakers, Eric-Jan. 2007. A practical solution to the pervasive problems of p values. *Psychonomic Bulletin & Review* 14(5). 779–804. https://doi.org/10.3758/BF03194105.

Dominic Schmitz, Julia Elisabeth Blessing-Plötner, Nazire Cinar, Nguyet Minh Dang, Henrike Hoffmanns, Aaron Luther, Imran Peksen, and Tomma Lilli Robke

Form identity and gendered associations: L2 English -*er* facilitates the bias of L1 German -*er*

Abstract: This study investigates the transfer of gender biases from L1 German to L2 English, specifically examining whether the male bias associated with German role nouns ending in –*er* is activated when German speakers encounter English role nouns also ending in –*er*. We address two primary research questions. First, is the male bias of L1 German role nouns transferred to L2 English role nouns? Second, does the –*er* suffix in English role nouns facilitate this bias transfer? To explore these questions, we conducted two tasks with 65 participants, all of whom were L1 German speakers of L2 English. The first experiment involved a story continuation task in which participants continued stories initiated by English prompts containing role nouns ending in –*er*. The second experiment required participants to translate English role nouns, some ending in –*er* and others not, into German. Results indicate that the male bias present in German role nouns is indeed transferred to English, and that the –*er* suffix in English role nouns significantly contributes to this bias transfer.

Keywords: bias transfer, generic masculine, male bias, role nouns, second language

1 Introduction: Gender in English and German

Modern English is a *notional* or *pronominal* gender language (Nevalainen and Raumolin-Brunberg 1993; McConnell-Ginet 2015; Siemund 2008). That is, gender is primarily marked in the English pronominal system and rarely or not at all elsewhere (Huddleston and Pullum 2002: 485). Modern German, on the contrary, is a *grammatical* gender language (Hekanaho 2020). The gender of a given noun influences the grammatical form of articles, attributive adjectives, ordinal numbers,

---

Dominic Schmitz, Julia Elisabeth Blessing-Plötner, Nazire Cinar, Nguyet Minh Dang, Henrike Hoffmanns, Aaron Luther, Imran Peksen, and Tomma Lilli Robke, Department of English Language and Linguistics, Heinrich Heine University Düsseldorf, e-mail: dominic.schmitz@uni-duesseldorf.de

Open Access. © 2025 the author(s), published by De Gruyter. This work is licensed under the Creative Commons Attribution 4.0 International License.
https://doi.org/10.1515/9783111388694-008

participles, adjectival, relative and question pronouns, and third-person singular pronouns (Jarnatowskaja 1968).

Both English and German overwhelmingly follow a *natural gender rule* for non-derived nouns denoting humans (Mills 1986). For example, German *die Tante* 'the aunt' is grammatically feminine, while *der Onkel* 'the uncle' is grammatically male. In English, one will most likely refer to an *aunt* using the grammatically feminine pronouns *she*, *her*, and *hers*, while one will most likely refer to an *uncle* using the grammatically masculine pronouns *he*, *him*, and *his*.

However, this clear mapping between grammatical gender and referent gender is violated in specific cases. In English, for instance, some inanimate objects are referred to using feminine pronouns, e.g., ships (Siemund 2008). In German, grammatically masculine role nouns with grammatically feminine counterparts may be used to refer to referents irrespective of their gender (Diewald 2018), see Examples (1-a) to (1-e) below. This usage is described as generic. Using a grammatically masculine role noun for a referent or group of referents of any gender, the role noun supposedly loses its male semantics. Instead, the role noun is assumed to be gender-neutral.

While this is the traditional grammarian idea of this usage, an array of linguistic studies have shown that generically used masculine role nouns are apparently not gender-neutral. Instead, this type of usage comes with a rather clear male bias (e.g. Braun et al. 1998; Heise 2000; Stahlberg and Sczesny 2001; Stahlberg et al. 2001; Rothmund and Scheele 2004; Gygax et al. 2008; Irmen and Kurovskaja 2010; Misersky et al. 2019; Keith et al. 2022; Schunack and Binanzer 2022; Körner et al. 2022; Zacharski and Ferstl 2023; Schmitz 2024). That is, even though generically used masculine role nouns may be intended as gender-neutral, this intention is not translated by the language user. Studies explained this male bias with the form identity of generically and non-generically used masculine forms (cf. Schmitz et al. 2023).

Form identity is also at issue when it comes to L1 German speakers of L2 English. Both English and German share the *-er* suffix used to derive role nouns. For example, *work* + *-er* = *worker* and, analogously, *Arbeit* + *-er* = *Arbeiter*. While in English this form is used for referents of any gender and, indeed, there is no competition with a closely related form, in German, there is. The grammatically masculine *Arbeiter* can be used to specifically refer to male referents, see Example (1-a). Its feminine counterpart *Arbeiterin* is used to specifically refer to feminine referents, as illustrated by Example (1-e). *Arbeiter*, however, can also be used generically to refer to referents of any gender, as is shown in Example (1-b), while *Arbeiterin* cannot, as given in Examples (1-c) and (1-d). As there is ample evidence for generic masculines in German to carry a male bias, one may assume that such a male bias is carried over in L2 contexts in which the morphology resembles the morphology of German role nouns. One such case presents itself in the *-er* suffix in English.

(1) a. *Alle der Arbeiter sind Männer.*
'All of the workers [specific masculine] are men.'
b. *Viele der Arbeiter sind Frauen.*
'Many of the workers [generic masculine] are women.'
c. * *Viele der Arbeiterinnen sind Männer.*
'Many of the workers [specific feminine] are men.'
d. ? *Viele der Arbeiterinnen sind Frauen.*
'Many of the workers [specific feminine] are women.'
e. *Alle Arbeiterinnen sind Frauen.*
'All of the workers [specific feminine] are women.'

The transfer of gender biases from an L1 to an L2 does not pose a novel idea. Previous studies have, for example, shown that Russian L1 speakers may struggle with processing English gendered pronouns that do not align with the grammatical gender of the corresponding nouns in Russian (Cook 2018). Koster and Loerts (2020) found that learners of German and Dutch as L2s often confuse the gender classes for nouns. Sabourin et al. (2016) demonstrated that L1 English speakers perform worse in gender assignment in German and Romance languages, which have grammatical gender systems, compared to native speakers. Sato et al. (2013) discovered that stereotypicality affects the gender assignment of English L1 speakers of French as L2. French learners of L2 English tend to transfer a male-dominant bias from the French gender system, and this effect diminishes with higher L2 proficiency. Since French, like German, has a male bias in its gender system, it is reasonable to expect a similar effect with German L1 speakers in gender assignment in L2 English.

The present paper, therefore, sets out to answer the following research questions:

RQ1: Is the male bias of L1 German role nouns transferred to L2 English role nouns?
RQ2: Does the *-er* suffix in English role nouns facilitate this bias transfer?

We attempt to answer these questions using two types of experimental paradigms. First, participants were asked to continue three short stories in German, with the initial contextualizing sentence being given in English. This initial sentence contained an English role noun ending in *-er*. Role nouns differed by their stereotypicality: They were either stereotypically male, female, or neutral. Second, participants were asked to translate role nouns from English to German. Role nouns were presented without contexts and differed by their endings. Half of them ended in *-er*, while the other half did not. Again, role nouns with male, female, and neutral stereotypicality were used.

Besides grammatically masculine and feminine forms for role nouns, e.g., *Arbeiter* and *Arbeiterin*, participants might have also used more gender-inclusive forms. To include both binary genders, i.e., male and female, participants may, for example, use the pair form, *Arbeiterin und Arbeiter*, the capital I form, *ArbeiterIn*, or a slash, *Arbeiter/-in*. To include genders beyond the binary, participants might have made use of several special symbols. That is, the asterisk, the column, and the underscore may be used in combination with a following *in* to constitute a new morpheme: *Arbeiter*in, Arbeiter:in, Arbeiter_in* (Völkening 2022 and Völkening in this volume). In the singular, the special symbol forms commonly refer to non-binary individuals when used to refer to a specific person as in the story continuation task. For non-specific singulars and in the plural, these forms commonly refer to individuals of any gender. Finally, participants might have also used gender-neutral paraphrases. For example, instead of *Arbeiter*, one could use *arbeitende Person* 'working person'. Both tasks will allow insight into which forms are used by L1 speakers of German when confronted with role nouns in their L2 English.

In the following, first the story continuation task and its results are presented and briefly discussed. Then, the translation task and its results are introduced. Finally, the results of both tasks are discussed, and a conclusion is drawn.

2 Experiments

2.1 Participants

Overall, 65 participants took part in both experiments. Their mean age was 29.6 years (SD 10.9), their median age was 25 years. The youngest participant was 18 years old, the oldest participant was 59 years old. All participants had German as only or one of their L1s and English as only or one of their L2s. Besides German, 14 other languages were provided as L1s, and besides English, 21 other languages were provided as L2s.

Participants were asked about their *Geschlecht*, without further specifying whether this asked for sex or gender. There were no predefined options given. Instead, participants were allowed to enter whatever information they deemed appropriate. Overall, 54 participants provided *weiblich* 'female' and 9 participants provided *männlich* 'male' as information. Furthermore, 1 participant provided *divers* 'diverse' as information and 1 participant did not provide an answer. Due to the low number of data points for the latter two categories, these participants and their data points were removed from the data set used for the analyses. Where further data points were removed for the respective analyses, this will be mentioned in the relevant sections.

Finally, participants were asked their attitude towards different ways of referring to individuals in German. On a 5-point Likert scale ranging from *sehr gut* 'very good' to *sehr schlecht* 'very bad', they had to indicate their stance towards generic masculines (e.g., *Lehrer*) 'teacher', pair forms (e.g., *Lehrer und Lehrerin* 'teacher (male) and teacher (female)'), neutral forms (e.g., *Lehrperson* lit. 'person who teaches'), participles (e.g., *Lehrende* lit. 'those who are teaching'), and gender star forms (e.g., *Lehrer*in* 'teacher (of any gender)').[1] The choices were introduced using the same examples as in the present paragraph. Additionally, participants were able to choose *kenne ich nicht / keine Meinung* 'I don't know this / no opinion' for each form. Overall, participants showed a median attitude of 2 towards the generic masculine and a median attitude of 4 towards all other forms. An overview of the responses is given in Figure 1.

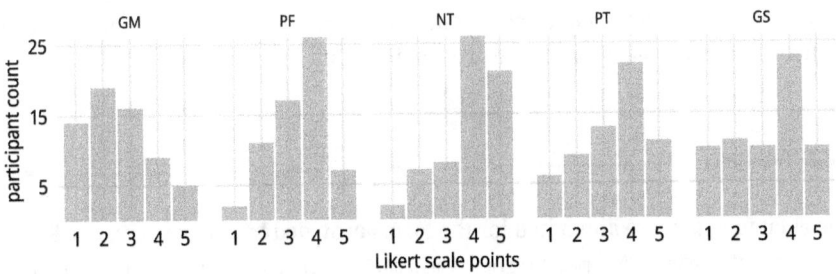

Fig. 1: Participant attitudes towards generic masculines (GM), pair forms (PF), neutral alternatives (NT), participles (PT), and gender star forms (GS).

2.2 Experiment 1: Story continuation task

2.2.1 Method

The first experiment was inspired by the study conducted by Stein and Schneider (same volume). Following their *short story approach*, participants were instructed to write three short stories with at least five sentences. For each short story, participants were prompted with a first sentence. This first sentence was given in English and contained one of three target role nouns. The role nouns were *hairdresser*, *programmer*, and *singer*, whose stereotypicality is female, male, and neutral, re-

---

1 The term *gender star* is used in this chapter and in the chapter by Völkening, while Ochs & Rüdiger in their chapter refer to the same concept as 'asterisk'.

spectively. Stereotypicality was considered as a variable as it commonly included in similar investigations; stereotypicality judgements were adopted from Misersky et al. (2014). The prompts that were used were simple sentences, they are given in Examples (2), (3), and (4).

(2) The **hairdresser** woke up late today.
(3) The **programmer** needs a new computer.
(4) The **singer** works on a new song.

Participants were instructed as follows: *Bitte verfasse eine Fortsetzung aus mindestens 5 Sätzen auf Deutsch für den folgenden Kontext:* 'Please write a continuation for the following context of at least 5 sentences in German'. That is, while the prompt sentences were given in English, i.e., with no gender information in the role noun, participants were asked to continue the story in German and hence had to decide on a grammatical gender (masculine, feminine) or novel form (e.g., with an asterisk) for the respective role noun. There was no time limit for this task.

2.2.2 Analysis

The elicited data were annotated for the forms provided by the participants. Possible form categories were masculine, feminine, neutral (i.e., gender-neutral paraphrases), non-binary (i.e., the use of a novel non-binary suffix), and unknown (i.e., no gendered forms referring to the role noun were used).

In 19 cases (5 for female, 6 for male, and 8 for neutral stereotypicality), participants avoided using the role noun in their sentences. In 1 stereotypically male case, a gender star form was used. In 9 cases (3 per stereotypicality), neutral paraphrases were used. Neutral, non-binary, and unknown forms were removed for the analysis, as they were too infrequent for allowing any generalizations.

The remaining data were analyzed using a generalized linear mixed effects regression model with the *lme4* package (Bates et al. 2015) in *R* (R Core Team 2023). The chosen forms were predicted by the fixed effects STEREOTYPICALITY, participant GENDER, participant AGE, and by the participants' attitude towards the generic masculine ATTGM, the pair form ATTPF, neutral alternatives ATTNT, participles ATTPT, and gender star forms ATTGS. Participant ID, L1s, and L2s were introduced as random effects. Differences between levels of a variable in the fitted model were analyzed using Bonferroni-corrected pairwise comparisons implemented by the *em-*

means package (Lenth 2024). Effects were plotted using the packages *visreg* (Breheny and Burchett 2017) and *ggplot2* (Wickham 2016).[2]

2.2.3 Results

Overall, masculine forms were used 103 times (29 for female, 51 for male, and 23 for neutral stereotypicality) and feminine forms were used 62 times (27 for female, 4 for male, and 31 for neutral stereotypicality).

A summary of the generalized linear mixed effects regression model fitted to these data is given in Table 1. Type II Wald chi-square tests on the generalized linear mixed effects model revealed a significant effect of STEREOTYPICALITY ($p < 0.001$). The other fixed effects did not reach significance. Taking a closer look at the effect of STEREOTYPICALITY, we found significant differences in chosen forms between stereotypically female and male forms and between stereotypically male and neutral forms. The difference between stereotypically female and neutral forms is not significant. As is shown in Figure 2, for the stereotypically male role noun *programmer*, masculine forms are most probable. For the stereotypically feminine role noun *hairdresser* and the stereotypically neutral role noun *singer*, masculine and feminine forms are more or less equally probable.

Tab. 1: Model summary for the generalized linear mixed effects regression model fitted to the story continuation task data.

	Estimate	Std. Error	z-value	p-value
Intercept	2.099	1.355	1.548	0.122
STEREOmale	2.562	0.594	4.310	<0.001
STEREOneutral	-0.384	0.395	-0.973	0.331
GENDERfemale	-0.971	0.570	-1.704	0.088
AGE	-0.014	0.019	-0.720	0.471
ATTGM	0.141	0.181	0.777	0.437
ATTPF	-0.033	0.193	-0.173	0.863
ATTNT	-0.181	0.209	-0.867	0.386
ATTPT	-0.134	0.158	-0.846	0.398
ATTGS	0.012	0.158	0.077	0.939

---

2 The R script and data are available at https://osf.io/96qxr, accessed: 27 February 2025.

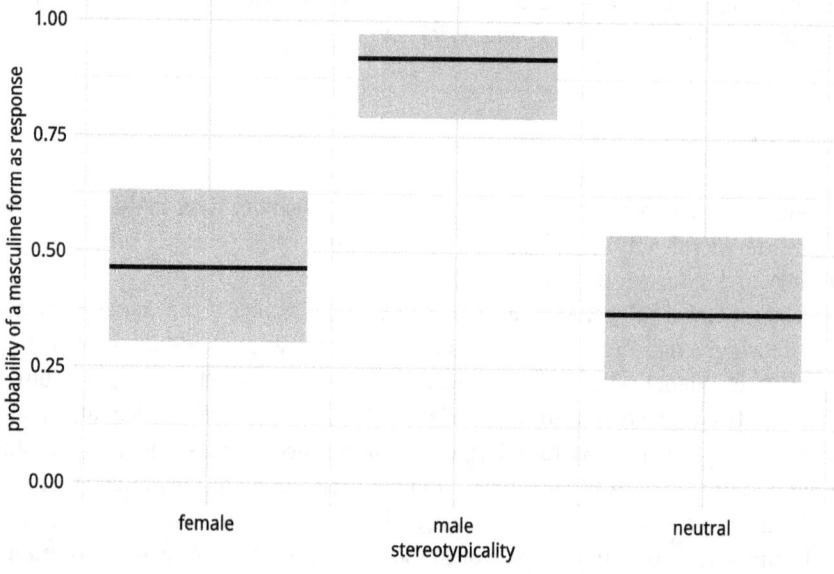

Fig. 2: The partial effect of stereotypicality as found in the generalized linear mixed effects regression model.

2.2.4 Interim Discussion

For the stereotypically male role noun, the present findings are little surprising. A role noun associated with male referents is translated into German using masculine forms. Similarly, the result for the stereotypically neutral role noun is what one would likely expect, similar numbers for masculine and feminine forms. The result for the stereotypically female role noun, however, is rather unexpected. That is, if stereotypicality was the main factor of influence, one would assume that the majority of German forms used to translate *hairdresser* were feminine. Instead, masculine forms were used as often as feminine forms. As *hairdresser* ends in the *–er* suffix, the question arises whether this suffix does indeed overwrite the female stereotypicality to some extent. The following experiment will investigate this idea more closely.

2.3 Experiment 2: Translation task

2.3.1 Method

The second experiment consisted of a simple translation task. Role nouns of either male, female, or neutral stereotypicality were given in alphabetical order below each other on one site. Stereotypicality information was again adopted from Misersky et al. (2014). Participants were asked to translate each word from English to German, following their first intuition rather than overthinking their translations. They were told that the experiment was not looking for perfect answers, that errors were not an issue, and that they were allowed to skip words they do not know. For each stereotypicality group, 8 items were used. Within the 8 items per stereotypicality group, 4 ended in *-er* and 4 did not. Table 2 provides an overview of all items.

Tab. 2: Items used in the translation task grouped by their stereotypicality.

male	female	neutral
programmer	hairdresser	singer
publisher	wedding planer	customer
killer	primary school teacher	designer
football player	fortune teller	piano player
magician	assistant	author
mechanic	flight attendant	journalist
professor	receptionist	astrologist
inspector	florist	biologist

2.3.2 Analysis

The elicited data were again annotated for the forms provided by the participants. Possible categories were masculine, feminine, binary (i.e., pair forms), non-binary (i.e., the use of a novel non-binary suffix), and not usable (i.e., a translation too far away from the actual meaning or no translation). For the following analysis, not usable data points were removed. Table 3 and Figure 3 summarize the data.

The remaining 1,463 data points were analyzed using multinomial regression as implemented by the *nnet* package (Venables and Ripley 2002). The translated forms were predicted by the fixed effects STEREOTYPICALITY and the forms' ENDINGS

(-er vs. not -er) in interaction, by participant GENDER, participant AGE, and participants' attitudes towards the different form options, i.e., ATTGM, ATTPF, ATTNT, ATTPT, and ATTGS. Random effects were not introduced, as the current implementations of multinomial regression in R do not support random effect structures. Differences between levels of a variable in the fitted model were analyzed using Bonferroni-corrected pairwise comparisons implemented by the *emmeans* package Lenth (2024). Effects were plotted using the packages *visreg* (Breheny and Burchett 2017) and *ggplot2* (Wickham 2016).[3]

Tab. 3: Distribution of forms (rows) by stereotypicality groups (columns) in the translation task data.

	male	female	neutral
feminine	10	39	17
masculine	311	268	310
binary	63	77	79
non-binary	99	99	91

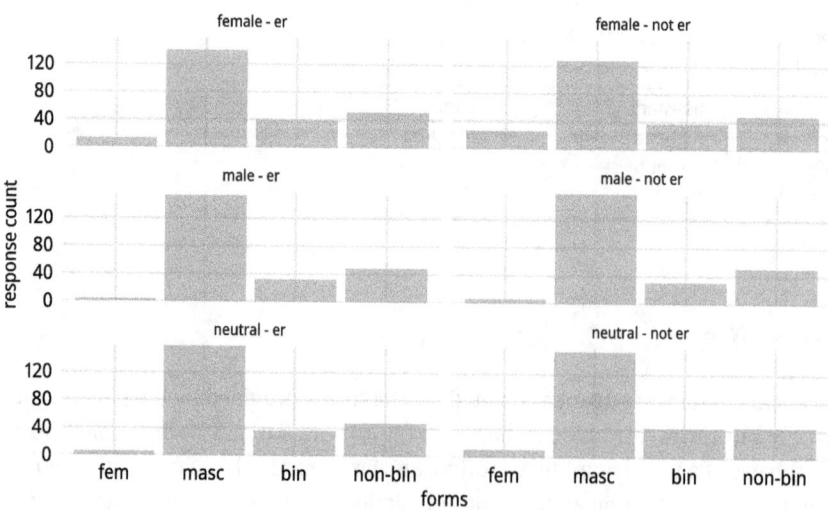

Fig. 3: Distribution of forms by stereotypicality groups and endings in the translation task data. 'fem' = feminine, 'masc' = masculine, 'bin' = binary, and 'non-bin' = non-binary.

---

[3] The R script and data are available at https://osf.io/96qxr, accessed: 27 February 2025.

2.3.3 Results

In sum, masculine forms were used 889 times, feminine forms were used 66 times, binary forms were used 219 times, and non-binary forms were used 289 times. Their distribution between items ending in *-er* and not ending in *-er* is given in Table 4.

Tab. 4: Distribution of forms by stereotypicality groups and endings in the translation task data.

	MALE		FEMALE		NEUTRAL	
	-er	not -er	-er	not -er	-er	not -er
feminine	4	6	13	26	6	11
masculine	153	158	140	128	158	152
binary	48	31	40	37	36	43
non-binary	32	51	51	48	47	44

The fitted multinomial regression model revealed significant effects for GENDER, AGE, ATTGM, ATTPF, ATTNT, ATTPT, and ATTGS, and for the interaction of STEREOTYPICALITY and items' ENDINGS. An overview of the model is given in Table 5.

Tab. 5: Type II Anova table for the multinomial regression model fitted to the translation task data.

	LR χ^2	df	*p*-value
STEREO	1.35	6	0.969
ENDING	6.86	3	0.076
GENDER	73.51	3	<0.001
AGE	28.95	3	<0.001
ATTGM	51.40	3	<0.001
ATTPF	259.21	3	<0.001
ATTNT	11.25	3	0.010
ATTPT	128.26	3	<0.001
ATTGS	320.92	3	<0.001
STEREO:ENDING	29.59	6	<0.001

For participant GENDER, female participants overall use feminine, binary, and non-binary forms more often than male participants, whereas male participants make use of masculine forms more often. This effect is displayed in Figure 4.

As for AGE, the probability of using masculine and binary forms decreases with age, while the probability of using feminine and non-binary forms increases. The effect of AGE is given in Figure 5.

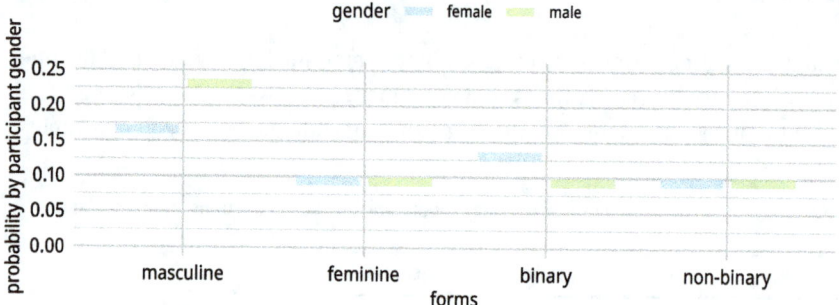

Fig. 4: The partial effect of participant GENDER as found in the multinomial regression model.

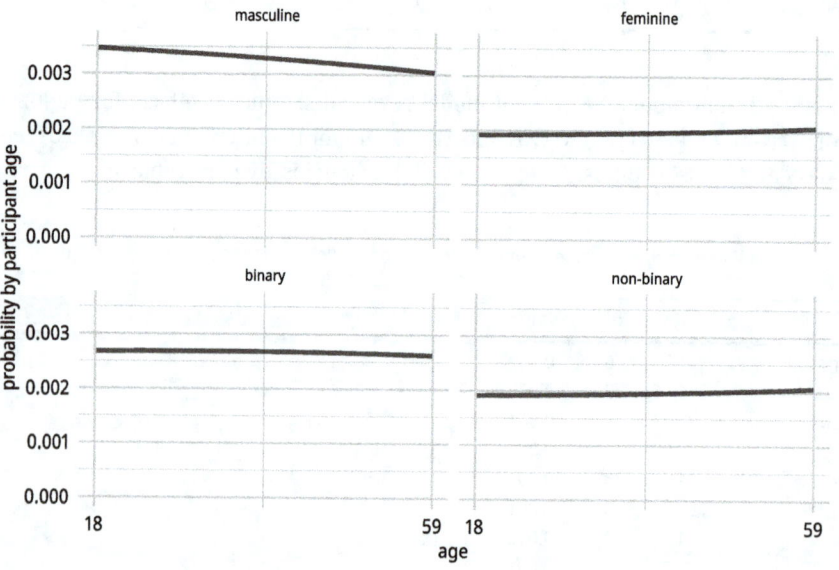

Fig. 5: The partial effect of participant AGE as found in the multinomial regression model.

The effect of the different notions of attitude is illustrated in Figure 6. Notably, participants chose translations following their attitudes. That is, participants in favor of generic masculines used most masculine forms, participants in favor of pair forms used binary forms, and participants in favor of gender star forms used non-binary forms for their translations. Further, binary forms are predominantly used by participants who are not in favor of gender star forms and generic masculines, whereas for feminine forms, attitudes play almost no role at all.

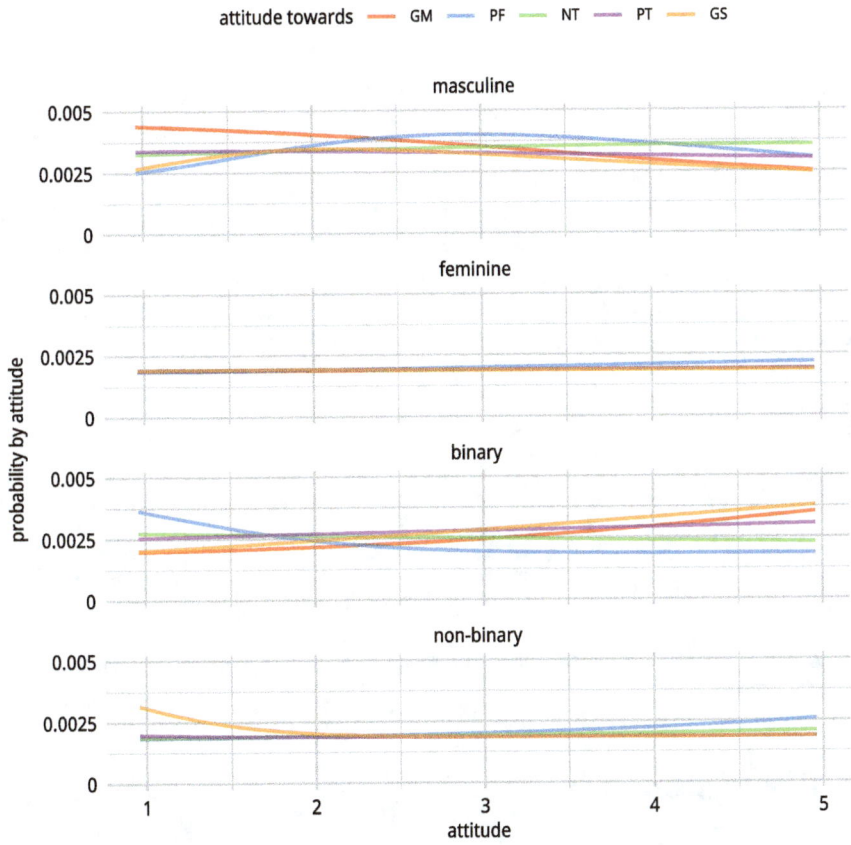

Fig. 6: The partial effect of participant ATTITUDE towards generic masculines (GM), pair forms (PF), neutral alternatives (NT), participles (PT), and gender star forms (GS) as found in the multinomial regression model.

Finally, using Bonferroni-corrected pairwise comparisons for the interaction of STEREOTYPICALITY and ENDINGS, it is found that significantly different forms are used for stereotypically female forms not ending in *-er* in comparison to stereotypically male forms ending in *-er*, stereotypically neutral forms ending in *-er*, stereotypically male forms ending not in *-er*, and stereotypically neutral forms not ending in *-er*. The partial effects of the interaction are visualized in Figure 7.

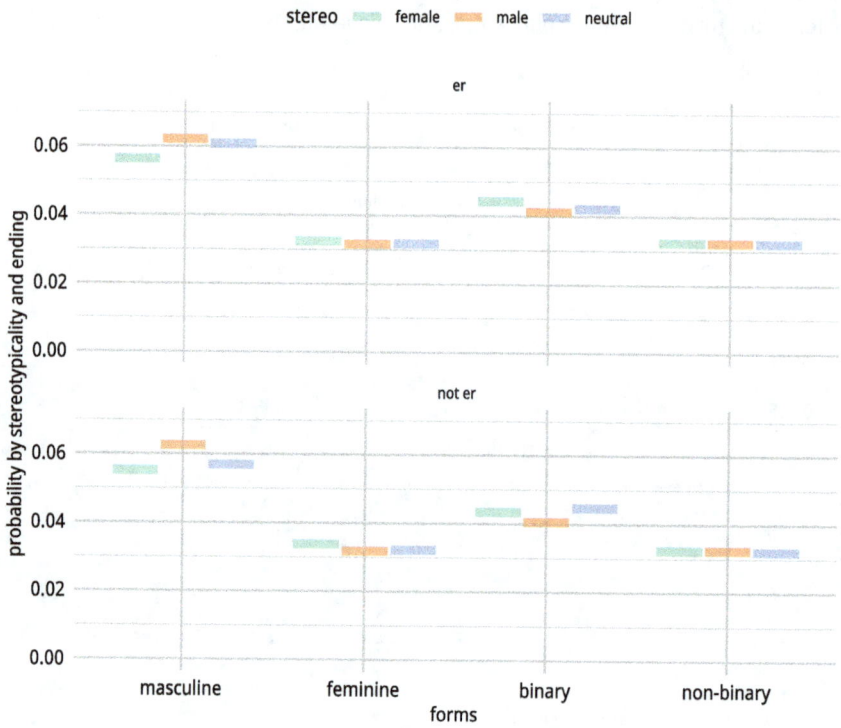

Fig. 7: The partial effect of the interaction of STEREOTYPICALITY and ENDING as found in the multinomial regression model.

3 Discussion

The present study set out to find answers to two research questions on L1 to L2 bias transfer. The first question, *RQ1*, was concerned with whether the male bias of German role nouns in transferred to English role nouns by L1 German speakers of L2 English. Using a story continuation task, it was found that the stereotypically female role noun *hairdresser* was translated to German using as many grammatically masculine as feminine forms. This finding offers room for speculation, as a very limited set of only three target words was tested. The present findings may be particular to the tested items or a bias found in story-telling as such. To investigate whether a male bias surfaces in a larger set of target words and is influenced by morphological similarities between the L1 and the L2, i.e., in the present study the *-er* suffix, a second experiment was conducted.

For the second experiment, *RQ2* asked whether the *–er* suffix in English role nouns facilitates the transfer of the L1 German male bias. Using a simple translation task, participants were asked to translate English role nouns ending and not ending in *–er* to German. Role nouns were equally distributed between male, female, and neutral stereotypicality. Results showed that, indeed, the *–er* suffix appears to make a difference. Stereotypically male and stereotypically neutral forms ending in *–er* showed significantly more masculine translations than stereotypically female forms not ending in *–er*. Additionally, stereotypically male forms not ending in *–er* also showed significantly more masculine translations than stereotypically female forms not ending in *–er*. The results suggest that stereotypically female role nouns not ending in *–er* are 'least male', while stereotypically male forms, no matter their ending, are 'most male'. Neutral forms ending in *–er* are also significantly 'more male' than the former female forms.

One point that should be mentioned even if a full discussion is outside the scope of the present study is that of markedness. If generic masculines are unmarked, as generic forms supposedly are, participants using them in a simple translation task is a non-surprising finding. However, if this were the case, one should not find differences between role nouns ending in *–er* and those not ending in *–er*. Hence, it appears that markedness may be but one potentially influencing factor in this regard. That is, assumably role nouns ending in *–er* are less marked than those not ending in *–er*.

Taking the results of both tasks together, it appears that the *–er* suffix in English role nouns does lead to a male bias transfer from L1 German to L2 English. These results are in line with previous findings, for example in L1 French and L2 English (cf. Sato et al. 2013). Even stereotypically neutral role nouns ending in *–er* are overwhelmingly translated using masculine forms. Hence, L1 speakers of German transfer the male bias of their L1 to L2 English, even though the English role nouns used in the present tasks are not grammatically gendered.

4 Conclusion

Using a story continuation task and a translation task, the present study provided novel insight into the transfer of the male bias in generic masculine role nouns from L1 German to L2 English. This transfer apparently does happen and is facilitated by the suffix *–er*, as this suffix is present in both German and English, while at the same time also subject to modulation by stereotypicality. In other words, form identity does indeed increase gendered associations.

At the same time, this observation raises a potential question for future research: Why does the *-er* suffix show the observed effect, but other suffixes or pseudo-suffixes found in both English and German do not? For instance, both languages know role nouns ending in *-or* and *-ist*. Similar investigations with pertinent items are required to allow answers to this question. Further, the question of the influence of markedness as raised in the discussion should be investigated to shed further light on potential influences on language inherent biases and to inform the concept of markedness in generic forms altogether. Finally, future research should investigate other combinations of L1s and L2s with differing gender systems and differing suffixes or derivational systems.

In sum, the present study brought forward evidence for a male bias transfer from L1 German to L2 English role nouns. A bias caused by variant mappings between grammatical and referent gender in German is transferred to English, a language without such a variant mapping in role nouns. The *-er* suffix facilitates this L1 to L2 bias transfer, as it is present in both languages and closely connected to the male bias in German role nouns.

References

Bates, Douglas, Martin Mächler, Ben Bolker and Steve Walker. 2015. Fitting linear mixed-effects models using lme4. *Journal of statistical software* 67(1). 1–48. https://doi.org/10.18637/jss.v067.i01.

Braun, Friederike, Anja Gottburgsen, Sabine Sczesny and Dagmar Stahlberg. 1998. Können Geophysiker Frauen sein? Generische Personenbezeichnungen im Deutschen. *Zeitschrift für Germanistische Linguistik* 26. 265–283. https://doi.org/10.1515/zfgl.1998.26.3.265.

Breheny, Patrick and Woodrow Burchett. 2017. Visualization of regression models using visreg. *The R Journal* 9(2). 56–71.

Cook, Svetlana V. 2018. Gender matters: From L1 grammar to L2 semantics. *Bilingualism: Language and Cognition* 21(1). 13–31. https://doi.org/10.1017/S1366728916000766.

Diewald, Gabriele. 2018. Zur Diskussion: Geschlechtergerechte Sprache als Thema der germanistischen Linguistik – exemplarisch exerziert am Streit um das sogenannte generische Maskulinum. *Zeitschrift für germanistische Linguistik* 46. 283–299. https://doi.org/10.1515/zgl-2018-0016.

Gygax, Pascal, Ute Gabriel, Oriane Sarrasin, Jane Oakhill and Alan Garnham. 2008. Generically intended, but specifically interpreted: When beauticians, musicians, and mechanics are all men. *Language and Cognitive Processes* 23(3). 464–485. https://doi.org/10.1080/01690960701702035.

Heise, Elke. 2000. Sind Frauen mitgemeint? Eine empirische Untersuchung zum Verständnis des generischen Maskulinums und seiner Alternativen. *Sprache & Kognition* 19. 3–13. https://doi.org/10.1024//0253-4533.19.12.3.

Hekanaho, Laura. 2020. *Generic and nonbinary pronouns: Usage, acceptability and attitudes*. Helsinki: University of Helsinki dissertation.

Huddleston, Rodney and Geoffrey K. Pullum. 2002. *The Cambridge grammar of the English language*. Cambridge: Cambridge University Press. https://doi.org/10.1017/9781316423530.

Irmen, Lisa and Julia Kurovskaja. 2010. On the semantic content of grammatical gender and its impact on the representation of human referents. *Experimental Psychology* 57. 367–375. https://doi.org /10.1027/1618-3169/a000044.

Jarnatowskaja, V. E. 1968. Die Kategorie des Genus der Substantive im System der deutschen Gegenwartssprache. *Deutsch als Fremdsprache* 5. 213–219.

Keith, Nina, Kristine Hartwig and Tobias Richter. 2022. Ladies first or ladies last: Do masculine generics evoke a reduced and later retrieval of female exemplars? *Collabra: Psychology* 8. https://doi.org /10.1525/collabra.32964.

Koster, Dietha and Hanneke Loerts. 2020. Food for psycholinguistic thought on gender in Dutch and German: A literature review on L1 and L2 production and processing. In Gunther De Vogelaer, Dietha Koster and Torsten Leuschner (eds.), *German and Dutch in contrast: Synchronic, diachronic and psycholinguistic perspectives*, 329–356. Berlin, Boston: De Gruyter. https://doi.org/10.1515/ 9783110668476-012.

Körner, Anita, Bleen Abraham, Ralf Rummer and Fritz Strack. 2022. Gender representations elicited by the gender star form. *Journal of Language and Social Psychology* 41. 553–571. https://doi.org /10.1177/0261927X221080181.

Lenth, Russell V. 2024. emmeans: Estimated marginal means, aka least-squares means. https://CRAN.R-project.org/package=emmeans. R package version 1.10.0.

McConnell-Ginet, Sally. 2015. Gender and its relation to sex: The myth of 'natural' gender. In Greville G. Corbett (ed.), *The expression of gender*, 3–38. Berlin, Boston: De Gruyter.

Mills, Anne E. 1986. *The acquisition of gender*. Berlin, Heidelberg: Springer. https://doi.org/10.1007/978-3-642-71362-0.

Misersky, Julia, Pascal M. Gygax, Paolo Canal, Ute Gabriel, Alan Garnham, Friederike Braun, Tania Chiarini, Kjellrun Englund, Adriana Hanulikova, Anton Öttl, Jana Valdrova, Lisa Von Stockhausen and Sabine Sczesny. 2014. Norms on the gender perception of role nouns in Czech, English, French, German, Italian, Norwegian, and Slovak. *Behavior Research Methods* 46(3). 841–871. https: //doi.org/10.3758/s13428-013-0409-z.

Misersky, Julia, Asifa Majid and Tineke M. Snijders. 2019. Grammatical gender in German influences how role-nouns are interpreted: Evidence from ERPs. *Discourse Processes* 56. 643–654. https: //doi.org/10.1080/0163853X.2018.1541382.

Nevalainen, Terttu and Helena Raumolin-Brunberg. 1993. Its strength and the beauty of it: The standardization of the third person neuter possessive in Early Modern English. In Dieter Stein and Ingrid Tieken-Boon van Ostade (eds.), *Towards a standard English*, 171–216. Berlin, Boston: De Gruyter. https://doi.org/10.1515/9783110864281.171.

R Core Team. 2023. R: A language and environment for statistical computing. http://www.R-project.o rg. Accessed: 9 March 2025.

Rothmund, Jutta and Brigitte Scheele. 2004. Personenbezeichnungsmodelle auf dem Prüfstand. *Zeitschrift für Psychologie / Journal of Psychology* 212. 40–54. https://doi.org/10.1026/0044-3409.212.1.40.

Sabourin, Laura, Laurie A. Stowe and Ger J. De Haan. 2016. Transfer effects in learning a second language grammatical gender system. *Second Language Research* 22(1). 1–29. https://doi.org /10.1191/0267658306SR259OA.

Sato, Sayaka, Pascal M. Gygax and Ute Gabriel. 2013. Gender inferences: Grammatical features and their impact on the representation of gender in bilinguals. *Bilingualism* 16(4). 792–807. https: //doi.org/10.1017/S1366728912000739.

Schmitz, Dominic. 2024. Instances of bias: The gendered semantics of generic masculines in German revealed by instance vectors. *Zeitschrift für Sprachwissenschaft* 43(2). 295–325. https://doi.org/10.1515/zfs-2024-2010.

Schmitz, Dominic, Viktoria Schneider and Janina Esser. 2023. No generic address in sight: An exploration of the semantics of masculine generics in German. *Glossa Psycholinguistics* 2. https://doi.org/10.5070/G6011192.

Schunack, Silke and Anja Binanzer. 2022. Revisiting gender-fair language and stereotypes – A comparison of word pairs, capital I forms and the asterisk. *Zeitschrift für Sprachwissenschaft* 41(2). 309–337. https://doi.org/10.1515/ZFS-2022-2008.

Siemund, Peter. 2008. *Pronominal gender in English: A study of English varieties from a cross-linguistic perspective*. London: Routledge.

Stahlberg, Dagmar and Sabine Sczesny. 2001. Effekte des generischen Maskulinums und alternativer Sprachformen auf den gedanklichen Einbezug von Frauen. *Psychologische Rundschau* 52. 131–140. https://doi.org/10.1026//0033-3042.52.3.131.

Stahlberg, Dagmar, Sabine Sczesny and Friederike Braun. 2001. Name your favorite musician: Effects of masculine generics and of their alternatives in German. *Journal of Language and Social Psychology* 20. 464–469. https://doi.org/10.1177/0261927X01020004004.

Venables, W. N. and B. D. Ripley. 2002. *Modern applied statistics with S*. 4th edn. New York: Springer.

Völkening, Lena. 2022. Ist Gendern mit Glottisverschlusslaut ungrammatisch? Ein Analysevorschlag für das Suffix [ʔɪn] als phonologisches Wort. *Zeitschrift für Wortbildung / Journal of Word Formation* 6(1). 58–80. https://doi.org/10.3726/zwjw.2022.01.02.

Wickham, Hadley. 2016. *ggplot2: Elegant graphics for data analysis*. New York: Springer.

Zacharski, Lisa and Evelyn Ferstl. 2023. Gendered representations of person referents activated by the nonbinary gender star in German: A word-picture matching task. *Discourse Processes* 60(4–5). 294–319. https://doi.org/10.1080/0163853X.2023.2199531.

Zaal Kikvidze
Gender-inclusive or not? Covert gender patterns in Georgian

Abstract: This chapter seeks to find out whether various occupational terms are gender-inclusive or not, and, hence, whether and how the gendered division of labor is reflected in Georgian as a genderless language. In genderless languages, that is, those having no grammatical gender, we can investigate covert gender. This approach assumes that a referent of a generic animate noun, denoting a human being, and related semantic markers may be regularly associated with only (or mainly) either a male or female individual. The analysis is based on a pilot study applying a questionnaire including twenty Georgian stimulus terms (occupational terms with neither word-formation nor semantic clues to disclose a possible gender of a referent). The main results are the following: (1) male and female interpretations of the stimulus terms have demonstrated whether and how gender-inclusive they are; (2) a genderless grammar does not necessarily provide for gender neutrality in the perception of personal nouns; (3) languages may be similar in terms of having genderless grammars; however, words of these languages with identical referential meanings may not be readily associated with one and the same gender and may or may not be gender-inclusive.

Keywords: covert gender, gender-inclusive, genderless language, Georgian, occupational terms

1 Introduction

All the four Kartvelian (South Caucasian) languages are genderless, Georgian (ISO 639–3: geo/kat; Glottolog: nucle1302) among them. However, a genderless grammar does not necessarily provide for gender neutrality in the perception of personal nouns and for them being gender-inclusive. Hence, one is likely to observe covert gender in such languages. This is to say that a referent of a generic animate noun, denoting a human being, may be regularly associated with only (or mainly) either a male or a female person. Therefore, identification of pertaining associations will allow relating them to linguistic dimensions of gendered division of labor in a respec-

---

Zaal Kikvidze, Department of General Linguistics, Akaki Tsereteli State University, e-mail: zaalk@yahoo.com

∂ Open Access. © 2025 the author(s), published by De Gruyter. [(cc) BY] This work is licensed under the Creative Commons Attribution 4.0 International License.
https://doi.org/10.1515/9783111388694-009

tive language community, as well as whether and which generic nouns are inclusive or not.

The chapter focuses on covert gender patterns in Georgian as a genderless language, describing a pilot study. The study is based on a questionnaire including twenty Georgian stimulus terms, lexical items referring to human beings (occupational terms) with neither morphological nor semantic clues to refer to a possible gender of a referent. Its results display both male-only and female-only interpretations, as well as mixed ones. These interpretations correspond to the actual gendered division of labor in the Georgian-speaking community, since male- or female-only and mixed interpretations are an outcome of the presence of statistically significantly more men or women in respective professions. The fact that the stimulus terms are generic does not imply that they are necessarily gender-inclusive.

In order to find out whether the interpretations are associated with referential (denotational) meanings of individual stimulus terms or something else, I contrasted the data with those from Turkish as a genderless language. With respect to both similarities and distinctions between the interpretations of the same occupational terms in the two languages, I arrived at the finding that words with the same referential meaning are not readily associated with the same gender in different genderless languages and are not equally inclusive or inclusive at all.

2 Gender-related linguistic items: In-/exclusive

2.1 Gender marking and the dominance effect

Irrespective of the fact that textbooks try to warn their readers against associating the grammatical category of gender and socio-culturally constructed gender, when we look at common nouns referring to human beings, what we witness is that these two phenomena do associate with each other in a host of cases (cf. Khaznadar 2002).

Moreover, the grammatical category of gender has been regarded to have its origins in the ancient mythological thought. For instance, back in 1772, in his *On the Origin of Human Language,* Herder deemed the grammatical category of gender to pertain to the primitive animist worldview. In the scholar's opinion, when primitive humans tried to understand the essence of the world and of their own being, they personified animals, plants, earth, stones, water, natural and supra-natural forces into men and women, into kind and evil, gods and goddesses (1966: 133). Some contemporary scholars too dwell upon similar relations and associations with respect to gender bias and sexism in language (for an overview, see Durrer, 2002).

However, can grammars tell us anything about the communities their speakers live in? Some answers to this question can be traced to the intersectionality between grammatical gender and social gender. In almost all languages with sex-based classes of nouns, the feminine has been analyzed as playing a secondary role in the gender system, that is, the masculine is presented as unmarked while the feminine is presented as marked (thus, it is derived from the supposed masculine base) (Baron 1986). The phenomenon in point has been referred to as 'dominance' since medieval Arabic grammarians have introduced this term (see, for instance, Suleiman, 1999; Guellouz, 2016).

This dominance effect has manifested itself in different areas, notably with the use of the so-called generic masculine to refer to mixed groups. It can also be visible in case-marking. For instance "Modern Standard German and its dialects including Pennsylvania Dutch and closely related Yiddish" lacks "any morphological distinction between nominative and accusative cases for feminines" (Krifka 2009: 141) and this is described as "remarkable": "This is not only unique within Germanic languages, but also quite remarkable from a typological and functional viewpoint, *under the plausible assumption that feminine NPs do not differ in animacy from masculine NPs*" (Krifka 2009: emphasis added).

His detailed and rigorous discussion of the loss of the nominative/accusative distinction for feminines (Krifka 2009: 9–27) envisions all the diachronic steps and possible explanations for this disappearance. He concludes that grammatically speaking the category 'female human beings' functions in the same way as the category 'inanimate', possibly because of hegemony: "In any case it is quite possible that an element of sexism played a role in these developments and influenced a core part of the grammar" (Krifka 2009: 31).

Another sexist view on grammar is evidenced in widespread instances of the markedness-unmarkedness relations in various languages as far as word-building is concerned (Beard 1995). As a normative rule, an unmarked form is thought as a base denoting predominantly male referents (or may have a generic meaning), whereas feminine ones are then considered to be derived from them.

2.2 Gendered division of labor in language

Another case in point is the opposition between the masculine-feminine for various occupations. The differences go beyond grammatical gender, since we argue that social gender and sex roles influence word meaning and word formation. Therefore, we are very likely to come across the term *working wife* but much less often, if ever, than *working husband*: "The language also still bears traces of the cultural norm of women as house-wives and men as workers outside the home; thus *working wife* and *working mother* are, to say the least, more likely to occur than *working husband* and *working father*" (Malmkjaer 2002: 306).

As for social gender and professions, I have to turn to instances of what is called *default gender*, whenever words, marked as masculine and feminine, refer to different social values. For example, if we consider the Russian pairs *akušer*.MASC/*akušerka*.FEM 'obstetrician'/'midwife' and *texnik*.MASC/*texnička*.FEM 'technician'/'cleaning woman', the prestige attached to male professions is obvious. Even though this imbalance between the patterns of lexical and referential gender can be subject to change over time, a number of nominal profession pairs in various languages demonstrate a certain hierarchy in the gendered division of labor, i.e., male = superior vs. female = inferior.

It is noteworthy how Georgian displays almost the same hierarchy of duties and domains when referring to male and female beings, albeit it is a genderless language. Indeed, similar morphological patterns (noun + noun) bear a different social value depending on whether respective words refer to male or to female beings, as is illustrated in Examples (1) and (2):

(1) mama- saxl- is- i
    father- house- GEN- NOM
    'headman, monitor'

(2) dia- saxl- is- i
    mother- house- GEN- NOM
    'housewife'

These two examples are typical linguistic representations of how labor was/is divided in terms of gender in respective language communities.

It is worthwhile to quote Otto Jespersen: "in Munda-Koh it is considered indecent to speak of a married woman except in the dual. She is, as it were, not to be imagined as being without her husband" (Jespersen 2006: 194, footnote 1). Truly enough, a number of publications have recorded the tendency to refer to women according to their relation to men, but less frequently vice versa (for instance, Lakoff, 1973; Pauwels, 1996): "a majority of (modern) industrialized societies, including English- and Dutch-speaking societies operate with a patrimonial system of naming and of marking ancestry (...). The practice of marking women as 'property' of men culminated in the naming conventions used by and for married women, especially in English-speaking countries, i.e., 'Mrs John Smith', in which a woman was merely identified as the 'mistress of a certain man'" (Pauwels 1996: 154f).

Thus, the fact that languages, despite their genetic affiliations, typological features, and/or area-based characteristics, reflected existing division of labor between genders to a certain extent, can be considered a widespread phenomenon.

3 Covert gender in Georgian as a genderless language

Georgian is one of the Kartvelian (South Caucasian) languages. Like its genetic sisters (Megrelian, Laz, and Svan), there is no grammatical gender in the Georgian language; even the 3rd person pronouns are gender-neutral. According to the Language Index of Grammatical Gender Dimensions developed by a group of scholars (Gygax et al. 2019), there are five basic language groups: 1. grammatical gender languages, 2. languages with a combination of grammatical gender and natural gender, 3. natural gender languages, 4. genderless languages with few traces of grammatical gender, 5. genderless languages. Georgian, pertaining to Group 5, lacks most of the grammatical devices available in languages of the other groups; however, this in no way implies that it is neutral in terms of gender equality.

Based on the contrastive study of typologically very distinct languages (i.e., Standard Average European English vs. Amerindian), Whorf distinguished between overt and covert categories, referring to them as pheno- and cryptotypes, respectively (Whorf 1945: 5). Phenotypes are classical morphological categories with explicit grammatical meaning and formal indication, that is, a morpheme, while cryptotypes are covert categories, being based upon the semantic and syntactic features of words with no explicit morphological expression, but essentially instrumental for the construction and understanding of utterances; they influence the collocation of a given word with other ones in a sentence. "Another type of covert category is represented by English gender. Each common noun and personal given name belongs to a certain gender class, but a characteristic overt mark appears only when there is occasion to refer to the noun by a pronoun in the singular number" (Whorf 1945: 3).

As for genderless languages (such as Georgian, Hungarian, Finnish, Turkish, Japanese, etc.), one is likely to observe covert gender. This is to say that, as already stated above, a referent of a generic animate noun, denoting a human being, may be regularly associated with only (or mainly) either a male or a female person; therefore, identification of pertaining associations will allow us to relate them to linguistic dimensions of gendered division of labor in a respective language community, as well as whether and which generic nouns are gender-inclusive or not.

In order to have a clear-cut and well-documented view of the aforementioned dimensions, and with respect to some preceding investigations on covert gender patterns in genderless languages (see, for instance, Braun 1997, 1998, 1999; Engelberg 2002; Vasvári 2011), I launched a pilot study of a new dataset from Georgian.

4 The pilot study: Data and analysis

Since the present chapter is aimed at identifying covert gender patterns in Georgian which is a genderless language, it is important to note that the data (selected from *Explanatory Dictionary of the Georgian Language* in eight volumes Chikobava 1950–1964) include words referring to human beings (occupational terms) with neither morphological nor semantic clues to refer to a possible gender of a referent. Hence, words similar to Example (1), Example (2), as well as to the following in Examples (3) and (4) were not included:

(3) med-   da-   ∅
     med[icine]- sister- NOM
     'nurse'

(4) k'ar- is-   k'ac- i
     door- GEN- man-   NOM
     'butler'

Twenty stimulus terms were selected. The questionnaire was organized as presented in Table 2. The study was conducted in Tbilisi, the capital city of Georgia, in 2014–2021. There were one hundred subjects (61 females and 39 males) with an age range between 22 and 70 years.

As a cover story, the participants were told that the occupation terms were from a screenplay and that their task was to first-name the characters. Along the stimulus terms there were two columns for Variant 1 and Variant 2 in order to allow both male and female interpretations. The detailed results are presented in Table 3.

The results show that 10 items were given a male-only interpretation (see 4), while 4 items received female-only interpretations (see 5). The rest of them received both male and female interpretations (6 items, cf. Table 1). This demonstrates that speakers display to have very clear stereotypes regarding who should have which professional occupation in society. Overall, more social roles are readily assigned to men than women. Hence, the stimulus terms are generic but hardly gender-inclusive.

Tab. 1: Distribution of female, male, and female and male interpretations.

item	translation	female int.	male int.	both int.
p'olicieli	'police officer'	2%	92%	6%
garemovač're	'street vendor'	61%	28%	11%
menežer	'manager'	45%	41%	14%
ekimi	'(medical) doctor'	15%	9%	76%
mocek'vave	'dancer'	24%	8%	68%
molare	'cashier'	99%	0%	1%

Not surprisingly, male-only interpretations included items such as *t'aksis mʒǧoli* 'taxi driver', *mesaate* 'watch-maker', or *inžineri* 'engineer', while female-only interpretations concerned items such as *masc'avlebeli* 'teacher', *mdivani* 'secretary', or *damlagebeli* 'cleaning person'.

Once again, these interpretations correspond to the actual gendered division of labor in the Georgian-speaking community, since male- or female-only interpretations are an outcome of the presence of statistically significantly more men or women in the respective professions. More teachers are female than male and more men are employed as engineers than women, for instance. Typical mixed interpretations include professions which used to be traditionally less open to females, such as *menežeri* 'manager' and *ekimi* '(medical) doctor', as we see in Table 1. This indicates that perception does evolve with fluctuating gender roles in a particular community.

In order to find out whether the interpretations are associated with denotational meanings of individual terms or something else, a contrastive analysis of these data with those from other genderless languages may yield notable results. Turkish seems to be an appropriate counterpart for several reasons: (i) Turkish and Georgian are both genderless languages; (ii) Turkish- and Georgian-speaking communities have long lived side by side, and they have much in common (alongside with differences). Indeed, Braun (1997) launched a study on Turkish, her questionnaire including some occupational terms, and a comparison of both studies can therefore inform us about differences in social gender representations in two grammatically genderless languages.

What I want to shed light on is that words with the same referential meaning cannot be readily associated with the same gender in different genderless languages; e.g., in Braun's study: "[o]ne group of stimulus-terms involved occupations which represent typically male domains", e.g., "*police officer, street vendor, taxi-driver*". These terms were interpreted as male by the majority of the respondents. The stimulus *polis* 'police officer', was interpreted as male by 98% of the subjects, and both male and female by only 1%. Similarly, *işportacı* 'street vendor' was interpreted as male by 94% of the subjects and as inclusive by only 1% (Braun 1999: 192).

However, in my data, *p'olicieli* 'police officer' appeared to be slightly more inclusive (female 2%, male 92%, both 6%) than the Turkish equivalent noun; while *garemovač're* 'street vendor', the Georgian equivalent of the Turkish *işportacı*, had received predominantly female interpretations (female 61%, male 28%, both 11%). Such findings shed more light on peculiarities of the gendered division of labor in respective communities, and, hence, in-/exclusiveness of respective terms.

5 Concluding remarks

What can be inferred from the discussion above should be spelled out as the following:
1. Male and female interpretations of the stimulus terms have demonstrated whether and how gender-inclusive individual stimulus terms are.
2. A genderless grammar does not necessarily provide for gender neutrality in the perception of personal nouns, particularly, of occupational terms, as far as there may always be some gender-based divisions of labor in society, and, hence, it is somehow reflected in language.
3. Languages may be similar with respect to having genderless grammars; however, this does not imply that words of these languages, with identical referential meanings, will be readily associated with one and the same gender and will (not) be gender-inclusive.

The present survey and its results are in no way exhaustive; however, it will serve as a platform for future, more in-depth explorations of the problem in point. For instance, it is interesting to find out how participant gender affected the results. Based on the "self-imagery hypothesis" (Martyna 1978; McKay and Fulkerson 1979), we know that individuals frequently interpret generics to agree with their own gender. Therefore, in my further surveys, I will consider not only gender but also age, educational and rural/urban backgrounds of the participants alongside various statistical data.

6 Appendix

Tab. 2: Questionnaire, transcribed and translated version.

no.	item and translation	variant 1	variant 2
1.	*masc'avlebeli* 'teacher'		
2.	*okromč'edeli* 'goldsmith'		
3.	*p'olicieli* 'police officer'		
4.	*garemovač're* 'street vendor'		
5.	*menežeri* 'manager'		
6.	*mdivani* 'secretary'		
7.	*damlagebeli* 'cleaning person'		
8.	*t'aksis mʒğoli* 'taxi driver'		
9.	*ekimi* '(medical) doctor'		
10.	*arkit'ekt'ori* 'architect'		
11.	*durgali* 'carpenter'		
12.	*mocek'vave* 'dancer'		
13.	*moč'idave* 'wrestler'		
14.	*ektani* 'paramedic'		
15.	*mesaate* 'watch-maker'		
16.	*inžineri* 'engineer'		
17.	*pexburteli* 'footballer'		
18.	*avt'obusis mʒğoli* 'bus driver'		
19.	*molare* 'cashier'		
20.	*mok'rive* 'boxer'		
	Age:		
	Gender:		
	Full name (not mandatory):		

Tab. 3: Questionnaire, general results.

no.	item and translation	female int.	male int.	both int.
1.	*masc'avlebeli* 'teacher'	100%	0%	0%
2.	*okromč'edeli* 'goldsmith'	0%	100%	0%
3.	*p'olicieli* 'police officer'	2%	92%	6%
4.	*garemovač're* 'street vendor'	61%	28%	11%
5.	*menežeri* 'manager'	45%	41%	14%
6.	*mdivani* 'secretary'	100%	0%	0%
7.	*damlagebeli* 'cleaning person'	100%	0%	0%
8.	*t'aksis mʒğoli* 'taxi driver'	0%	100%	0%
9.	*ekimi* '(medical) doctor'	15%	9%	76%
10.	*arkit'ekt'ori* 'architect'	0%	100%	0%
11.	*durgali* 'carpenter'	0%	100%	0%
12.	*mocek'vave* 'dancer'	24%	8%	68%
13.	*moč'idave* 'wrestler'	0%	100%	0%
14.	*ektani* 'paramedic'	100%	0%	0%
15.	*mesaate* 'watch-maker'	0%	100%	0%
16.	*inžineri* 'engineer'	0%	100%	0%
17.	*pexburteli* 'footballer'	0%	100%	0%
18.	*avt'obusis mʒğoli* 'bus driver'	0%	100%	0%
19.	*molare* 'cashier'	99%	0%	1%
20.	*mok'rive* 'boxer'	0%	100%	0%

Tab. 4: Questionnaire, items with male interpretations only.

no.	item	translation
2.	okromč'edeli	'goldsmith'
8.	t'aksis mʒğoli	'taxi driver'
10.	arkit'ekt'ori	'architect'
11.	durgali	'carpenter'
13.	moč'idave	'wrestler'
15.	mesaate	'watch-maker'
16.	inžineri	'engineer'
17.	pexburteli	'footballer'
18.	avt'obusis mʒğoli	'bus driver'
20.	mok'rive	'boxer'

Tab. 5: Questionnaire, items with female interpretations only.

no.	item	translation
1.	masc'avlebeli	'teacher'
6.	mdivani	'secretary'
7.	damlagebeli	'cleaning person'
14.	ektani	'paramedic'

References

Baron, Denis L. 1986. *Grammar and gender*. New Haven: Yale University Press.
Beard, Robert. 1995. *Lexeme-morpheme base morphology: A general theory of inflection and word formation*. Albany: SUNY Press.
Braun, Friederike. 1997. Genderless = gender-neutral? Empirical evidence from Turkish. In Friederike Braun and Ursula Pasero (eds.), *Kommunikation von Geschlecht – communication of gender*, 13–29. Pfaffenweiler: Centaurus.
Braun, Friederike. 1998. Prototype theory and covert gender in Turkish. In Jean-Pierre Koenig (ed.), *Discourse and cognition: Bridging the gap*, 113–122. Stanford: Center for the Study and Information.
Braun, Friederike. 1999. Gender in a genderless language: The case of Turkish. In Yasir Suleiman (ed.), *Language and society in the Middle East and North Africa: Studies in variation and identity*, 190–203. Richmond: Curzon.
Chikobava, Arnold (ed.). 1950–1964. *Explanatory dictionary of the Georgian language, 8 volumes*. Tbilisi: Georgian Academy of Sciences.
Durrer, Sylvie. 2002. Les femmes et le langage selon charles bally: "des moments de décevante inadvertance"? *Linguistik Online* 11(2). doi:10.13092/lo.11.916.

Engelberg, Mila. 2002. The communication of gender in Finnish. In Marlis Hellinger and Hadumod Bussmann (eds.), *Gender across languages: The linguistic representation of women and men*, volume 2, 109–132. Amsterdam and Philadelphia: John Benjamins. https://doi.org/10.1075/impact.10.11eng.
Guellouz, Mariem. 2016. Gender marking and the feminine imaginary in Arabic. In Julie Abbou and Fabienne H. Baider (eds.), *Gender, language and the periphery: Grammatical and social gender from the margins*, 47–64. Amsterdam and Philadelphia: John Benjamins. https://doi.org/10.1075/pbns.264.03gue.
Gygax, Pascal M., Daniel Elmiger, Sandrine Zufferey, Alan Garnham, Sabine Sczesny, Lisa von Stockhausen, Friederike Braun and Jane Oakhill. 2019. A language index of grammatical gender dimensions to study the impact of grammatical gender on the way we perceive women and men. *Frontiers in Psychology* 10. Article 1604. doi:10.3389/fpsyg.2019.01604.
Herder, Johann G. 1966. *On the origin of language*. New York: Ungar.
Jespersen, Otto. 2006. *The philosophy of grammar*. London, New York: Routledge.
Khaznadar, Edwige. 2002. *Le féminin à la française: académisme et langue française*. Paris: Harmattan.
Krifka, Manfred. 2009. Case syncretism in German feminines: Typological, functional and structural aspects. In Patrick O. Steinkrüger and Manfred Krifka (eds.), *On inflection*, 141–172. Berlin, New York: Mouton De Gruyter. https://doi.org/10.1515/9783110198973.141.
Lakoff, Robin T. 1973. Language and woman's place. *Language in Society* 2(1). 45–79. https://doi.org/10.1017/S0047404500000051.
Malmkjaer, Kirsten. 2002. Language and gender. In Kirsten Malmkjaer (ed.), *The linguistics encyclopedia*, 302–307. London, New York: Routledge. https://doi.org/10.4324/9780203432860.
Martyna, Wendy. 1978. What does 'he' mean? Use of the generic masculine. *Journal of Communication* 28. 131–138. https://doi.org/10.1111/J.1460-2466.1978.TB01576.X.
McKay, Donald G. and David C. Fulkerson. 1979. On the comprehension and production of pronouns. *Journal of Verbal Learning and Verbal Behavior* 18. 661–673. https://doi.org/10.1016/S0022-5371(79)90369-4.
Pauwels, Anne. 1996. Feminist language planning and titles for women: Some cross-linguistic perspectives. In Marlis Hellinger and Ulrich Ammon (eds.), *Contrastive sociolinguistics*, 151–167. Berlin and New York: Mouton De Gruyter. https://doi.org/10.1515/9783110811551.251.
Suleiman, Yasir. 1999. *The Arabic grammatical tradition: A study in Ta'lil*. Edinburgh: Edinburgh University Press. https://doi.org/10.1515/9781474472920.
Vasvári, Louise O. 2011. Grammatical gender trouble and Hungarian gender[lessness]. Part I: Comparative linguistic gender. *AHEA: E-journal of the American Hungarian Educators Association* 4. http://ahea.net/e-journal/volume-4-2011/17. Accessed: 8 January 2025.
Whorf, Benjamin L. 1945. Grammatical categories. *Language* 21. 1–11.

Francesca Panzeri and Martina Abbondanza
Gender-inclusive language and male bias: Task matters!

Abstract: The use of the generic masculine has been claimed to evoke masculine representations. Specifically, job offers adopting generic masculine to describe the ideal candidate have been defined as discouraging possible female candidates. Most studies, however, base this hypothesis on responses to questions that explicitly mention the gender of the ideal candidate. The present study aims at testing whether the use of the generic masculine in a text that describes a job offer or that advertises leisure activities lead participants (N = 245) to perceive the described environment as less inclusive. Job offers and advertisements were presented in Italian in three forms. The first form involved the use of the generic masculine and the other two involved gender-inclusive strategies: the feminization strategy (i.e., adding the feminine counterpart of each gender-marked element of the sentence) and the neutralization strategy (i.e., substituting words' final morpheme with the schwa symbol). Results showed that the use of generic masculine did not make participants feel less motivated, connected, included and satisfied. Moreover, no difference was observed between the two gender-inclusive strategies, raising questions about the idea that the activation of the male bias is directly imputable to the choice of linguistic forms.

Keywords: gender-inclusive language, generic masculine, male bias, perception of inclusion

1 Introduction

Languages differ regarding gender morphological marking. Genderless languages (e.g., Finnish, Turkish, Chinese and Swahili), provide no gender marking on nouns and other linguistic expressions; in natural gender languages, such as English, even if (most) nouns have no grammatical marking of gender, pronouns show a gender distinction (as in *A girl entered the room. She was holding a mug of beer*); in grammatical gender languages (e.g., Russian, German and Spanish), all nouns are assigned a feminine or masculine (or sometimes neuter) gender (Prewitt-Freilino et al. 2012). Italian belongs to this last class: The large majority of nouns are marked

---

Francesca Panzeri and Martina Abbondanza, Department of Psychology, University of Milan – Bicocca, e-mail: francesca.panzeri@unimib.it

ⓐ Open Access. © 2025 the author(s), published by De Gruyter. (cc) BY This work is licensed under the Creative Commons Attribution 4.0 International License.
https://doi.org/10.1515/9783111388694-010

for gender and there is morphosyntactic agreement between nouns and the words or elements that depend on them (Hockett 1958; Corbett 2014). Thus, for instance, in Italian not only nouns but also pronouns, determiners, adjectives, past participles (in both singular and plural forms) and, partially, numerals and quantifiers are either marked as feminine or masculine, as in Examples (1) and (2).

(1) (Lei)   è la   mia   candidata   preferita.
    (She.FEM) is the.FEM mine.FEM candidate.FEM preferred.FEM
    'She is my favorite candidate.'

(2) Alcuni   degli   studenti   sono partiti.
    Some.MASC of-the.MASC students.MASC are left.MASC
    'Some of the students have left.'

In the case of nouns which refer to individuals who can be biologically male or female (such as *candidate* or *student*), the feminine form is considered to be marked, in the sense that it can refer only to female individuals, whereas the masculine form is unmarked because it can be used to refer to female referents as well. This is illustrated by the contrast in Examples (3) versus (4), adapted from Jakobson (1984: 1–2), where the Italian masculine form of donkey, *asino*, in (3) covers also female exemplars, whereas the feminine form *asina* in (4) is restricted to biologically feminine donkeys (see also Bobaljik and Zocca 2011):

(3) a. È un   asino?
       Is a.MASC donkey.MASC?
       'Is that a donkey?'
    b. Sì, di fatto è un'   asina.
       Yes, by fact is a.FEM donkey.FEM
       'Yes, actually, it is a jenny (female donkey).'

(4) a. È un   asina?
       Is a.FEM donkey.FEM?
       'Is that a donkey?'
    b. *Sì, di fatto è un   asino.
       Yes, by fact is a.MASC donkey.MASC
       'Yes, actually, it is a (male) donkey.'
    c. No, è un   asino.
       No, is a.MASC donkey.MASC
       'No, it is a (male) donkey.'

When referring to a person whose gender is unknown (or irrelevant) or to a mixed gender plurality of persons, Italian (and other grammatical gender languages) resort to the generic masculine. For instance, in (5) and (6), the noun *candidate* is morphologically marked with masculine gender, but it can refer to female candidates as well, that is, (5) asserts that also a woman can pose a question and (6) that female candidates are invited as well:

(5) Se un candidato ha una domanda, può farla.
If a.MASC candidate.MASC has a question, can do-it
'If a candidate has a question, he can pose it.'

(6) I candidati sono invitati a entrare.
The.MASC candidates.MASC are invited.MASC to enter
'The candidates are invited to come in.'

Even if most linguists view masculine gender as unmarked, and thus as being able to refer indistinctly to both male and female referents, many scholars argue that the use of masculine forms evokes male referents and obscures the presence of women (Sczesny et al. 2016). This has also been found to be the case for a natural gender language such as English: As the English translation of (5) illustrates, to refer to a previously introduced referent (*candidate*, which is not marked for gender in English), the masculine pronoun *he* represents the prescriptive choice (Hellinger and Bußmann 2003).

It has been claimed, though, that resorting to the masculine form activates a *male bias*: The mental representations evoked by this form tend to be male, rather than female or neutral (Gastil 1990), and this has been attested since childhood (Hyde 1984). In grammatical gender languages, moreover, the generic masculine in role nouns (especially occupational titles) has been found to strongly associate with male individuals, compared to other gender-inclusive forms, in German (e.g., Gabriel and Mellenberger 2004; Gygax et al. 2008; Körner et al. 2022; Glim et al. 2025), French (e.g., Gygax and Gabriel 2008; Gygax et al. 2008, 2012; Irmen 2007; Kim et al. 2023), and Italian (Horvath et al. 2016).

These considerations prompted the adoption of a gender-neutral language,[1] that is, according to the guidelines issued by the European Parliament in 2018, [2] a language that avoids "word choices which may be interpreted as biased, discriminatory or demeaning by implying that one sex or social gender is the norm", with

---

[1] In the European Parliament's guidelines, the term *gender-neutral language* is viewed as a "generic term covering the use of non-sexist language, inclusive language or gender-fair language". We will here use these terms interchangeably, even if it has been claimed that there are differences among them.
[2] https://www.europarl.europa.eu/cmsdata/151780/GNL_Guidelines_EN.pdf, accessed: 07 February 2025.

the purpose of reducing gender stereotyping.[3] Particular attention has been paid to personal pronouns: To avoid male bias, several strategies have been proposed, such as feminization (adding the feminine pronoun, as in *If a candidate has a question, he/she can pose it*), or neutralization strategies, substituting the gendered pronoun with *they* or other forms (see Ludbrook 2022 and others). The concept of inclusiveness in the workplace has been extensively investigated, since it has been found that an inclusive work environment has a positive impact on the perception of a climate of trust, affective and organizational commitment, job satisfaction, and employee well-being (see Wolfgruber et al. 2021 and references therein). In this field, the inclusion/exclusion dichotomy is "conceptualized as a continuum of the degree to which individuals feel a part of critical organizational processes" (Mor Barak 1999: 52).

Several studies investigated the use of gender-fair language in job advertisements, with the purpose of ascertaining whether the use of a gender-fair language has an impact on the perception of inclusiveness in the workplace. In particular, it has been hypothesized that resorting to the generic masculine (an "exclusive language" option, since it would obscure the mental representation of women and non-binary individuals) might lead addressees to experience a sense of ostracism, perceiving the work environment as less inclusive. To address this issue, in some studies, participants were asked to evaluate the suitability of male and female candidates for positions that were advertised with or without the explicit mention of the feminine gender. Horvath and Sczesny (2015) focused on German, a grammatical gender language, and found that when the generic masculine was used, women were perceived to fit less with high-status positions compared to male applicants, even if they were seen as equally competent. On the other hand, if the job description explicitly mentioned women (i.e., *Geschäftsführerin/Geschäftsführer*, 'CEO.FEM/CEO.MASC'), the perceived suitability of female applicants became analogous to that one of men. Nevertheless, similar results were found also in natural gender languages such as English and Swedish, in which the gender-neutral neutral noun *the applicant* (*den sökande* in Swedish) still perpetrated the male bias (Lindqvist et al. 2019). The fact that women appear to be underrepresented also in languages that do not mark grammatical gender on nouns suggests that this effect is not imputable to the use of the generic masculine per se but to a more general androcentric worldview where men constitute the norm. This is argued for by Renström et al. (2023), who found evidence for male bias even in grammatical genderless languages such as Turkish and Finnish.

---

[3] In the last years, awareness has been raised concerning the importance of adopting gender-inclusive language relatively to not only gender identity, but also race, disability, sexuality, and geography (Hudley et al. 2024).

In a pertinent study, Stout and Dasgupta (2011) asked participants to read a job offer and then to answer questions assessing their perception of the working environment: When the job description was written using the masculine form intended as generic, also referred to as "gender-exclusive language" across their study, both men and women perceived the environment as sexist, but only women demonstrated less belongingness: They felt excluded, they identified less with the job position, and they felt less motivated. Keener and Kotvas (2023) replicated Stout and Dasgupta's (2011) study, with some modifications: Besides the exclusive-language version of the job offer (with the masculine pronoun *he*), two different inclusive-language versions were presented, one with the feminization strategy (as in Stout and Dasgupta 2011 with the binary pronouns *he* or *she*), and a new one with a neutralization strategy, substituting the gendered pronoun with the gender-neutral pronoun *they*. The rationale behind this choice is that the feminization strategy is viewed as overemphasizing gender binarism, triggering gender stereotypes (Hyde et al. 2019), and excluding people whose gender identity is not binary. The results are comparable to those of Stout and Dasgupta: For both men and women, texts with generic masculine were felt to be sexist; for the indicators of belongingness, only women obtained scores that depended on the language style, with generic masculine texts leading women to anticipate more ostracism, less identification and less motivation. No significant difference emerged for the two gender-fair strategies (binary and non-binary pronouns).

The studies mentioned so far, however, openly reveal their purpose by explicitly asking participants to evaluate the gender dimension, either by indicating the gender of an ideal candidate or by assessing how sexist an environment is. This might not reflect the actual perception of environments in relation to the linguistic form used, considering that participants' attention is, in some way, guided beforehand. Furthermore, to date, there is no study investigating the effect of using the masculine form as a generic in Italian job advertisements and, more importantly, no research compares the use of the masculine form with more recent strategies of gender-fair and inclusive language.

2 The present study

We carried out a study that tested whether using the generic masculine or gender-fair and gender-inclusive strategies in advertising texts impacts participants' conceptualization, leading them to perceive the described environment as more or less inclusive. In this study, the notion of inclusiveness in the workplace is operationalized as sense of belongingness, personal motivation and general satisfaction in the workplace.

The study was conducted in Italian, a grammatical gender language in which most nouns, together with all the elements agreeing with them, are morphologically marked with respect to gender. Besides the language, other modifications were introduced to the previously mentioned studies of Stout and Dasgupta (2011) and Keener and Kotvas (2023). We prepared four different advertising texts: A job offer from a communication agency, and three other ones that advertise leisure activities, that is, a gym offering courses suitable for everyone, a cultural association organizing film clubs, theater performances, and art events, and an association that proposes leisure and personal development courses. We hypothesized that also in these cases, if language styles influence participants' sense of belongingness, similar results to job offers should be obtained, possibly with a less pronounced sense of exclusion, since ostracism in a workplace is more harmful. Moreover, we decided to eliminate the questions assessing the perceived sexism of the environment. In Stout and Dasgupta (2011) and Keener and Kotvas (2023), there were three questions assessing perceived sexism, with explicit mention of the writing style, and of gender issues (e.g., "Do you think that the writing style in the job description favored one gender over the other?"). These explicit questions might have led participants to answer in a more deliberate way, that does not necessarily reflect the initial conceptualization of the working environment, and that might be the by-product of voluntary reasoning, possibly influenced by a social desirability bias. Finally, we added a question that assessed the participant's interest in the job or activity that was advertised, before reading the text. It has been found that girls' lower interest in enrolling in STEM courses is influenced by stereotypes against women (Master et al. 2016), so we aimed to check whether the level of interest could influence the perception of inclusion.[4]

3 Method

3.1 Participants

Two hundred and forty-five Italian-speaking adults (213 females, 25 males, 7 who do not identify with a specific gender), aged 18 to 52 years, and with a mean age of 26 years (SD = 6.15) participated in the study. Some participants were involved through

---

[4] All the materials, data and analyses are stored and publicly available in the OSF repository at: https://osf.io/z8qn4, accessed: 10 March 2025.

the Sona System of the University of Milan-Bicocca and received credit for their participation, others were reached through social media and personal contacts.

Tab. 1: Example of a trial, in this case: *Gym*.

part	text
introduction	Now imagine that you want to join a gym. Read carefully the ad we present below, try to foreshadow the environment of this gym, and then answer to the questions you find just after the ad.
interest question (1 – *no interest*, 7 – *much interest*)	Before you read the ad, however, we ask you what your interest is in gyms, and gym classes, in general.
advertisement text (excerpt)	...If you're looking for an engaging way to reach your health goals, you've come to the right place! At our Energy Fit gym, we offer a wide range of classes suitable for **[tutti]**M **[tutti/e]**M/F **[tuttɜ]**SCHWA ('everyone') and for any skill level and physical condition. ... Whether you are **[un principiante o un esperto]**M **[un/una principiante o un/una esperto/a]**M/F **[unə principiante o unə espertə]**SCHWA (='a beginner or an expert'), you will receive the attention and support you need to progress...
inclusion questions	I am inspired to attend this environment. I think people in this environment can notice me and include me. This environment can motivate me. I could gain personal satisfaction by attending this environment. I would feel a sense of connection in this environment. I would feel a sense of appreciation in this environment. I would feel a sense of acceptance in this environment. I would feel a sense of welcome in this environment.

3.2 Manipulations and measures

We prepared four advertising texts for a job in a communication agency (*Job*), a gym (*Gym*), a cultural association (*Culture*), and for in-presence and online courses (*Courses*). The texts were presented in three versions: One version was with the generic masculine (M), and two other versions were using inclusive-language styles. With the feminization strategy (M/F), the feminine version of each noun (and expressions agreeing with it) was added to the masculine one, thus mentioning both genders. In the neutralization strategy (SCHWA), the gender morphological markings (typically, *–o*.SG and *–i*.PL for the masculine and *–a*.SG and *–e*.PL for the feminine) were substituted with the schwa symbol (/ə/ for the singular and /ɜ/ for the plural). Even if the schwa is not part of the phonemic repertoire of Italian, this option has been recently proposed as a gender-inclusive linguistic strategy in Italian (Boschetto 2015; Gheno 2021; Baiocco et al. 2023). Importantly, this proposal has been strongly opposed both for ideological reasons (it would nullify gender binarism), a criticism made mainly by people with a right-wing political orientation, and for practical reasons (since schwa is not a symbol belonging to the standard Italian inventory, its adoption may cause reading difficulties in people with reading disorders). To exemplify the different writing styles, the noun candidate in the sentence "we are looking for a candidate who..." was presented with the generic masculine (*un.*MASC *candidato.*MASC)M, or with the feminization strategy (*un.*MASC/*una.*FEM *candidato.*MASC/a.FEM)M/F, or with the neutralization strategy (*una candidatə*)SCHWA.

The main measure was the self-reported sense of belongingness in the described environment. Participants were asked 8 questions assessing the perception of inclusion (i.e., the reverse of being ostracized), how motivated they would be in that place, and how they would identify with it (Table 1). These items used 7-point response scales ranging from 1 – *I do not agree at all* to 7 – *I completely agree*. The Inclusion score was obtained by the sum of the scores recorded in each response for each participant, thus ranging from 8 to 56. Before presenting each of the advertising texts, participants were asked how much they were interested in each of the proposed activities (Interest question), and had to answer indicating a value from 1 – *no interest* to 7 – *much interest*. See Table 1 for one example.

3.3 Procedure

The questionnaire was implemented on Qualtrics, a platform for online surveys. Participants had to consent to participate, and then answered to a series of questions regarding their age, gender, educational level, and political orientation (on a scale ranging from 1 – *extreme left* to 7 – *extreme right*). Participants were then randomly assigned to three different lists, and presented with each of the advertising texts (*Job, Gym, Culture,* and *Courses*), written in one of the manipulated styles (M, M/F, and SCHWA).

3.4 Hypothesis

We hypothesize that, if the use of the masculine form as generic leads to a male bias, participants, particularly women, would perceive the environments as less inclusive (i.e., with lower inclusion scores) after reading the text with the generic masculine (M) compared to texts written with gender-fair forms, that is with feminization (M/F) or neutralization (SCHWA) strategies. Since the neutralization strategy is debated, this option might be less favored by participants, especially by those with a more conservative political orientation.

4 Results

We analyzed the results in the R environment (R Core Team 2023) using linear mixed-effects models with the package lme4 (Bates et al. 2015). The *p*-values reported in the outputs of the models are based on the Satterthwaite approximation to the denominator degrees of freedom, as implemented in the lmerTest package (Kuznetsova et al. 2017). We visually inspected the distribution of participants' responses to ensure that none of them answered randomly, for example, by consistently assigning the same value to every response.

To test whether the use of the generic masculine leads to a perception of the environment as less inclusive, we set contrasts to compare the texts involving generic masculine to the texts that involved the other two gender-inclusive strategies. Moreover, we were interested in comparing the two inclusive language strategies with each other. The contrast schema is reported in Table 2.

Tab. 2: Contrast schema set for the analysis.

linguistic form	contrast 1	contrast 2
generic masculine M	2/3	0
feminization M/F	-1/3	+1/2
neutralization SCHWA	-1/3	-1/2

We were also interested in exploring whether the working environment was overall perceived as less inclusive with respect to leisure activities. In order to answer this question, we set contrasts [5] to compare the perception of inclusiveness in response to texts containing job advertisements and texts that promoted leisure activities. We also tested whether there are differences in the perception of inclusiveness among texts promoting leisure activities. We then ran a model which contained the inclu-

---

[5] Considering that the levels of the variable *Type of advertisement* involved the levels *Courses, Culture, Gym, Job*, the contrast schema adopted was: c(-1/4,-1/4,-1/4,+3/4), c(-0.5,+0.5,0,0), c(0,-0.5,+0.5,0).

sion score as dependent variable, the linguistic strategy together with the type of advertisement, the interest score toward the activities, participants' political orientation, age and self-declared gender as predictors, and participants' IDs as random intercept. The output of the model is reported in Table 3.

Tab. 3: Fixed-effects of the model including the inclusion score as dependent variable, the linguistic strategy together with the type of advertisement, the interest score, participants' political orientation, age and self-declared gender as predictors and participants' IDs as random intercept.

	estimate	standard error	t-value	df	p-value
(Intercept)	3.594	0.061	58.703	287.970	0.001
Strategy (contrast 1)	0.001	0.016	0.063	749.674	0.949
Strategy (contrast 2)	-0.002	0.019	-0.120	748.288	0.904
Adv (Job vs others)	-0.047	0.018	-2.564	738.944	0.011
Adv (Cours. vs Cult.)	0.063	0.026	2.409	740.922	0.016
Adv (Cult. Vs Gym)	-0.129	0.025	-5.184	719.153	0.001
Interest value	0.064	0.005	12.888	906.340	0.001
Political orientation	-0.015	0.011	-1.325	234.123	0.187
Age	-0.008	0.002	-4.537	233.953	0.001
Gender	-0.034	0.036	-0.949	233.836	0.344

Results from the first contrast showed that the use of generic masculines did not result in the environment being perceived as less inclusive compared to the two gender-inclusive language strategies. Results from the second contrast showed no difference in the perception of inclusiveness due to the different inclusive strategies adopted (feminization and neutralization). Results from the comparison of the types of advertisements showed that, indeed, texts that advertise job offers are perceived to be the absolute least inclusive, compared to those that advertise leisure activities. On the other hand, participants felt generally more included when responding to an advertisement from a cultural association with respect to the other leisure activities (Figure 1).

Interestingly, results showed that the interest in the target activity strongly predicted the perception of inclusiveness of such an environment (Figure 2, left panel), independently of the linguistic forms used. Lastly, we observed an effect of participants' age on the perception of the inclusiveness of the environment, showing that the older the participants, the less included they felt (Figure 2, right panel).

No effect of participants' political orientation and self-declared gender was observed.

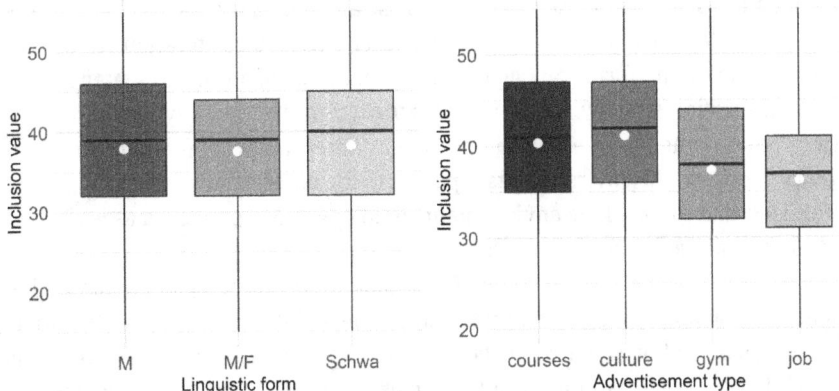

Fig. 1: Mean values of perceived inclusiveness based on the linguistic form adopted (left) and type of advertisement (right). White dots represent the means, while black bars represent the medians.

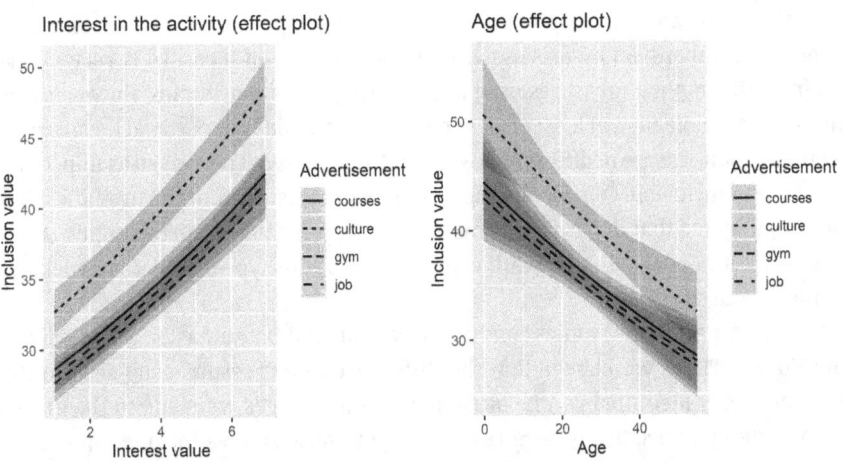

Fig. 2: Effect plots of interest value (left panel) and age (right panel) split per advertisement type.

5 Discussion

The present study aimed at testing whether the use of the masculine generic within advertisements led to a decrease of the perception of inclusiveness (measured asking participants to imagine how they would feel motivated, satisfied, accepted, and so on), with respect to the use of gender-fair strategies. As gender-inclusive strategies we included the feminization strategy, which involves the iteration of the masculine and feminine forms on each gender-marked element of the sentence, and the neutralization strategy, which involves the use of the schwa symbol as gender neutral morpheme. We were also interested in observing whether there were differences between the environments reported in the different ads, especially we hypothesized that the working environment could have been perceived as less inclusive in general, regardless of language form.

Results show that there is no evidence that the use of the generic masculine impact participants' perception of the inclusiveness of the environment. No difference was observed between the texts that adopted the two gender-inclusive forms as well. Hence, the use of the so-called exclusive-language (generic masculine) or inclusive-language strategies (feminization or neutralization) did not have an effect on how participants felt motivated, connected, included and satisfied. This result is particularly interesting considering that the great majority of our participants was constituted by women (87%) and hence, if the use of masculine tended to exclude women, it should have strongly emerged in women's judgment.

In this study, we used an explicit measure of the perception of inclusion in a given environment, and we acknowledge that this type of measure is very different from the implicit measures used in language processing studies. However, it is interesting to note that, at least at an explicit and potentially superficial level of conceptualization, the use of different linguistic strategies is not perceived as impacting the sense of inclusion. Our results show, at the very least, in contrast to studies that have highlighted that the use of the masculine triggers a male representation (Glim et al. 2025; Kim et al. 2023; Horvath et al. 2016), that this type of effect may depend on the task used.

With respect to the studies conducted by Stout and Dasgupta (2011) and Keener and Kotvas (2023), we believe that the difference in our results compared to the male bias they identified can be attributed to the changes we made to the experimental design. Specifically, as already pointed, those studies included questions that directed participants' attention to the writing styles of the texts (e.g., Keener and Kotvas 2023 asked "To what extent do you think the writing style favored men [favored women] [was gender inclusive]?"). To provide an answer, participants are invited to reflect upon linguistic strategies, and this might have led to less spontaneous and more reflective responses (also for social desirability reasons). On the other hand, those studies found an effect of gender-unfair language styles on the other tested dimensions (anticipated ostracism, identification, and motivation), in which no explicit mention of writing strategies or gender was made. It seems unlikely that the diverging results could be imputed to differences in social or cultural factors, since in Italy there is a lively debate about the need for linguistic strategies that do not exclude anyone. Probably the key difference between our study and the studies reported is the absence of explicit reference to sexism and language forms. Indeed, when investigating the effect of linguistic forms on inclusion, making explicit reference to gender or sexism might bias the results and not show the actual perception.

With respect to the other variables that influenced participants' perception of inclusion, their (initial) interest in the advertised job or activity strongly predicted the results. Indeed, the more they declared to be interested, the more they perceived a sense of belongingness to the environment. This result may seem trivial, as it is predictable that the more a person is interested in an activity, the more likely they are to feel included by an advertisement promoting it. However, the truly interesting aspect of this finding is that, for someone who is already interested in the activity beforehand, the way the advertisement is presented does not influence the perception of inclusion in any way. Age influenced the perception as well: The older the participants, the less they felt included. This finding may be linked to the type of activities proposed, which were probably more suitable for a younger segment of the population.

The present study shows some limitations that might be considered as starting points for future research. For instance, the gender and age distribution of the participants is unbalanced, with a significant overrepresentation of women and younger participants. More importantly, the proposed activities (job in a communication agency, a gym, and cultural association) can be considered to be truly open to female presence. It would be interesting to see whether different results might be obtained in case of advertising texts for stereotypically masculine environments (e.g., a job as software developer, or a boxing gym): It could be that in these cases the use of gender-fair language, and in particular the feminization strategy, might contribute to make women more visible and even open up new opportunities (Hiller 2023).

6 Conclusion

Our main result is that when participants declare to be highly interested in a specific activity (a job position, a gym, an association organizing cultural activities or courses), they will foresee that environment in positive terms, anticipating a sense of inclusion. Indeed, in the present study we report that the linguistic forms adopted do not impact how participants felt motivated, connected, included and satisfied. Overall, these findings do not support the idea that generic masculine per se obscures the presence of women, who will therefore feel ostracized. In other words, the male bias that has been attested in other studies that investigated the perception of the workplace after reading a job advertisement has possibly emerged in relation to specific features of society and social relations (i.e., a general androcentric worldview, Renström et al. 2023), rather than in relation to the linguistic forms used. It has to be acknowledged, though, that the existence of a male bias triggered by the use of masculine generic in German has been attested using other techniques (discriminative learning), showing that this form resembles explicit masculine form and differs from explicit feminine forms, independently of societal stereotypes (Schmitz et al. 2023), and thus further research is needed.

References

Baiocco, Roberto, Fau Rosati and Jessica Pistella. 2023. Italian proposal for non-binary and inclusive language: The schwa as a non-gender-specific ending. *Journal of Gay & Lesbian Mental Health* 27(3). 248–253. https://doi.org/10.1080/19359705.2023.2183537.

Bates, Douglas, Martin Mächler, Ben Bolker and Steve Walker. 2015. Fitting linear mixed-effects models using lme4. *Journal of statistical software* 67(1). 1–48. https://doi.org/10.18637/jss.v067.i01.

Bobaljik, Jonathan David and Cynthia Levart Zocca. 2011. Gender markedness: The anatomy of a counter-example. *Morphology* 21. 141–166. https://doi.org/10.1007/s11525-010-9156-3.

Boschetto, Luca. 2015. Proposta per l'introduzione della schwa come desinenza per un italiano neutro rispetto al genere, o italiano inclusivo. http://bit.ly/italianoneutro. Accessed: 25 January 2025.

Corbett, Greville G. 2014. Gender typology. In Greville G. Corbett (ed.), *The expression of gender*, 87–130. Berlin: De Gruyter.

Gabriel, Ute and Franziska Mellenberger. 2004. Exchanging the generic masculine for gender-balanced forms. The impact of context valence. *Swiss Journal of Psychology* 63(4). 273–278. https://doi.org/10.1024/1421-0185.63.4.273.

Gastil, John. 1990. Generic pronouns and sexist language: The oxymoronic character of masculine generics. *Sex Roles* 23. 629–643. https://doi.org/10.1007/BF00289252.

Gheno, Vera. 2021. *Femminili singolari: il femminismo è nelle parole*. Firenze: Effequ.

Glim, Sarah, Anita Körner, Holden Härtl and Ralf Rummer. 2025. An ERP-based comparison of gender representations elicited by generic masculine role nouns and the German gender star form. *Journal of Neurolinguistics* 73. 101231. https://doi.org/10.1016/j.jneuroling.2024.101231.

Gygax, Pascal and Ute Gabriel. 2008. Can a group of musicians be composed of women? generic interpretation of french masculine role names in the absence and presence of feminine forms. *Swiss Journal of Psychology* 67(3). 143–151. https://doi.org/10.1024/1421-0185.67.3.143.

Gygax, Pascal, Ute Gabriel, Arik Lévy, Eva Pool, Marjorie Grivel and Elena Pedrazzini. 2012. The masculine form and its competing interpretations in French: When linking grammatically masculine role names to female referents is difficult. *Journal of Cognitive Psychology* 24(4). 395–408. https://doi.org/10.1080/20445911.2011.642858.

Gygax, Pascal, Ute Gabriel, Oriane Sarrasin, Jane Oakhill and Alan Garnham. 2008. Generically intended, but specifically interpreted: When beauticians, musicians, and mechanics are all men. *Language and Cognitive Processes* 23(3). 464–485. https://doi.org/10.1080/01690960701702035.

Hellinger, Marlis and Hadumod Bußmann. 2003. Engendering female visibility in German. In Marlis Hellinger and Hadumod Bußmann (eds.), *Gender across languages: The linguistic representation of women and men. Volume 3*, 141–174. Amsterdam, Philadelphia: John Benjamins Publishing Co.

Hiller, Gundula Gwenn. 2023. How language use can empower women: The discourse on gender-equitable language in Germany. In Claude-Hélène Mayer, Elisabeth Vanderheiden, Orna Braun-Lewensohn, Gila Chen, Kiyoko Sueda, Brightness Mangolothi, Saba Safdar and Soyeon Kim (eds.), *Women's empowerment for a sustainable future: Transcultural and positive psychology perspectives*, 677–692. Cham: Springer. https://doi.org/10.1007/978-3-031-25924-1_42.

Hockett, Charles F. 1958. *A course in modern linguistics*. New York: The Macmillan Company. https://doi.org/10.1111/j.1467-1770.1958.tb00870.x.

Horvath, Lisa K., Elisa F. Merkel, Anne Maass and Sabine Sczesny. 2016. Does gender-fair language pay off? The social perception of professions from a cross-linguistic perspective. *Frontiers in Psychology* 6. 2018. https://doi.org/10.3389/FPSYG.2015.02018.

Horvath, Lisa Kristina and Sabine Sczesny. 2015. Reducing women's lack of fit with leadership positions? Effects of the wording of job advertisements. *European Journal of Work and Organizational Psychology* 25(2). 316–328. https://doi.org/10.1080/1359432X.2015.1067611.

Hudley, Anne H. Charity, Christine Mallinson and Mary Bucholtz. 2024. *Inclusion in linguistics*. Oxford: Oxford University Press.

Hyde, Janet Shibley. 1984. Children's understanding of sexist language. *Developmental Psychology* 20(4). 697–706. https://doi.org/10.1037/0012-1649.20.4.697.

Hyde, Janet Shibley, Rebecca Bigler, Daphna Joel, Charlotte Chucky Tate and Sari van Anders. 2019. The future of sex and gender in psychology: Five challenges to the gender binary. *American Psychologist* 74(2). https://doi.org/10.1037/amp0000307.

Irmen, Lisa. 2007. What's in a (role) name? Formal and conceptual aspects of comprehending personal nouns. *Journal of Psycholinguistic Research* 36. 431–456. https://doi.org/10.1007/s10936-007-9053-z.

Jakobson, Roman. 1984. *Structure of the Russian verb*. Berlin: Mouton De Gruyter.

Keener, Emily and Kourtney Kotvas. 2023. Beyond he and she: Does the singular use of "they, them, their" function generically as inclusive pronouns for cisgender men and women? *Gender Issues* 40(1). 23–43. https://doi.org/10.1007/s12147-022-09297-8.

Kim, Jonathan, Sarah Angst, Pascal Gygax, Ute Gabriel and Sandrine Zufferey. 2023. The masculine bias in fully gendered languages and ways to avoid it: A study on gender neutral forms in Québec and Swiss French. *Journal of French Language Studies* 33(1). 1–26. https://doi.org/10.1017/S095926952200014X.

Kuznetsova, Alexandra, Per B. Brockhoff and Rune Haubo Bojesen Christensen. 2017. lmertest package: Tests in linear mixed effects models. *Journal of Statistical Software* 82(13). https://doi.org/10.18637/jss.v082.i13.

Körner, Anita, Bleen Abraham, Ralf Rummer and Fritz Strack. 2022. Gender representations elicited by the gender star form. *Journal of Language and Social Psychology* 41. 553–571. https://doi.org/10.1177/0261927X221080181.

Lindqvist, Anna, Emma Aurora Renström and Marie Gustafsson Sendén. 2019. Reducing a male bias in language? establishing the efficiency of three different gender-fair language strategies. *Sex Roles* 81(1–2). 109–117. https://doi.org/10.1007/s11199-018-0974-9.

Ludbrook, Geraldine. 2022. From gender-neutral to gender-inclusive English. The search for gender-fair language. *DEP. DEPORTATE, ESULI, PROFUGHE* 48. 20–30.

Master, Allison, Sapna Cheryan and Andrew N. Meltzoff. 2016. Computing whether she belongs: Stereotypes undermine girls' interest and sense of belonging in computer science. *Journal of Educational Psychology* 108(3). 424–437.

Mor Barak, Michàl E. 1999. Beyond affirmative action: Toward a model of diversity and organizational inclusion. *Administration in Social Work* 23(3–4). 47–68.

Prewitt-Freilino, Jennifer L., T. Andrew Caswell and Emmi K. Laakso. 2012. The gendering of language: A comparison of gender equality in countries with gendered, natural gender, and genderless languages. *Sex Roles* 66(3–4). 268–281. https://doi.org/10.1007/s11199-011-0083-5.

R Core Team. 2023. R: A language and environment for statistical computing. http://www.R-project.org. Accessed: 9 March 2025.

Renström, Emma A., Anna Lindqvist, Gulcin Akbas, Laura Hekanaho and Marie Gustafsson Sendén. 2023. Are gender-neutral pronouns really neutral? Testing a male bias in the grammatical genderless languages Turkish and Finnish. *Journal of Language and Social Psychology* 42(4). 476–487.

Schmitz, Dominic, Viktoria Schneider and Janina Esser. 2023. No generiaddress in sight: An exploration of the semantics of masculine generics in German. *Glossa Psycholinguistics* 2. https://doi.org/10.5070/G6011192.

Sczesny, Sabine, Magda Formanowicz and Franziska Moser. 2016. Can gender-fair language reduce gender stereotyping and discrimination? *Frontiers in Psychology* 7. 25. https://doi.org/10.3389/fpsyg.2016.00025.

Stout, Jane G. and Nilanjana Dasgupta. 2011. When he doesn't mean you: Gender-exclusive language as ostracism. *Personality and Social Psychology Bulletin* 37(6). 757–769.

Wolfgruber, Daniel, Lina Stürmer and Sabine Einwiller. 2021. Talking inclusion into being: Communication as a facilitator and obstructor of an inclusive work environment. *Personnel Review* 51(7). 1841–1860.

Laura Vela-Plo and Marina Ortega-Andrés
Theoretical and empirical basis for gender-fair language use: The case of Spanish

Abstract: The use of so-called gender-fair language (GFL) strategies has increased in light of a much heated and complex theoretical, social and political debate. However, there is still: (i) a crucial need for clarification of the actual consequences (positive and negative) of the use of diverse GFL strategies, and (ii) a lack of comprehensive analyses that systematically contrast the prejudices, arguments against and in favor, and theoretical assumptions underlying GFL with the results of empirical research on the topic conducted in the last decades. For this reason, this chapter first critically analyses the underlying feminist theories that support GFL use and then comprehensively examines those arguments in favor or against their use, focusing particularly on the case of Spanish, a language with grammatical gender marking where masculine grammatical gender is habitually used for mixed-gender reference. Empirical evidence from several languages serves to categorize those arguments against or in favor of GFL that are empirically grounded from those which are not. Therefore, this chapter helps clarify what appear to be prejudices against a potential language change from actual (linguistic and social) consequences of the choice of one or other strategy to refer to people.

Keywords: feminist theories, gender-fair language, linguistic relativism, male bias, masculine generics, Spanish, stereotypes

Laura Vela-Plo, Department of Philology and History, University of the Basque Country UPV/EHU, e-mail: laura.vela@ehu.eus
Marina Ortega-Andrés, Department of Linguistics and Basque Studies, University of the Basque Country UPV/EHU, e-mail: marina.ortega@ehu.eus

Open Access. © 2025 the author(s), published by De Gruyter. This work is licensed under the Creative Commons Attribution 4.0 International License.
https://doi.org/10.1515/9783111388694-011

1 Introduction

Gender-fair language (GFL) comprises those linguistic strategies that aim at reducing gender stereotyping[1] and discrimination (Sczesny et al. 2016).[2] In recent years, the use of GFL has spread in different contexts (especially in social media and institutions; see Guerrero Salazar 2012, 2020 regarding Spanish). These alternative uses of language aim at avoiding the effects of sexism, that is, discrimination or bias towards a particular sex or social gender, and androcentrism in language: The perspective according to which the masculine and men are taken as the standard norm for humanity (cf. Sczesny et al. 2016).

Two main GFL strategies have been used to make languages more inclusive in terms of a more symmetrical treatment of gender:

1. *Neutralization*, when using (i) epicene nouns such as Spanish *la persona* 'the.FEM person' or *el alumnado* 'the.MASC student.body'; (ii) gender-neutral pronouns such as *quien solicite...* 'whoever applies for...'; (iii) recently formed pronouns to avoid gender binarism in a given language (e.g., *elles* in Spanish, *ze* in English, or *iel* in French); (iv) elided nominals, when possible, as in *Se atenderá en orden de llegada* '(customers) will be assisted in order of arrival'; (v) or the use of letters or special symbols that can only be reproduced in written texts (*lxs alumnxs* or *l@s alumn@s* 'the students').

2. *Gendering*, particularly, feminization, is based on the explicit inclusion of women. Several strategies follow under the latter category, such as (i) gender-splits or pair coordination in *las y los antropólogos* 'the.FEM and the.MASC anthropologists.MASC' in Spanish (or *emakume eta gizon antropologoak* 'female and male anthropologists' in genderless languages such as Basque); or (ii) the use of abbreviated forms with slashes (as in German *Elektriker/in* 'electrician.m/f' or Spanish *el/la autor/a* 'the.MASC/FEM author.MASC/FEM'). Although its application is rather limited and politicised, some speakers also choose to refer to mixed-gender groups and/or to themselves with (iii) grammatically feminine terms in clear opposition to the more extended use of masculine forms for generic statements and mixed-gender groups (*Estamos todas reunidas hoy...* '(We) are all.FEM gathered.FEM here...').

---

[1] In the field of person perception within social psychology, stereotypes have been shown to play a central role in shaping how listeners construe social meaning in context (e.g., Macrae and Bodenhausen 2001; Greenwald et al. 2002). Following Levon (2014), stereotypes can be defined as cognitive structures that link group concepts with collections of both trait attributes and social roles.

[2] This article focuses on the linguistic representation of women and men. Theoretical and experimental studies on the representation of gender identities outside this binary approach are still scarce, and future research should address this relevant issue.

The use of some of these strategies has increased in light of a heated and complex debate. Many arguments against sexist uses of language seem to apply to different conceptions about the relationship between language, mind and society. To better understand the discussion about GFL strategies in Spanish, we find it necessary to distinguish three different kinds of approaches in favor of feminist language reforms: [1] *Whorfianist/Relativist* proposals defend the idea that language shapes the way we think; [2] the *Invisibility approach*: Some language uses contribute to women's invisibilization;[3] and [3] the *Pro-change approach*: Speakers of a language in a given speech community can change society, actively choosing and reproducing some particular language uses (and, maybe, avoiding others). Although these three approaches are different, they are not mutually exclusive, as we will show in Section 2.

The chapter is organized as follows. Section 2 comprehensively examines the most relevant theories and notions behind the promotion of GFL strategies. We will clarify the main arguments against and in favor of Whorfianist or Relativist approaches to GFL in Section 3, and against and in favor of Invisibility and Pro-change approaches to GFL in Section 4, focusing on the case of Spanish. Importantly, throughout this chapter, we will critically analyze the empirical evidence presented so far in favor and against these different theories. Section 5 concludes with a summary of most relevant results.

2 Main theories behind the use of GFL strategies

Sexist language reforms have been argued to be built based on Whorfianism or the Sapir-Whorf theory (Gil 2020). Sapir (1929) and Whorf (1956/2012) are considered the precursors of the following claims: that language determines thought, or fixes it in some way ('Strong' versions of Whorfianism), or that language at least influences or shapes thought (as 'Weak' versions state). Within the latter group, *Linguistic Relativity* (LR) or *Neowhorfianism* are weak Whorfianist approaches to language that postulate that the way in which individuals think depends on the language they normally speak. These theories are cognitive theories about how specific grammatical and semantic features of a given language shape the way speakers conceptualize the words and, consequently, how they behave and interact with the world.

---

[3] In this work, we define 'invisibility' as the fact of being ignored, not noticed, or not considered, and 'visibility' in turn refers to the opposite situation, that is, being acknowledged, noticed, or recognized.

Under a *Neowhorfianist/LR* approach to GFL, for instance, one could think that constantly speaking about carpenters using the masculine expression *los carpinteros* ('the.MASC carpenters.MASC') in a generic statement may shape how we learn the concept of *carpenter* as children. People learn what the typical carpenter is by their experiences with carpenters and through the image of carpenters that speakers of their community transmit. Following this logic, language could be one of the possible causes that explain why we have specific expectations about the gender of carpenters, and why the prototypical carpenter in our mental imagery is likely to be male.

Regarding *(in)visibility*, most defenders of GFL claim that language invisibilizes women because they are very rarely mentioned explicitly in our habitual language uses. Although the main tenet behind the invisibility approach differs from Neowhorfianist claims, these two approaches share some important ideas. According to defenders of this approach, language may not directly shape the way people think, but it can favor a male imagery and make women "invisible" in society.

While Neowhorfianism focuses on how language modulates thought, that is, causes a tendency to conceptualize the world in a specific way, proponents of the invisibility approach do not necessarily commit to the idea that language is the cause of gender inequality. Aside from this relevant difference, these two theories are quite intertwined. Defenders of the invisibility approach also claim that how we speak influences the construction of social mental images that make us envision how reality is shaped. In a society where men seem to be everywhere, particularly in positions of power, the message transmitted will be interpreted as females being out of these positions in the collective worldview or social imagery. This line of thought has inspired many published language guides in favor of non-sexist language uses. Bengoechea (2003) claims that, during childhood, women learn to be invisible and construct their identity as being the invisible ones; and, according to her, language has an important role in this process (see also Gygax et al. 2009 for a discussion on the formal learning of grammatical gender in French, and Gygax et al. 2019 for the interpretation of masculine forms by French children).

At this point, it is important to analyze the possible meanings of the term *invisibility*. We distinguish three different perspectives to this notion. First, invisibility can be a synonym of *non-existence*:[4] Every time a group (that is relevant in a specific

---

[4] In English, for instance, the finding that grammatically masculine words can be used to refer to either women or men (*Everyone views his grammar rules as written in stone*) has been interpreted as making women invisible, and to embody and transmit a sexist view of social relations (McConnell-Ginet 1984; Silveira 1980). Moreover, the idea that "What is not named does not exist", attributed to the philosopher George Steiner, has been used as an argument in defense of GFL.

context) is not mentioned in that context, the presence of that particular group is somehow negated, i.e., it does not exist.

Secondly, invisibility can be understood as a consequence of a cognitive bias: The way we speak can perpetuate this sexist bias that the audience already has. In this sense, language is not the cause of the sexist bias; society is. For example, if the prototypical surgeon is a man, when one utters the masculine expression *los cirujanos* ('the.MASC surgeons.MASC'), the stereotype of a male surgeon is perpetuated. In contrast, when uttering *los (cirujanos) y las cirujanas* ('the.MASC [surgeons.MASC] and the.FEM surgeons.FEM'), the speaker is breaking the stereotype, making the audience think about female surgeons as well.

Thirdly, language can be thought of as a tool for (or against) visibilization. This approach takes the notion of invisibility as a cognitive bias a step further and claims that GFL can make the presence of women evident through language, given that women are normally invisible for social reasons. Defenders of this approach will agree that language is not sexist, but comprehenders are. The relevant point in this terminological difference is that the only way to make parsers think about the invisible group is by making their presence explicit, and this may help change people's prejudices and cognitive biases. Every time we utter *los y las cirujanas*, we are explicitly saying that surgeons may be female and potentially counterbalancing an existing sexist prejudice.

Accordingly, the only way to avoid the invisibility of women in our collective imagery is to make explicit that women are present, and one can reach that aim by making some specific linguistic choices that unambiguously evidence women's presence. Therefore, one may consider not using grammatically masculine forms as generic (*masculine generic*; henceforth, MG) in Spanish, since their meaning is ambiguous. For example, one could utter the sentence *Espere a que un médico le llame* 'Wait for some.MASC doctor.MASC to call you' without knowing what the gender of the doctor will be. In this generic statement, the expression *un médico*, thus, may refer to a female doctor or to a male doctor, theoretically. However, people seem to typically interpret these ambiguous expressions as if they referred to men only (Guerrero Salazar 2012; Aliaga Jiménez 2018); i.e., they show a male bias.

The so-called male bias in language use refers to the biased perception of terms that name people without defining their gender as belonging solely to the masculine gender (Stahlberg et al. 2007). Existing studies on this sexist bias have found that it is a robust and frequent phenomenon across different languages (Hamilton 1991; Stahlberg et al. 2007; Garnham et al. 2012: a.o.; see Section 4.2). Androcentrism is considered one of the possible causes of male bias in language. From an androcentric perspective, men are considered to be the subject of reference in general statements about human beings and women are left invisible or excluded from those statements.

One of the most controversial linguistic strategies due to its asymmetric treatment of gender is the use of MG in so-called generic uses to refer to both women and men. Take, for example, grammatically masculine linguistic forms like *exministro* 'ex-minister.MASC' or masculine quantifiers like *todo* 'all.MASC' in Example (1). These masculine forms can be used: a) with specific gender reference to name a group of men, or b) generically to refer to mixed groups or people whose gender is irrelevant or unknown.

(1) *Todos los que vivimos en una ciudad grande...*
     'All of us (in masculine in Spanish) who live in a big city...'

Should the use of generic masculine terms be considered sexist? Does it entail an asymmetry when referring to men and women? García Meseguer (1994) pointed out that there is a difference between the use of MG in Example (1), not considered sexist, and phrases like Example (2), which he did consider clearly sexist for imposing an undoubtedly androcentric vision in a general statement about human beings:

(2) Even the most important events in our lives, such as choosing our wife or our career, are determined by unconscious influences.[5]

The question currently being debated is whether the use of some forms not considered sexist by experts in linguistics or grammar until now, such as the use of MG in Spanish, can entail a cognitive gender bias that perpetuates the existing inequalities in the social sphere. That is, even if they do not involve a sexist use of language explicitly or consciously, do they entail a gender bias implicitly or unintentionally?

Finally, with respect to the *Pro-change approach* (linguistic change as social change theory), it should be noted that any proposal of language reform seems to be based on the thesis of social change: A sociolinguistic approach to language planning (e.g., Fasold 1984) emphasizes that language reforms are directed at achieving social change, especially of the kind that promotes greater equality, equity and access to resources. This approach is based on the idea that our linguistic choices can influence society. A large body of empirical work has shown (e.g., in ethnic revival movements and situations of intergroup conflict) that language can become a powerful symbol of group identity and cultural pride, and thus can acquire social significance far beyond its function as a medium of communication (Lambert 1967). Defenders of GFL agree on the idea that language is not only a symbol, but also a tool for social change.

---

5 From the Spanish: "Hasta los acontecimientos más importantes de nuestra vida, como elegir nuestra esposa o nuestra carrera, están determinados por influencias inconscientes." (García Meseguer 1994).

3 Arguments in favor and against Determinist and Neowhorfianist/Relativist approaches to GFL

Argument against GFL use: Communities with feminine generics should be more egalitarian, but they are not.

Against a strong Determinist approach to GFL, many linguists and experts have argued that there is no causal relation between social inequality and language. For example, Grijelmo (2018) argues that this relationship is not a causal one, since many societies that use generic feminine forms (which, in principle, may suggest a social asymmetry in favor of women) are patriarchal societies. Some other researchers (Bosque 2012; Gil 2020) have claimed that GFL can be used in patriarchal societies to express sexist messages, and that we may use non-GFL to express very gender-inclusive ideas. These authors hence defend the notion that some uses of language may be sexist, but sexism is not an essential part of language per se, but of the things that people say.

In some regions of the world, there are languages whose structure shows a systematic bias towards the feminine grammatical gender (Alpher 1987; Motschenbacher 2010b).[6] This situation has been documented for certain Australian Aboriginal languages (such as Kala Lagaw Ya, a Pama-Nyungan language), Native American languages (such as the Iroquoian languages Oneida and Seneca; Chafe 1977; in Motschenbacher 2010b) and African languages (Maasai, a Nilotic language spoken in Kenya; Tucker and Mpaayei 1955). Kala Lagaw Ya, for instance, possesses a grammatical gender system with two classes: feminine and masculine. The masculine class is restricted to nouns denoting men, male animals and the moon, exclusively, and all other nouns are feminine. Feminine gender is the default choice for noun classification, and it can function generically for plural personal reference (for groups, even if they comprise males only; Bani 1987). Similarly, in Maasai, the feminine grammatical gender is used for generic reference, whereas masculine agreement is male-specific (the sentence *Ainai na-ewuo?* can mean either the generic 'Who has come?' or the feminine-specific 'Which woman has come?'; Tucker and Mpaayei 1955: 27).

As noted by Alpher (1982; in Motschenbacher 2010b), this systematic bias towards the feminine grammatical gender as the unmarked gender category happens in the languages of cultures in which women have, or have had, a relatively high status. Oneida, an Iroquoian language, is cited as an example of this phenomenon. The first relevant question in the light of our research is whether there is higher so-

---

6 There is a major cross-linguistic asymmetry, as the masculine default is more frequently used across languages compared to the feminine default (Motschenbacher 2010a).

cial equality, or either female or male-oriented sexism, in those communities where a language with feminine generics is spoken. Although there are still no systematic studies that clarify this question, Grijelmo (2018) notes that languages with feminine generics do not seem to correspond to more egalitarian nor matriarchal societies. Zayse, for example, is spoken by a multilingual community of around 30,000 speakers in southwestern Ethiopia, a community characterized by a marked patriarchal social organization (Marqueta 2016). However, other languages with feminine generics, such as Mohawk (now 3,000 speakers in the US and Canada), did occur in societies with notable matriarchal features (Grijelmo 2018).

Following a strong linguistic determinism hypothesis, female-biased languages (such as those with feminine generics) should be female-dominated. This prediction does not seem to hold, as a language systematically and traditionally having the feminine as the default or generic grammatical gender does not assure its community to be clearly female-dominated or more egalitarian in general terms.

Argument against GFL use: Languages without grammatical gender marking should be more egalitarian.

One could also wonder whether users of languages without gender marking are less sexist than those who speak a language with feminine/masculine grammatical gender contrasts. Wasserman and Weseley (2009) conducted two surveys at a New York high school where participants had to read a text in either a gender marking language (Spanish or French) or a language without grammatical gender marking (English), and then complete a survey of sexist attitudes. 74 students who were enrolled in Spanish language classes participated in the Spanish-English study (they were mostly monolingual English speakers, but also some L1 Spanish and some English-Spanish bilingual speakers). 85 students at the same school participated in the French-English study (mostly monolingual English speakers, but also a few L1 French and English-French bilingual speakers). The results of these two studies show that participants who had read a passage in a language with grammatical gender distinctions expressed more sexist attitudes than those that had read the same passage in English. In their discussion of the results, Wasserman and Weseley suggest that, since they constantly differentiate between the masculine and feminine, languages with this grammatical gender contrast may contribute to a more general belief that men and women are different.

However, considering that empirical research has shown that there is a foreign language effect in decision-making, we should be cautious about the abovementioned results. Concretely, research has found that people do not make the same decisions in a foreign language as they would in their native tongue (Costa et al. 2014; Hayakawa et al. 2017; a.o.). In this light, since most participants were L1 English speakers, the results of the two above-mentioned studies could be showing a difference in performance because participants completed a task either in their native language (English) or in a foreign language (Spanish or French).

Second, Prewitt-Freilino et al. (2012) observed a correlation between countries in which a language with a grammatical masculine-feminine contrast is the predominant language and lower gender equality compared to countries in which a language is spoken that does not show such a contrast, or only distinguishes gender in third-person pronouns. The authors found such an effect even when other potentially influential factors on gender equality (such as geographic region, religious tradition, political system, overall development) were apparently controlled for. Prewitt-Freilino et al. (2012) find that countries that speak gender-marked languages evidence less gender equality than countries that speak languages without grammatical gender marking. However, as it will become clear later, languages without grammatical gender marking can include seemingly gender-neutral terms that in fact connote a male bias (just as gender-marked languages). Hence, a strong deterministic approach to the social consequences of our linguistic uses should be questioned and still further investigated.

Argument against GFL use: Languages do not influence people's mental representations.[7]

At this point, it is important to have in mind that the GFL version of Neowhorfianism/LR is a much softer version of the original deterministic hypothesis. Nowadays, most defenders of the former claim that language does not determine the way people think, but it can shape how we create some concepts and how we think about them (Boroditsky 2001; Levinson 2003). However, Neowhorfianists do not predict that communities in which people use more inclusive strategies will be more feminist. They claim that linguistic differences may modulate how speakers of different languages categorize reality and, therefore, their thought and their performance may differ (Levinson 2003).

---

7 As Gygax and Gabriel (2011) discuss, a common assumption underlying linguistic comprehension is that both explicit information as well as extracted implicit information form what is called a mental representation or a mental model of the text (Broek et al. 1998; Graesser et al. 1994). A mental model is composed by (i) the exact words and syntax; (ii) all text propositions and elements needed for text cohesion; and (iii) a more elaborate level that conveys the situation portrayed in the text. This third level is argued to embrace information about people, settings, actions and events described explicitly or implicitly by the text (Garnham and Oakhill 1996), which are included in readers' mental model through the process of inference making (McKoon and Ratcliff 1992; Graesser et al. 1994) (see Gygax and Gabriel 2011 for further discussion on the notion of mental representation).

Some Neowhorfianists have claimed that the grammatical gender assigned to an object by a language influences how people think of that object (Boroditsky et al. 2003). Flaherty (2001), for instance, investigated the influence of grammatical gender on the way children perceive the world by investigating Spanish, a gender-marked language, and English, a non gender-marked language. In one of the experiments, English-speaking and Spanish-speaking participants of different ages (5–7 years, 8–10 years and adults) had to assign gender and to put typical male or female names to different objects presented in cartoons. Older Spanish participants (8–10 and adults) were inclined to assign gender and names according to the grammatical gender of the object, whereas older English participants assigned gender according to specific perceived gender attributes. Both 5–7-year-old English and Spanish participants assigned gender according to their own gender more than older participants. Flaherty's (2001) main conclusion was that grammatical gender enabled Spanish participants to assign gender and gender attributes for older participants; whereas younger participants had not yet fully acquired the principles of grammatical gender. Most importantly, this study showed that acquiring a language with or without grammatical gender marking can influence cognitive processing and the gender attributes assigned to referents.

Argument against GFL use: Grammatical gender is arbitrary and has completely innocuous or neutral consequences.

In the specific context of Spanish language, the debate has been very much focused on the use of MG to refer to groups that include men and women. For example, masculine expressions such as *los alumnos* ('the.MASC students.MASC') are generally used to refer to mixed-gender groups or to a group of people whose gender is irrelevant or unknown. According to many feminists, the use of MG contributes to invisibilizing or excluding non-males.

Contrary to this idea, it has been argued that GFL defenders confuse grammatical gender with conceptual/social gender (Escandell-Vidal 2020; Mendívil-Giró 2020; Gil 2020). That is, that there is a false matching between social gender and grammatical gender, since grammatical gender and social gender or sex do not always converge. For example, the Spanish word *lámpara* ('lamp') is feminine and the word *suelo* ('floor') is masculine. There is nothing in these two objects that make them masculine or feminine. The assignment of one grammatical gender or another seems to be arbitrary. When we speak about gendered individuals, Spanish mostly uses masculine and feminine terms that coincide with their social gender or biological sex, but this does not occur in many cases, such as generics, groups, epicene nouns (*la persona* 'the.FEM person') etc. These expressions carry grammatical gender cues, but they are not related to the social gender of the referent.

Despite the proposals just presented, empirical research has shown that the presence of grammatical cues is a relevant factor for interpreting a given expression, and that grammatical gender marking does not have completely arbitrary or neutral consequences for parsers, even when talking about inanimate objects (cf. Boroditsky et al. 2003; Bassetti 2007). For instance, in Konishi (1993), German and Spanish speakers rated a set of nouns on the dimension of potency (a dimension highly associated with masculinity). Half of the nouns were grammatically masculine in German and feminine in Spanish, and the other half were opposite. Results showed that both Spanish and German speakers judged the word for *man* to be more potent than that for *woman*. Interestingly, they also judged grammatically masculine nouns in their native language to be more potent (stronger, bigger or heavier) than feminine ones, even though all tested nouns referred to objects or entities that had no biological gender. The author concluded that words carry connotations of femininity and masculinity depending on their grammatical gender.

Sera et al. (2002) also tested Spanish, French and English adults and children (aged 6, 8, and 10) using a voice attribution task. Participants attributed either a female or a male voice to pictures of artifacts (e.g., plane and book), animals (e.g., spider and bat), and naturally occurring objects (e.g., corn and star). Results showed that the grammatical gender of the word for each entity affected the voice attributions of French and Spanish adults and children above age eight. When natural kinds and artifacts had the same gender in the two languages, French and Spanish speakers attributed them either feminine or masculine voices depending on the grammatical gender of the word for that entity. And when they had opposite gender, French and Spanish children attributed opposite voices to natural kinds, depending on the grammatical gender of the word in each language (although this effect was not found with artifacts).

The results from these studies show that, even if the assignment of one grammatical gender or another to a given word may be arbitrary, grammatical gender marking can influence how people perceive the referent of a word (for a more detailed review, see Boroditsky et al. 2003 and Bassetti 2007). That is, despite being arbitrary, grammatical gender marking has an impact on how people categorize and conceptualize the referent of a given word. Therefore, it may be possible for words marked with a particular grammatical gender (as in the case of MGs) to influence the way people conceptualize the referent of those words.

4 Arguments in favor and against Invisibility and Pro-change approaches to GFL

4.1 Stereotypicality in gender roles and the interpretation of (ambiguous) masculine forms

Argument against GFL use: The potential ambiguity of MG is effectively resolved, since they can easily be interpreted as mixed-gender (generic), or male-exclusive depending on the context.

Against the Invisibility approach to GFL, it has also been claimed that MG forms are only theoretically ambiguous, but not in their real use. Escandell-Vidal (2020) and Mendívil-Giró (2020) defend that comprehenders normally understand whether an ambiguous masculine expression has an interpretation inclusive to all genders or not. These authors argue that it is the exclusive (male-only) interpretation that requires further specification. For example, the phrase *el empleado* has different meanings in Examples (3-a) and (3-b): It can refer to any employee (female or male) in (3-a); or to a particular male employee in (3-b).

(3)   a.   *El empleado que se ausente será despedido (, sea hombre o mujer).*
              'Any(the.MASC) employee.MASC who gets absent will be fired, be they a man or a woman.'
    b.   *El empleado que se ausentó fue despedido (?, fuera hombre o mujer).*
              'The.MASC employee.MASC who was absent was fired, be they a man or a woman.'

Mendívil-Giró (2020) argues that MG are only potentially ambiguous, since a given context disambiguates their meaning; that is the reason why the continuation in parentheses in (3-a) is felicitous, but not in (3-b).

In contrast, following an invisibility approach, it is noted that the fact that context may sometimes help in disambiguating the meaning of an MG does not make these expressions non-ambiguous:

(4)   *Los empleados que se ausenten serán despedidos.*
       'Any(the.MASC) employees.MASC who get absent will be fired.'

Example (4) is ambiguous, just as the beginning of Example (3-a). While *sea hombre o mujer* in (3-a) disambiguates the sentence, making it explicit that some of the employees may be women, that may not be the case in sentences such as (4).

As Bosque (2012) claims, the use of MG to designate groups of women and men is firmly established in many grammars, such as that of Spanish. It is noteworthy that when we find an ambiguous word (that is, when we can have a male specific or mixed-gender interpretation) or when no explicit information about the gender of a referent is given (e.g., *the surgeons*), gender stereotypes rooted in our society often unconsciously disambiguate these expressions for us and make a prediction about the gender of the referent (that we may need to revise later on). Sanford (1985) and Carreiras et al. (1996) show that there is a tendency to consider ambiguous nouns as having male referents in English and Spanish, and argue that it is due to the use of MG and social stereotypes or sexist roles established in these speech communities. These authors suggest that information about gender stereotypes is reproduced in linguistic forms that do not have grammatical gender cues or which are ambiguous, thus maintaining social gender asymmetries.

With reference to stereotypes, on the one hand, Martyna (1978) observed that stereotypical gender roles affect the interpretation of nouns in English that do not specify the gender of the referent. In the study, participants had to complete sentence fragments such as *When an engineer makes an error in calculation....* She varied the content of the sentences, using male-related (as in *engineer* above), female-related, or non-gender-related antecedents, and found that participants' choices of pronouns were strongly affected by the socially rooted gender stereotype of the antecedent. So, for example, subjects were likely to write *an engineer..., he, a secretary..., she*, and *a human being..., they*, and both the pronouns used and the imagery (what images had come to people's minds as they completed the sentences) tended to match the antecedent's stereotypical gender (cf. also Garnham et al. 2002).

While socially rooted gender stereotypes seem to play an important role in the mental representation of gender in languages with gender-unmarked nouns such as English, in gender-marked languages, grammatical gender cues also come into play and at times seem to be predominant. In a systematic comparative study, Gygax et al. (2008) found that in gender marking languages grammatical gender generally outweighs social gender. Their results indicated that when role names were written in the masculine plural form in French and in German, grammatical cues overrode stereotype information in constructing a mental representation of gender. When no grammatical gender information was available, as in English, the mental representation of gender was solely based on stereotype information. From this, they concluded that the representation of gender is based on stereotypicality when no gender cues are provided, whereas it is based on the grammatical marking of gender if cues are provided.

In sum, information about gender stereotypes is reproduced in linguistic forms that do not show grammatical gender cues or which are ambiguous, as in the case of MGs. Therefore, those uses may reproduce prevailing social gender asymmetries.

In this light, it is also important to highlight a general conclusion in Gygax et al. (2019) based on previous empirical research on the processing of (ambiguous) masculine forms: Adults struggle to process masculine forms as generic, and tend to attribute male values to role nouns or occupations written in the masculine form, in most cases regardless of stereotype. This result was observed in Stahlberg et al. (2007) or Schmitz et al. (2023) in German; and Gygax et al. (2008), Gabriel et al. (2008), or Garnham et al. (2012) in French and German, among many other studies. In fact, many studies, using a variety of comprehension tasks, have consistently found that both terms such as *man* and *he* in English also tend to be interpreted as referring only to males, despite appearing in generic contexts (some early studies are Moulton et al. 1978; MacKay 1980; Martyna 1980; Crawford and English 1984).

In the case of Spanish, Perissinotto (1983) showed that sentences like *Todo hombre tiene derecho de entrar en la república y salir de ella* ('Every man has the right to get into and out of the republic') are naturally interpreted as referring not to every human being but to every man. The author claims that "Such high incidence of specific interpretations casts serious doubt on the whole notion of generic which, this research seems to show, is only useful when talking about self-monitored and guarded speech, hardly the most common mode" (Perissinotto 1983: 585). Thus, although it has been argued that MGs have a clear mixed-gender interpretation in generic contexts, numerous comprehension tasks have shown that, despite appearing in explicitly gender-neutral contexts, MGs tend to be interpreted as referring only to males (Perissinotto 1983; Schmitz 2024; Gygax et al. 2019: and references therein), thus supporting Invisibility theories to GFL.

4.2 GFL and reducing sexist cognitive biases

Argument against GFL use: GFL is unnecessary, as its strategies do not reduce the gender bias present in our society.

Since the 70s, studies into the mental imagery associated with MG have shown that the use of GFL reduced the maleness of the mental imagery. Most studies on gender biases in language use have been carried out for English or German. As far as English is concerned, evidence of a male bias can be found, for example, in studies by Moulton et al. (1978), Wilson and Ng (1988), Hamilton (1988, 1991), Khoroshahi (1989), Stahlberg et al. (2001) or Lindqvist et al. (2019), more recently. As Sczesny et al. (2016) claim, empirical findings about the disadvantages of MG have been ignored in political controversies and public discussions about GFL.

Most investigations in English and German found that, when GFL forms were used instead of MG, the cognitive inclusion of women was promoted and the male bias weakened. Although the effects of this bias varied in degree, and it was not confirmed in all the experimental conditions of all the empirical investigations, it is evident that it is the most general trend that has emerged in the cited empirical studies (Stahlberg et al. 2007: for a review). In Khoroshahi (1989), for instance, the results revealed differences in the mental imagery connected to MG or GFL only in the case of women who had reformed their language. She concluded that the adoption of GFL was only effective if there is personal awareness of the discriminatory nature of some expressions and there is personal commitment to change.

Already in 1975, Harrison and Passero observed a male bias in 8-year-old children when interpreting MG in English. Concretely, upon reading instructions like *Christmas is a time when [people/men] of goodwill gather to celebrate. Circle the following group or groups which show [people/men] of goodwill.*, only 3–31% of the children who saw the instructions with neutral words (*people*) circled males only. In contrast, it was 49–85% of the students who saw the instructions with MG (*men*) that circled male figures. This difference was statistically significant. The results suggest that children interpret masculine forms in generic contexts as if they referred to males only, not with a generic interpretation. This male bias is alleviated when using terms that do not specify the gender of the referent (*handmade/manmade, salesperson/salesman*).

More recently, Lindqvist et al. (2019) have run two experiments (English and Swedish) to measure the perception of different gender coding strategies and analyze the consequences of the use of neologisms that avoid the binary gender system. Participants had to read a text (a description of a candidate for a gender-neutral job position) and choose an image of the person who fitted the description best. Some sentences in these texts were written with either the doubling strategy (using gender-splits or couplets such as *he/she*); with new gender-neutral pronouns (the newly created English pronoun *ze* and Swedish *hen*); or without gender cues (as in *the applicant*). Importantly, the results of both experiments indicated that feminization by duplication and new gender-neutral pronouns were interpreted as if they referred to women more often than any other strategy; and the forms used traditionally and that lack gender marks were mostly interpreted as referring to men (male bias).[8]

---

[8] One of the limitations of this experiment is that the number of female and male participants was not balanced. Previous research has shown (Hamilton and Henley 1982; Martyna 1978) that men tend to have more male-biased imagery than women. Men's greater bias might be explained in several different ways. The most obvious but least charitable explanation is that men are simply more sexist than women. Other factors may contribute, however. Part of what goes into the creation of imagery for both men and women could be a projection of 'self' into the sentences. This idea comes from Silveira's (1980) *people = self bias*. Another possibility also suggested by Silveira is that

4.3 Comprehensibility, quality, economy and level of difficulty

Arguments against GFL use:
1. GFL is less comprehensible for parsers, and considered to be of less quality for both speakers and hearers.
2. GFL is less economical for both speakers and hearers.
3. GFL is difficult to use continuously for speakers.

It has been argued that some GFL strategies that visibilize women and non-binary people may require a high level of attention to grammar and that they may be very difficult to be processed or understood. For example, in order to use the non-binary neomorpheme -e in Spanish, speakers have to pay attention to all determiners, adjectives and nouns that refer to people. This observation has been used to develop an argument against the guidelines published by some institutions (Gil 2020): GFL requires speakers to be very self-conscious of their grammar, which may be particularly hard for non highly-qualified people. Moreover, it has been argued that it is very problematic for a particular group of people to decide that some expressions (that most speakers use every day) should be avoided (Bosque 2012; Martínez 2008). Bosque (2012) argues that if the linguistic strategies proposed in language reform guides were applied in their strictest terms, it would not be possible to speak; and that those proposals should not be applied to common language, but in official language uses only.[9]

Nevertheless, the purpose of GFL guides is not that of imposing a single way to speak, but to offer institutions and individuals some linguistic strategies to be more inclusive, and to raise awareness on sexist uses.

Regarding Spanish, one of the mostly criticized GFL strategies is pair coordination or gender-splits. As stated by Real Academia Española (responsible for regulations on the normative usage of the Spanish language), "Gender pair coordination is grammatical, even polite; but if applied without control, it creates discursive monsters" (Real Academia Española 2020: 56).[10] The sentence in (5) exemplifies a case of overuse of this strategy:

---

the people = self bias may be stronger for men than for women, in part due to repeated exposure to MG. A third possibility is that women are less able to project themselves into the sentence when they use MG than are men. These various explanations are not mutually exclusive.

9 For various responses to Bosque's (2012) work, see Moreno Cabrera (2012) and Guerrero Salazar (2012).

10 *Los desdoblamientos de género son gramaticales, e incluso corteses; pero, aplicados sin control, generan monstruos discursivos.*

(5) *Los empleados y las empleadas avisaron a los profesores y las profesoras de que sus hijos e hijas no podrían ir al colegio ese día.*
The.MASC employees.MASC and the.FEM employees.FEM notified the.MASC teachers.MASC and the.FEM teachers.FEM that their sons and daughters would not be able to go to school that day.

The critique seems obvious: Repetitions may feel exhausting to the speaker and audience. It has been argued not only that this strategy is too demanding, but also that it is against the principle of the economy of language (Real Academia Española 2020), which we will discuss below.

Against the idea that GFL is very difficult or demanding, empirical research has shown that reading a text that is written using GFL is not more demanding than reading a text that was not written using GFL (Parks and Roberton 1998). Text quality (Rothmund and Christmann 2002) and cognitive processing are not damaged by the use of GFL (Braun et al. 2007). GFL texts were compared to (generic) masculine texts, and there were no differences in readability and aesthetic appeal (Blake and Klimmt 2010). It is also important to have in mind that these experiments do not measure the cognitive effort from the point of view of the speaker, but only from the perspective of the parsers.

In 2002, the Académie Française, responsible for all regulations on the usage of the French language, explicitly stated that writing job titles in both masculine and feminine forms was "useless" and disruptive to normal reading. Gygax and Gesto (2007) replied and showed that, although the first encounter of alternative terms to the masculine-only in a text did indeed slow down reading (which they considered as a sign of hindering), there was a very fast habituation effect, leading to a perfectly normal reading pace. Gygax and Gesto (2007) showed five texts to participants, each describing an occupation (e.g., mechanic), and each comprising three mentions of the occupation. Some participants saw the texts with MG, whereas others read the text comprising alternatives to the masculine-only form (*mécanicienne-s* or *mécaniciens et mécaniciennes*). The authors monitored self-paced reading times and noticed that for the texts containing the alternative forms, although reading was slowed down by the first encounter of the occupation, participants achieved a normal reading speed at the second and third encounter of the occupation. Hence, Gygax and Gesto (2007) argued that people get used to alternative forms that only temporarily hinder reading.

Regarding the principle of economy of language (PE), according to Jespersen (1949) or Zipf (1949), linguistic economy is best achieved when both addressee's mental energy and speaker's articulatory energy are optimally economized when communicating a message. In this line, PE would not only be a matter of using fewer words, but also about reducing the mental energy of the interlocutors. Importantly, what all definitions of PE assume is that it is not a law that we must follow, but a descriptive rule that (as speakers) we typically comply with. Álvarez Mellado (2018) claims that, although people generally have an inclination towards linguistic economy, PE is not a mandatory rule that language users and languages must always obey. And, in many cases, speakers do not follow PE, for example, due to expressive reasons. An audience typically expects a speaker to be clear and precise, which usually requires the speaker to use a larger amount of information units to make themselves understood in a given context.

In this spirit, Vervecken et al. (2013) investigated how employing either MGs or duplications for job descriptions impacts children's perception and interest regarding traditionally male occupations, concretely, among girls who spoke two languages with grammatical gender marking systems, Dutch and German. Participants had to read a set of sentences in generic masculine (*Firemen are people who extinguish fires*) or using a coordination of feminine and masculine forms (*Firewomen and firemen...*). In a first experiment, participants had to imagine that they were directors of a film and had to choose who was going to play in that film. Results show that those participants who read the sentences in GFL chose more female actors than participants in the generic masculine condition. Girls were asked who they think was more successful in the given jobs and which job they would like to have when they got older. Importantly, Vervecken et al. found that participants in the GFL condition were more likely to say that women would be more successful and that they would like to work as one of the mentioned jobs.

In the light of the results of Vervecken et al. (2013), a speaker may find expressive or other reasons to use GFL, even if there are "more economical" options. It may not be necessary to use GFL strategies every time there is a human reference in our discourse, but its use in some particular contexts may be notably effective at avoiding ambiguity and male imagery (although still more research is necessary on this point). In this sense, reform guides tend to recommend avoiding the overuse of MGs, not a complete abandonment.

4.4 Feminization strategies and the importance of time

Argument against GFL use: The use of some feminine terms can have negative social consequences.

Moving to the Pro-change hypothesis, Escandell-Vidal (2020) questions the idea that language change and the use of GFL will promote gender equality. This author worries about the potentially negative consequences for women of several feminization strategies. For example, if we insist on making it explicit that a candidate for a job is a woman, that could have a negative impact on her, because some people will not hire her. Following this line of thought, instead of visibilizing and empowering women, the effect could be that of devaluating the job.

Regarding empirical research on the topic, masculine job titles have been found to be associated with higher competence (McConnell and Fazio 1996), higher status (Merkel et al. 2012), and higher professional opportunities (Formanowicz et al. 2013) than feminine forms. Merkel et al. (2012) show that the feminine job title *avvocatessa* ('lawyer.FEM') in Italian leads to a lower valuation of the status of some jobs. In a similar study, Formanowicz et al. (2013) included an ideological test before the evaluation task and showed that participants who considered themselves politically conservative showed a greater tendency to negatively evaluate women who wrote their job title in the feminine, in comparison to those participants who considered themselves progressivists.

It is important to note that the implementation of GFL is often associated with negative reactions and hostile attacks on people who propose a change, particularly in the case of neopronouns. This was also the case in Sweden in 2012, when a third gender-neutral pronoun (*hen*) was proposed as an addition to the already existing Swedish pronouns *hon* 'she' and *han* 'he' (Gustafsson Sendén et al. 2015). The pronoun *hen* can be used both generically, when gender is unknown or irrelevant, and as non-binary pronoun for people who want to avoid gender binarism. From 2012 to 2015, this third gender-neutral pronoun reached the broader population of language users; this makes the situation in Sweden unique. According to Gustafsson Sendén et al. (2015), in 2012 the majority of the Swedish population had a negative attitude towards the neopronoun, but already in 2014 there was a significant shift towards more positive attitudes. Importantly, time was one of the strongest predictors for a change in attitudes, and the actual use of the word *hen* also increased in this period, although to a lesser extent than the attitudes shifted. Gustafsson Sendén et al. (2015) conclude that, although new words challenging the binary gender system may evoke hostile and negative reactions, attitudes may normalize rather quickly.

5 Conclusion

It is often argued that GFL may be useless (as gender inequality goes far beyond grammar) or even impossible (as speakers' resistance defies linguistic planning). Moreover, it seems to us that visibilizing women through language (being acknowledged, noticed, or recognized) may not be enough to achieve a positive social change for women and gender equality, since it is still mandatory that we change long-established gender stereotypes (cognitive structures that link group concepts with collections of both trait attributes and social roles) and prejudices. However, studies such as Gustafsson Sendén et al. (2015) in Sweden or Vervecken et al. (2013), among many others, have shown that visibilizing is both possible and that it can have active positive effects on language attitudes and behavior. Most importantly, in Sections 3 and 4 we have reviewed extensive evidence of the impact of grammatical gender on the perception of reality, and the role of MGs and GFL in either reproducing a male bias and gender stereotypes, or avoiding them. Concretely, we have seen that acquiring a language with or without grammatical gender marking can influence cognitive processing, and, although the assignment of grammatical gender may be arbitrary, gender marking was observed not to be meaningless nor neutral, as it may have social consequences (Section 3). Additionally, Section 4.3 showed that GFL is not more difficult, nor of less quality for the listener, and that both economy and expressivity should be taken into consideration for choosing one or another strategy to codify gender. Still, more research on the consequences of using GFL from the point of view of the speaker is necessary.

In addition, gender stereotypes have been shown to influence our interpretation of genderless ambiguous nouns (Section 4.1). But, importantly, ambiguous MG tend to be interpreted as male only due to a sexist cognitive bias, even in clearly generic contexts. In order to avoid such a cognitive bias, some GFL strategies have been shown to avoid or reduce this general male bias (Section 4.2).

Finally, whereas some feminization strategies may show potential negative consequences in the beginning, time is an important factor for changing attitudes and uses (Section 4.4). The empirical evidence in favor of the Neowhorfianist/Linguistic Relativity approach and the Invisible approach suggest that language can be one (of many) vehicles towards social change.

6 Acknowledgements

This research has been partially funded by the linguistics research group *HiTT Hizkuntzalaritza Teorikorako Taldea* (IT1537–22) at the University of the Basque Country UPV/EHU and by *Emakunde – Basque Institute for Women* with a Grant for research on equality between women and men for the year 2023 (2023-BTI1-TE-05). The authors would like to thank two anonymous reviewers that helped improve this manuscript, as well as Marta De Pedis for her valuable comments on a previous version of the manuscript.

References

Aliaga Jiménez, José Luis. 2018. *Lenguaje inclusivo con perspectiva de género*. Zaragoza: Gobierno de Aragón.

Alpher, Barry. 1987. Feminine as the unmarked grammatical gender. *Australian Journal of Linguistics* 7(2). 169–187. https://doi.org/10.1080/07268608708599380.

Álvarez Mellado, Elena. 2018. Más allá de la economía del lenguaje. https://www.eldiario.es/opinion/zona-critica/alla-economia-lenguaje_129_2019252.html. El País, Online. Accessed: 9 March 2025.

Bani, Ephraim. 1987. Garka a ipika: Masculine and feminine grammatical gender in Kala Lagaw Ya. *Australian Journal of Linguistics* 7(2). 189–201. https://doi.org/10.1080/07268608708599381.

Bassetti, Benedetta. 2007. Bilingualism and thought: Grammatical gender and concepts of objects in Italian-German bilingual children. *International Journal of Bilingualism* 11(3). 251–273. https://doi.org/10.1177/1367006907011003010.

Bengoechea, Mercedes. 2003. *El lenguaje instrumento de igualdad*. Madrid: Iniciativa Comunitaria.

Blake, Christopher and Christoph Klimmt. 2010. Geschlechtergerechte Formulierungen in Nachrichtentexten. *Publizistik* 55. 289–304. https://doi.org/10.1007/s11616-010-0093-2.

Boroditsky, Lera. 2001. Does language shape thought? Mandarin and English speakers' conceptions of time. *Cognitive Psychology* 43(1). 1–22. https://doi.org/10.1006/cogp.2001.0748.

Boroditsky, Lera, Lauren A. Schmidt and Webb Phillips. 2003. Sex, syntax, and semantics. In Dedre Gentner and Susan Goldin-Meadow (eds.), *Language in mind: Advances in the study of language and thought*, 61–79. The MIT Press. https://doi.org/10.7551/mitpress/4117.003.0010.

Bosque, Ignacio. 2012. *Sexismo lingüístico y visibilidad de la mujer*. Madrid, España: Real Academia Española.

Braun, Friederike, Susanne Oelkers, Karin Rogalski, Janine Bosak and Sabine Sczesny. 2007. How masculine generics and alternative forms affect the cognitive processing of a text. *Psychologische Rundschau* 58. 183–189. https://doi.org/10.1026/0033-3042.58.3.183.

Broek, Paul Van den, Michael Young, Yuhtsuen Tzeng and Tracy Linderholm. 1998. The landscape model of reading: Inferences and the on-line construction of a memory representation. In Susan R. Goldman and Herre van Oostendorp (eds.), *The construction of mental representation during reading*, 71–98. Mahwah: N.J. Erlbaum.

Carreiras, Manuel, Alan Garnham, Jane Oakhill and Kate Cain. 1996. The use of stereotypical gender information in constructing a mental model. *The Quarterly Journal of Experimental Psychology* 49(3). 639–663. https://doi.org/10.1080/713755647.

Costa, Albert, Alice Foucart, Inbal Arnon, Melina Aparici and Jose Apesteguia. 2014. "piensa" twice: On the foreign language effect in decision making. *Cognition* 130(2). 236–254. https://doi.org/10.1016/j.cognition.2013.11.010.

Crawford, Mary and Linda English. 1984. Generic versus specific inclusion of women in language: Effects on recall. *Journal of Psycholinguistic Research* 13. 373–381. https://doi.org/10.1007/BF01068152.

Escandell-Vidal, M. Victoria. 2020. En torno al género inclusivo. *Igualdades* 2(2). 223–249. https://doi.org/10.18042/cepc/IgdES.2.08.

Fasold, Ralph. 1984. *Language policy and change: Sexist language in the periodical news media*. Washington DC: Georgetown UP.

Flaherty, Mary. 2001. How a language gender system creeps into perception. *Journal of Cross-Cultural Psychology* 32(1). 18–31. https://doi.org/10.1177/0022022101032001005.

Formanowicz, Magdalena, Sylwia Bedynska, Aleksandra Cisłak, Friederike Braun and Sabine Sczesny. 2013. Side effects of gender-fair language: How feminine job titles influence the evaluation of female applicants. *European Journal of Social Psychology* 43(1). 62–71. https://doi.org/10.1002/ejsp.1924.

Gabriel, Ute, Pascal Mark Gygax, Oriane Sarrasin, Alan Garnham and Jane Oakhill. 2008. Au pairs are rarely male: Norms on the gender perception of role names across English, French, and German. *Behavior Research Methods* 40(1). 206–212. https://doi.org/10.3758/BRM.40.1.206.

García Meseguer, Álvaro. 1994. *¿es sexista la lengua española?: Una investigación sobre el género gramatical*, vol. 4. Madrid: Editorial Paidós.

Garnham, Alan and Jane Oakhill. 1996. The mental models theory of language comprehension. In Bruce K. Britton and Arthur C. Graesser (eds.), *Models of understanding text*, 313–339. New York: NJ Erlbaum.

Garnham, Alan, Jane Oakhill and David Reynolds. 2002. Are inferences from stereotyped role names to characters' gender made elaboratively? *Memory & Cognition* 30(3). 439–446. https://doi.org/10.3758/BF03194944.

Garnham, Alan, Gabriel Ute, Oriane Sarrasin, Pascal Gygax and Jane Oakhill. 2012. Gender representation in different languages and grammatical marking on pronouns. *Discourse Processes* 49(6). 481–500. https://doi.org/10.1080/0163853X.2012.688184.

Gil, José Manuel. 2020. Las paradojas excluyentes del "lenguaje inclusivo". *Revista Española De Lingüística* 50(1). 65–84. https://doi.org/10.31810/RSEL.50.1.3.

Graesser, Arthur, Murray Singer and Tom Tabasso. 1994. Constructing inferences during narrative text comprehension. *Psychological Review* 101. 371–395. https://doi.org/10.1037/0033-295X.101.3.371.

Greenwald, Anthony, Mahzarin Banaji, Laurie Rudman, Shelly Farnham, Brian Nosek and Deborah Mellot. 2002. A unified theory of implicit attitudes: Stereotypes, self-esteem and self-concept. *Psychological Review* 109(3). 3–25. https://doi.org/10.1037/0033-295X.109.1.3.

Grijelmo, Alex. 2018. ¿invisibiliza nuestra lengua a la mujer? https://elpais.com/cultura/2018/11/28/actualidad/1543418937_639835.html. El País. Accessed: 9 March 2025.

Guerrero Salazar, Susana. 2012. La feminización del lenguaje en la sociedad de la información. In Ainara Larrondo-Ureta and Koldo Meso-Ayerdi (eds.), *Mujer y medios de comunicación*, 57–74. UPV/EHU.

Guerrero Salazar, Susana. 2020. El debate social en torno al lenguaje no sexista en la lengua española. *IgualdadES* 2. 201–221.

Gustafsson Sendén, Marie, Emma A. Bäck and Anna Lindqvist. 2015. Introducing a gender-neutral pronoun in a natural gender language. *Frontiers of Psychology* 6. 893. https://doi.org/10.3389/fpsyg.2015.00893.

Gygax, Pascal, Ute Gabriel, Oriane Sarrasin, Jane Oakhill and Alan Garnham. 2008. Generically intended, but specifically interpreted: When beauticians, musicians, and mechanics are all men. *Language and Cognitive Processes* 23(3). 464–485. https://doi.org/10.1080/01690960701702035.

Gygax, Pascal Mark and Ute Gabriel. 2011. Gender representation in language: More than meets the eye. In Ramesh Kumar Mishra and Narayanan Srinivasan (eds.), *Language and cognition: State of the art*, 72–92. München: Lincom AP.

Gygax, Pascal Mark, Ute Gabriel, Oriane Sarrasin, Jane Oakhill and Alan Garnham. 2009. Some grammatical rules are more difficult than others. *European Journal of Psychology of Education* 24. 235–246. https://doi.org/10.1007/BF03173014.

Gygax, Pascal Mark and Noelia Gesto. 2007. Lourdeur de texte et féminisation. *L'Année Psychologique* 107. 233–250.

Gygax, Pascal Mark, Lucie Schoenhals, Arik Lévy, Patrick Luethold and Ute Gabriel. 2019. Exploring the onset of a male-biased interpretation of masculine generics among French speaking kindergarten children. *Frontiers in Psychology* 10. 1225. https://doi.org/10.3389/fpsyg.2019.01225.

Hamilton, Mykol C. 1988. Using masculine generics: Does generic he increase male bias in the user's imagery? *Sex Roles* 19. 785–899. https://doi.org/10.1007/BF00288993.

Hamilton, Mykol C. 1991. Masculine bias in the attribution of personhood. People = male, male = people. *Psychology of Women Quarterly* 15. 393–402. https://doi.org/10.1111/j.1471-6402.1991.tb00415.x.

Hamilton, Mykol C. and Nancy M. Henley. 1982. *Detrimental consequences of generic masculine usage*. Paper presented at the meeting of the Western Psychological Association, Sacramento, CA.

Harrison, Linda and Richard N. Passero. 1975. Sexism in the language of elementary textbooks. *Science and Children* 12(4). 22–25.

Hayakawa, Sayuri, David Tannenbaum, Albert Costa, Joanna D. Corey and Boaz Keysar. 2017. Thinking more or feeling less? Explaining the foreign-language effect on moral judgment. *Psychological Science* 28(10). 1387–1397. https://doi.org/10.1177/0956797617720944.

Jespersen, Otto. 1949. *Efficiency in linguistic change* Det Kongelige Danske Videnskabernes Selskab. Copenhagen: Ejnar Munksgaard.

Khoroshahi, Fameteh. 1989. Penguins don't care, but women do: A social identity analysis of a Whorfian problem. *Language in Society* 18. 505–525. https://doi.org/10.1017/S0047404500013889.

Konishi, Toshi. 1993. The semantics of grammatical gender: A cross-cultural study. *Journal of Psycholinguistic Research* 22. 519–534. https://doi.org/10.1007/BF01068252.

Lambert, Wallace E. 1967. A social psychology of bilingualism. *Journal of Social Issues* 23. 91–109. https://doi.org/10.1111/j.1540-4560.1967.tb00578.x.

Levinson, Stephen. 2003. *Space in language and cognition*. Cambridge: Cambridge University Press.

Levon, Erez. 2014. Categories, stereotypes, and the linguistic perception of sexuality. *Language in Society* 43(5). 539–566. https://doi.org/10.1017/S0047404514000554.

Lindqvist, Anna, Emma Aurora Renström and Marie Gustafsson Sendén. 2019. Reducing a male bias in language? establishing the efficiency of three different gender-fair language strategies. *Sex Roles* 81(1–2). 109–117. https://doi.org/10.1007/s11199-018-0974-9.

MacKay, Donald G. 1980. Psychology, prescriptive grammar, and the pronoun problem. *American Psychologist* 35. 444–449. https://doi.org/10.1037/0003-066X.35.5.444.

Macrae, C. Neil and Galen Bodenhausen. 2001. Social cognition: Categorical person perception. *British Journal of Psychology* 92. 239–255. https://doi.org/10.1348/000712601162059.

Marqueta, Bárbara. 2016. El concepto de género en la teoría lingüística. In Miguel Ángel Cañete (ed.), *Algunas formas de violencia. Mujer, conflicto y género*, U.Zar.

Martyna, Wendy. 1978. What does 'he' mean? Use of the generic masculine. *Journal of Communication* 28. 131–138. https://doi.org/10.1111/J.1460-2466.1978.TB01576.X.

Martyna, Wendy. 1980. The psychology of the generic masculine. In Sally McConnell-Ginet, Ruth Borker and Nelly Furman (eds.), *Women and language in literature and society*, 69–78. New York: Praeger.

Martínez, Jose Antonio. 2008. *El lenguaje de género y el género lingüístico*. Oviedo: U. Oviedo.

McConnell, Allen R. and Russel H. Fazio. 1996. Women as men and people: Effects of gender-marked language. *Personality and Social Psychology Bulletin* 22. 1004–1013. https://doi.org/10.1177/01461672962210003.

McConnell-Ginet, Sally. 1984. The origins of sexist language in discourse. *Discourse in Reading and Linguistics* 123–135. https://doi.org/10.1111/j.1749-6632.1984.tb14764.x.

McKoon, Gail and Roger Ratcliff. 1992. Inferences during reading. *Psychological Review* 99. 440–446. https://doi.org/10.1037/0033-295X.99.3.440.

Mendívil-Giró, José Luis. 2020. El masculino inclusivo en español. *Revista Española de Lingüística* 50(1). 35–64. https://doi.org/10.31810/RSEL.50.1.2.

Merkel, Elisa, Anne Maass and Laura Frommelt. 2012. Shielding women against status loss: The masculine form and its alternatives in the Italian language. *Journal of Language and Social Psychology* 31. 311–320. https://doi.org/10.1177/0261927X12446599.

Moreno Cabrera, Juan Carlos. 2012. Acerca de la discriminación de la mujer y de los lingüistas en la sociedad. https://infoling.org/informacion/IG28.html. Infoling. Accessed: 9 March 2025.

Motschenbacher, Heiko. 2010a. Female-as-norm. In Markus Bieswanger, Heiko Motschenbacher and Susanne Mühleisen (eds.), *Language in its socio-cultural context*, 35–67. Frankfurt am Main: John Benjamins.

Motschenbacher, Heiko. 2010b. *Language, gender and sexual identity*. Amsterdam, Philadelphia: John Benjamins. https://doi.org/10.1075/impact.29.

Moulton, Janice, George M. Robinson and Cherin Elias. 1978. Sex bias in language use. *American Psychologist* 33. 1032–1036. https://doi.org/10.1037/0003-066X.33.11.1032.

Parks, Janet B. and Mary Ann Roberton. 1998. Contemporary arguments against nonsexist language. *Sex Roles* 39. 445–461. https://doi.org/10.1023/A:1018827227128.

Perissinotto, Giorgio. 1983. Spanish hombre: Generic or specific? *Hispania* 66(4). 581–586. https://doi.org/10.2307/341473.

Prewitt-Freilino, Jennifer L., T. Andrew Caswell and Emmi K. Laakso. 2012. The gendering of language: A comparison of gender equality in countries with gendered, natural gender, and genderless languages. *Sex Roles* 66(3–4). 268–281. https://doi.org/10.1007/s11199-011-0083-5.

Real Academia Española. 2020. Informe de la real academia española sobre el lenguaje inclusivo y cuestiones conexas. https://www.rae.es/sites/default/files/Informe_lenguaje_inclusivo.pdf. Real Academia Española. Accessed: 9 March 2025.

Rothmund, Jutta and Ursula Christmann. 2002. Auf der Suche nach einem geschlechtergerechten Sprachgebrauch. *Muttersprache* 112. 115–135.

Sanford, Anthony J. 1985. *Cognition and cognitive psychology*. London: Weidenfeld and Nicolson.

Sapir, Edward. 1929. The status of linguistics as a science. *Language* 5. 207–214. https://doi.org/10.2307/409588.

Schmitz, Dominic. 2024. Instances of bias: The gendered semantics of generic masculines in German revealed by instance vectors. *Zeitschrift für Sprachwissenschaft* 43(2). 295–325. https://doi.org/10.1515/zfs-2024-2010.

Schmitz, Dominic, Viktoria Schneider and Janina Esser. 2023. No generiaddress in sight: An exploration of the semantics of masculine generics in German. *Glossa Psycholinguistics* 2. https://doi.org/10.5070/G6011192.

Sczesny, Sabine, Magda Formanowicz and Franziska Moser. 2016. Can gender-fair language reduce gender stereotyping and discrimination? *Frontiers in Psychology* 7. 25. https://doi.org/10.3389/fpsyg.2016.00025.

Sera, Maria D., Chryle Elieff, James Forbes, Melissa Clark Burch, Wanda Rodríguez and Diane Poulin Dubois. 2002. When language affects cognition and when it does not: An analysis of grammatical gender and classification. *Journal of Experimental Psychology: General* 131(3). 377–397. https://doi.org/10.1037/0096-3445.131.3.377.

Silveira, Jeanette. 1980. Generic masculine words and thinking. *Women's Studies International Quarterly* 3(2–3). 165–178. https://doi.org/10.1016/S0148-0685(80)92113-2.

Stahlberg, Dagmar, Friederike Braun, Lisa Irmen and Sabine Sczesny. 2007. Representation of the sexes in language. In Klaus Fiedler (ed.), *Social communication. A volume in the series frontiers of social psychology*, 163–187. New York: Psychology Press.

Stahlberg, Dagmar, Sabine Sczesny and Friederike Braun. 2001. Name your favorite musician: Effects of masculine generics and of their alternatives in German. *Journal of Language and Social Psychology* 20. 464–469. https://doi.org/10.1177/0261927X01020004004.

Tucker, A. N. and J. Tompo Ole Mpaayei. 1955. *A Maasai grammar with vocabulary* African. London: Longmans, Green and Co.

Vervecken, Dries, Bettina Hannover and Ilka Wolter. 2013. Changing (s)expectations: How gender fair job descriptions impact children's perceptions and interest regarding traditionally male occupations. *Journal of Vocational Behavior* 82(3). 208–220. https://doi.org/10.1016/j.jvb.2013.01.008.

Wasserman, Benjamin D. and Allyson J. Weseley. 2009. ¿Qué? Quoi? Do languages with grammatical gender promote sexist attitudes? *Sex Roles* 61(9–10). 634–643. https://doi.org/10.1007/s11199-009-9696-3.

Whorf, Benjamin. 1956/2012. *Language, thought, and reality: Selected writings of Benjamin Lee Whorf.* Cambridge, Massachusetts: MIT Press.

Wilson, Elizabeth and Sik H. Ng. 1988. Sex bias in visuals evoked by generics: A New Zealand study. *Sex Roles* 18. 159–168. https://doi.org/10.1007/BF00287786.

Zipf, George Kingsley. 1949. *Human behavior and the principle of least effort.* Cambridge, MA: Addison Wesley Press.

Jeff Roxas
Teaching Spanish in the Philippines: A queer-decolonial pedagogy

Abstract: Spanish, a masculine-feminine language, is characterized by lexical and morphological features that heavily rely on the traditional gender binary. How, then, do Filipino teachers and learners whose mother tongues are relatively more gender-neutral negotiate these linguistic constraints in classes of Spanish as a foreign language? This autoethnographic study explores this question by sharing and reflecting on my experiences as a queer Spanish university professor in the Philippines. I position myself within the politics of ensuring that diverse gender and sexual identities are represented and celebrated in classroom discourses and materials, often shaped by heteronormative and Westcentric ideologies. The study begins by tracing the history of teaching Spanish in the Philippines in relation to our colonial history, and subsequently outlines the diachronic evolution of the Spanish language in light of gender-inclusive language. Drawing on language and gender theories, I argue that historicizing the linguistic development of gender-inclusive language attempts to: 1) interrogate deeply held and restricted language structures that influence our ideas of gender and sexuality; and 2) incorporate values of social justice and gender equality in classrooms thereby recognizing that the access to gender-inclusive language is a fundamental human right. Ultimately, the study foregrounds a paradigm shift to queer-decolonial pedagogy, an alternative approach to teaching Spanish in postcolonial contexts. Such an approach provides pedagogical guidelines for educators, students, scholars, and policymakers to design and to use gender-responsive and context-sensitive didactic materials in their classrooms.

Keywords: gender-inclusive language, language and gender, materials development, queer-decolonial pedagogy, teaching Spanish as a foreign language

1 Introduction

With over four years of experience in teaching Spanish as a foreign language to Filipino students, I give a testament to how beautiful it is to learn, to use, and to teach the language. I teach across different course levels from basic to intermediate, which means that students learn about family, colors, professions, Hispanic

---

Jeff Roxas, Department of European Languages, University of the Philippines – Diliman, e-mail: jbroxas2@up.edu.ph

Open Access. © 2025 the author(s), published by De Gruyter. This work is licensed under the Creative Commons Attribution 4.0 International License.
https://doi.org/10.1515/9783111388694-012

figures, among the many topics that usually carry deeply entrenched gendered ideologies. As a queer teacher, my classrooms are my entry point through which my students and I unlearn and break down harmful gender stereotypes, and reinterpret social realities using the power of another language. Yet, this presented another layer of discussion when one student asked me about the gender-neutral term for *hermano* to refer to her sibling who identifies as non-binary. I was put on the spot as I did not know how to approach the question. My first register was that there was no such thing, in that the language only offers binary choices: *hermana/hermano, madre/padre, tía/tío*. While some gender-neutral words (e.g., *estudiante, dentista*) do not explicitly imply one's gender, their use is limited to certain terms and fails to account for the complexities of gender identities that exist beyond the traditional notions of masculinity and femininity of identities. This dilemma prompted me to confront the tension between my identity as a Spanish teacher, who gets to say what is sayable, and what is not sayable, and as someone, who wishes for a gender-just world, which, then, led me to reflect: Why are these forms not allowed if such identities exist?

Gender-inclusive language (GIL), also referred to as language of inclusion, gender-fair, and gender-transformative language, encompasses linguistic choices, discourses, and materials, inclusive of and responsive to the realities of all gender and sexual identities. As one tool for genuine social transformation, GIL draws from linguistic theory to reform language, addressing social inequalities and patriarchal traits embedded in language (Papadopoulos 2021). The study, grounded in this premise, explores and critically examines the applicability of gender inclusivity to Spanish, a masculine-feminine language characterized by linguistic features of gender categorizations, labeling, and binary morphological systems. Such features, common in Romance languages, prove to present cross-linguistic challenges to Filipino learners whose known languages, that are of Austronesian origin, are gender-neutral (Sibayan-Sarmiento 2018). For instance, while Filipino uses the gender-neutral pronoun *siya*, and English has incorporated singular *they* in both formal writing and daily communication, Spanish remains constrained by the binary pronouns *ella* ('she') and *él* ('he'). This limitation creates linguistic barriers for nonbinary and genderqueer speakers who do not normally identify with the feminine nor the masculine (Papadopoulos 2021). As the language gains traction and acquires authority in discourse, learned morphosyntactic features might prompt users to negotiate or resist acquired and learned gendered truths. How could the Spanish language, then, be reconstructed in a way that makes gender self-expression available despite the constraints that hinder gender inclusivity? In other words, could the Spanish language have a potential to be gender-inclusive?

While the study explores Spanish as a site of potential linguistic transformation, it also places equal importance on the critical role of Spanish language classrooms in advancing gender justice. Language classrooms are not neutral; they (re)produce gender ideologies and values, often imposing heteronormative standards that marginalize identities outside the binaries (Endo et al. 2010; Nemi Neto 2018). Heteronormativity in educational spaces views heterosexuality as the default sexual identity for teachers and students. This ideology thrives in mainstream published materials, visual and textual, and classroom discourses and interactions (Bollas 2021). Sexually deviant students, those who do not believe in, agree to, or perform such essentialized gender stereotypes, then face "unconscious policing of identities" (Paiz 2017: 4). These practices restrict these students' productive skills, consider them as incapable language learners, and subject them to explicit and implicit punishments. Recent years, nonetheless, have witnessed concerted efforts of gender mainstreaming in language education, mostly in English (e.g., Tarrayo 2022; Tarrayo and Salonga 2022; Bollas 2021; Nemi Neto 2018; Paiz 2017). The initiatives recognize that schools are a critical avenue for advancing gender equality and women empowerment (United Nations Educational, Scientific, and Cultural Organization [UNESCO] 2018); as such, a language classroom has to acknowledge different social categories, such as gender and sexuality, as fundamental aspects of a student's lived experiences "primarily constructed and negotiated in and through the use of language" (Tarrayo and Salonga 2022: 2). It must capture the full, diverse experiences of gender and sexual minorities, women and LGBTQIA+ (lesbian, gay, bisexual, trans, queer, intersex, asexual, and more) individuals, whose identities are invisibilized in academic spaces.

The present study, then, acknowledges that both the Spanish language and its pedagogy can introduce gender perspectives in educational spaces. As in the Philippines, the language enjoys a prestigious linguistic status derived from its increasing global relevance by the number of speakers, employment and educational opportunities endowed to those capable communicating in the language, and the shared historical-linguistic ties between the Philippines and Spain (Blázquez-Carretero et al. 2023). Given the positive reception of Spanish among Filipino learners, the study seeks to build on that enthusiasm by embedding critical gender perspectives into language content and structure. Our classrooms not only enrich language learning but also promote wider social dialogues on gender, cultures, and identity.

Drawing on my experiences as a queer Spanish university professor, this autoethnographic study uses my experiences as a lens to understand the political and gendered dimensions of the Spanish language and its pedagogy. Guided by queer-decolonial pedagogy, the study ultimately attempts to advocate for the use of gender-inclusive language and queer-affirming methods of language teaching. I argue that these interventions denaturalize the relationship between gender, sex, and sexuality, and consequently ensure the representation and celebration of trans, gender non-conforming, and nonbinary identities. The next sections attempt to establish the link between language and gender through a structured discussion. It begins with an overview of Spanish language teaching in the Philippines (Section 2), followed by historicization of gender theories in Spanish language and their relation to gender-inclusive language (Section 3). Finally, it introduces queer-decolonial pedagogy as an alternative approach to teaching Spanish, alongside sample didactic materials (Section 4).

2 Teaching Spanish in Filipino classrooms: A history

The politics of teaching Spanish in the Philippines has always been intimately situated in the historical, cultural and linguistic relations between the Philippines and Spain. The colonial underpinnings of the language create tension, placing it at the intersection of ideologies: Spanish as the language of the motherland, of the colonizers, or of the global world (Argüelles 1964; Rodao 1997; Sibayan-Sarmiento 2018)? This debate raises a question about how Filipinos reconcile the language's colonial 'legacy' with its modern, globalized significance. While being the official language during the 333 years of Spanish colonial rule, Spanish was not widely spoken across the entire country by the 16th century. Its use was opposed by most religious orders who feared losing their power over indigenous groups and if used, the language was only available to the privileged elite minority for them to gain access to state and economic affairs. It was not until 1863 that the language was taught in Philippine public schools. Through a Royal Decree, there were 75 primary schools in the provinces and 23 in Metro Manila that included Spanish as a subject in basic education (Bautista 2004).

The American occupation of the islands in 1898 halted this short-lived, belated effort by changing the official language to English. Filipino elites, later, revived Spanish in classrooms through successive laws. In 1949, *Ley Sotto* made Spanish an elective subject in secondary schools; followed by *Ley Magalona* in 1952 that required university students to obtain 12 credits of Spanish before they graduate; finally, by *Ley Cuenco* in 1957 which doubled the 12 credits in university education. This was again interrupted after the Martial Law was lifted and the dictator Ferdinand Marcos was ousted from his presidential seat, prompting lawmakers to draft and ratify a new Philippine constitution in 1987. It was an opportune time for academics and university students to remove Spanish as one of the country's official languages. This was a way to support decolonization and national building of Filipino identity, which led to the removal of Spanish as an obligatory subject in the Philippine education system (Blázquez-Carretero et al. 2023). Subsequently, English eventually took the place of Spanish as the language of prestige, putting the latter in the peripheries.

After more than 20 years, Spanish was resurrected in Philippine basic education through two memorandums of agreement in 2010 and 2012 between the Philippine and Spanish governments. The language, along with five languages (i.e., Japanese, Mandarin Chinese, Korean, French, and German), is included in the high school curriculum through the Special Program in Foreign Language (SPFL) of the Philippine Department of Education (DepEd). The SPFL allows Grade 7 to 12 students, aged 12 to 18, to choose a foreign language elective and to achieve a B1 (threshold) proficiency after graduating from high school. The program is designed to "prepare students for meaningful interaction in a linguistically and culturally diverse global workplace" (DepEd, "DepEd Enhances Foreign Language Skills") following the Common European Framework of Reference for Languages (CEFR). At the university level, there is a growing number of adolescent and university learners, with 6,000 to 7,000 students currently enrolled in Spanish courses (Galvan-Guijo 2021). For instance, in UP Diliman where I teach, the Department of European Languages offers undergraduate and graduate study programs with a specialization in Spanish Philology. In addition to attaining a B2 level of proficiency, students specializing in Spanish are required to take courses in literature (e.g., Fil-Hispanic literature), history, translation, and cultural studies.

According to Blázquez-Carretero et al. (2023: 164), an estimated half-million people in the Philippines can communicate in and understand the language. The population includes students, speakers of Chavacano (a Spanish-based creole language spoken in different regions of the Philippines), native speakers of Spanish, and individuals over 50 years old who studied Spanish in the past. The linguistic and sociopolitical landscape – specifically, the increasing number of speakers and their growing interest in the language – shapes how they perceive and attach particular values to it (Kircher and Zipp 2022; Achugar and Pessoa 2009). While no scientific studies have examined language attitudes of Filipinos toward Spanish, current studies on Spanish language education in the Philippines suggest that Filipinos hold positive attitudes toward the language. Blázquez-Carretero et al. (2023) note that Filipinos view Spanish as an advantage, primarily for economic reasons. Similarly, Coyol-Morales (2023) highlights the rising interest in learning Spanish among Filipino university students. Beyond its historical significance, Coyol-Morales argues that Spanish, as one of the most widely spoken languages in the world, holds significant socio-political capital, offering employment and educational opportunities while also maintaining strong visibility in various media platforms. While the language is generally perceived in positive, "productive" terms, Sales (forthcoming, 2025) argues that its resurgence may also be linked to Hispanofilipino thought, which could evoke feelings of colonial nostalgia. He acknowledges that this perspective may pose challenges for a broader acceptance within Filipino society, but also advocates for reimagining Hispanofilipino thought as a space for counterhegemonic discourse.

3 Spanish evolves over time: How gender-inclusive Spanish came into being

All languages are, by nature, socially constructed and dynamic. Like other languages, Spanish has undergone diatopic (e.g., varieties of Spanish in Latin America and Equatorial Guinea), diachronic (e.g., conquests and reconquests, migration, rise of nation states, and increasing number of learners), and sociolinguistic changes (Penny 2009). From a social constructionist lens, Foucault argued that languages are not only products of historical and genealogical discourses – a group of signs and elements referring to contents of representations; they also refer to "practices that systematically form the objects of which they speak" (Foucault 1972: 49). Language, as a discourse, defines and produces the objects of our knowledge. As a mechanism of power, it creates and constitutes reality. Its form and its use influence how users view the world based on available linguistic resources and patterns of speech. In other words, the way how language is formed and used is a reflection of the political and gendered implications of language – one that constructs gender identities, and enables, as well as forecloses, certain ways of being.

Gender, as a prominent linguistic feature of Spanish, has always been a significant concept and a fundamental organizing principle in societies worldwide, leading to its codification in language. It manifests itself in the vocabulary of most, if not all, languages in the world and establishes a finite number of interpretations of the world which may either liberate or restrict identities (Heredero 2007). These realities are reified by gender categories and basic personhood (e.g., *transgenero, mujer, hombre*) and masculine/feminine social markers (e.g., *tío/tía, hermano/hermana*) based on traditional stereotypes on biological sex and social gender (Papadopoulos 2021). The evolution of modern Romance languages into masculine-feminine systems underscores the importance of gender as a primary axis of difference among its users. There is a significant alignment where words describing men are grammatically masculine and those describing women are grammatically feminine. Therefore, we understand that the terms "masculine" and "feminine" carry an inherent gender meaning, as these qualities are associated with human characteristics (Papadopoulos 2021).

Language as being characterized by its volatility is contrary to the essentialist understanding that frames language as prediscursive, pure, and innocent. Dominant discourses in linguistics weaponize this ideology by determining which speech style is correct and which is wrong. This politics of knowledge production causes the conflation of gender-inclusive language and grammatical incorrectness. I would argue that correctness is different from grammaticality. While grammaticality is a concept of how well an innovation/variation aligns with the internal rules of the linguistic system, correctness refers to social rules or traditions which dictate what is considered the "proper" and "appropriate" way to use the language. Failing to make the distinction between the two concepts leads to tag gender-inclusive language as "grammatically incorrect" even though it may follow the rules of the language. It results in trivializing and ridiculing language innovation and variation, often showing that speakers evaluate language users rather than the languages per se (Achugar and Pessoa 2009).

Such language policing faced backlash from feminist and queer language movements advocating for gender-inclusive Spanish. Their interventions questioned and exposed the androcentric and heteronormative nature of Spanish grammar, demonstrating how users can intervene in and rearrange the linguistic order of Spanish (Papadopoulos 2021). Their position is that no matter how structured and categorized the language may seem, there will always be exceptions that defy grammatical rules; moreover, grammar is not fixed, but is constantly (re)created through innovation and engagement with the descriptive realities of language use. Both movements exposed that the process is not natural, just as sex and gender are not strictly binary. More importantly, they critiqued the invisible power within prescriptive language regulation and hierarchy that privileges certain groups while marginalizing the socially deviant. Who created this conjunction of grammatical rules? Were they men or women? Whom do these rules favor? Why are masculine forms considered generic for all genders? Why were there no feminine words for certain professions like judge, pilot, and engineer (i.e., *jueza, pilota, ingeniera*) before? Queer and feminist linguists revealed existing structures by highlighting the process through which inequality and power-assymetries manifest in the language.

Global feminist linguists in the 1970's, on the one hand, challenged the default acceptance of masculine forms as inclusive of both masculine and feminine genders. They argued that this linguistic practice was sexist as it prescribes the use of masculine forms as a generic personal reference, thereby rendering women invisible in language use. As a result, *Real Academia Española* (RAE, hereafter) produced 366 feminized forms and more institutions and universities are encouraged to use masculine-feminine linguistic genders (e.g., *hermanos y hermanas, herman@s, hermanos/as* for 'brothers and sisters/siblings') over default masculine variants (*hermanos* for 'brothers'). However, queer linguists counterargued that this proposal remains framed in a cisgender, heteronormative sense, offering few to no solutions for nonbinary users. For instance, the use of the *at* sign (@), as *herman@s*, incorporates both the masculine (–o) and feminine (–a) morphemes through its orthographical combination, which still reflects a gender-binary structure (Nissen 2002). This heteronormative framing of the grammatical system perpetuates naturalizing the relationship among sex, gender, and sexuality, which has consequences in the present day for trans and queer individuals. Such language regulations could promote exclusionary practices, depriving learners of the opportunity to appreciate the full extent of gender and sexual experiences (Butler 1990).

3.1 Reimagining Spanish grammatical gender systems

Queer linguists have innovated gender-inclusive pronominal and morphological systems to accommodate identities that do not conform to traditional masculine and feminine categories such the trans, gender non-conforming, and nonbinary. Regarding pronominal gender, queer linguists introduced the personal pronouns, *elle* ['eje] and *ellx* ['eks], with the –*e* and –*x* morphemes. Following the principle of grammaticality, the rules of morphosyntax also dictate that parts of speech like adjectives, articles, nouns, among others, must also be consistent with its pronominal antecedent. The morphological gender system, therefore, utilizes the same morphemes. Tables 1 and 2 show the GIL reforms of Spanish using the –*e* and –*x* morphemes in different grammatical genders in comparison with those of gender-binary variants in masculine and feminine:

Tab. 1: Gender binary and inclusive grammatical gender system.

grammatical gender	binary language		inclusive language	
	masculine	feminine	–e	–x
personal pronouns	él	ella	elle	ellx
definite articles	el	la	le	lx
canonical nouns	hermano	hermana	hermane	hermanx
non-canonical nouns	profesor	profesora	profesore	profesorx
adjectives	latino	latina	latine	latinx
honorifics	Señor	señora	Señore	Señnorx

Among the remaining vowel letters (–*e*, –*i*, and –*u*), –*e* is commonly used in gender-neutral variants that can be either masculine or feminine in Standard Spanish (Papadopoulos 2021). The –*x* morpheme, on the other hand, connotes a political move to decolonize Spanish grammatical gender and incorporate the orthography of the indigenous languages of Latin America in Spanish grammar (Lugones 2008). Both morphemes challenge the coloniality of the practices of using Spanish. Contrary to the assumption that gendered innovations are Western impositions, its use could give justice to our gender-transitive predecessors (e.g., *bakla, bayoguin, binabae, babaylan*, among others) whose identities were deliberately obliterated in favor of the gender binary impositions of the Spaniards (Garcia 2013). Through GIL, we explore the possibility of claiming ownership of the language while questioning the inherent ambiguity not only of the gender-sexuality binary but also other oppositional identity categories (e.g., white/of color, adult/youth, citizen/undocumented, straight/queer, abuser/victim) that is historically Western Anglo-Christian (Sifuentes 2021: 2079). Below is a table that shows how to transform a binary sentence into an inclusive one:

Tab. 2: Morphosyntactic agreement with the grammatical gender. English translation: 'Mx. López, our professor, is very happy today. They are very affectionate.'

binary language	inclusive language	
-a	-e	-x
Señora López, nuestra profesora, está muy contenta hoy. Ella es muy cariñosa.	Señore López, nuestre profesore, está muy contente hoy. Elle es muy cariñose.	Señorx López, nuestrx profesorx, está muy contentx hoy. Ellx es muy cariñosx.

3.2 Gender-inclusive language as a human right

Access to GIL should be understood as a fundamental human right (Papadopoulos 2021). It rests on the premise to improve the social status of nonnormative gender and sexual identities, ensuring they are provided with linguistic resources that affirm their identities. The United Nations affirms that its use is 'a powerful way to promote gender equality and eradicated gender bias'. As Armas (as cited in Cornwall and Jolly 2006) states, rights to sexuality and to education go together, especially in schools where students experience and express their identities. It is relevant to confront issues like drop-outs, bullying, and discrimination based on sexual orientation, gender identity, gender expression, and sex characteristics (SOGIESC). Tarrayo (2022) emphasizes that the language used in classrooms influences students' academic performance, revealing the crucial role of language in governing learners' behavior and practices. GIL provides students expansive and meaningful linguistic resources and safe spaces to celebrate and recognize diverse identities in the classroom. Otherwise, if educational institutions refuse to recognize their identity, both their self-esteem and learning progress may be negatively affected (UNDP and USAID 2014). Access to GIL nurtures empathy and builds affective ties where students feel a sense of belonging, allowing them to feel present in their learning experiences. At the same time, its use in the classroom modeled by teachers may address heteronormative practices which may also benefit non-queer people by showing them how to view the world beyond cisgender, heteronormative representations in the classroom.

The University of the Philippines – Diliman takes the matter of gender inclusivity seriously, with numerous policies that protect the rights of genderqueer students in academic spaces. One of them is a memorandum providing guidelines on affirming transgender and gender-nonconforming (TGNC) students' lived names, pronouns and titles released in 2021 by the UP Center for Women's and Gender Studies (University of the Philippines Center for Women's and Gender Studies 2021). This was after cases of professors deadnaming, misgendering, and using wrong pronouns of TGNC students. Consequently, professors and administrators now take a closer look at student data in class lists to address them correctly with their lived names, pronouns, and honorifics. This raises important questions about how Spanish teachers can facilitate gender self-expression in the classroom despite these constraints.

4 Queer-decolonial pedagogy in the local contexts

Despite the growing scholarly attention on gender-inclusive Spanish, no concrete framework nor specific models have been provided to incorporate its use in teaching language content and structure. To address its dearth, I propose a paradigm shift to queer pedagogy, a teaching approach that seeks to develop gender-responsive, queer-affirming discourses, materials and methods that better engage and theorize issues of sexual orientation and gender identities especially of women and LGBTQI students in classrooms. Rooted in ideas of queer theory to oppose hegemony and normalization, queer pedagogy "seeks to contribute to practices of education, analyzing the fluidity and mobility of society and affirming that educational institutions should not attach themselves to one set model since these ideals end up alienating, even excluding certain individuals" (Nemi Neto 2018: 591). The approach grounds teachers in the duty to provide permissive spaces for all sexualities and peripheral identities, enabling queer subjectivities and practices in spaces where students learn about and experience themselves and others. Making classrooms queer, in addition, ensures that methods and materials are respectful of individual identities and critical of identity positions and subjectivities (Sifuentes 2021: 7).

Another interesting variable is the idea of coloniality which influences the dynamics of teaching Spanish in our country. The Philippines continues to endure colonial and neoliberal power structures engendered in contemporary foreign language education (Cabling et al. 2020). As such, a decolonial approach in language pedagogy will accommodate queer pedagogy by decentering knowledge from the canons that reinforce global linguistic hierarchies (Cabling et al. 2020: 185) and engaging local practices and experiences of Filipinos. Taking inspiration from critical pedagogies, the union of queer and decolonial pedagogies, or queer-decolonial pedagogy, critically examines and challenges the colonial, classed, racialized, and gendered norms that shape and sustain prevailing Euro-American teaching practices (Puar 2017). Queer-decolonial pedagogy confronts "narratives of linear human and identity development, oppositional binary thinking, competitive hierarchies, and mechanistic analyses of people, cultures, and environments" (Sifuentes 2021).

Specifically, I propose these guidelines for the creation and development of instructional materials that reflect a queer-decolonial approach and serve as points of reflection: 1) Do the materials reflect and validate the realities of women and LGBTQI communities in the region? 2) Do the materials problematize the representations of identities in the intersection of gender, sexuality, class, and race (Paiz 2017)?; 3) Do the materials encourage students to use their daily experiences as a starting point to express themselves in the target language while constructing vocabulary and structures (Nemi Neto 2018: 595)?; and 4) Are the materials and pedagogic tools context-sensitive to fit the diverse contexts of target learners (Cabling et al. 2020)?

4.1 Queering and decolonizing the Spanish class: Some examples

To further illustrate how a queer-decolonial pedagogy can be applied in the teaching of Spanish in localized contexts, I am sharing four examples that I use in my basic to intermediate Spanish classes. These examples include adaptations and revisions of textbook units as well as original sources I created myself, covering topics on family, daily routines, writing biographies, and verbs of household chores. The examples could serve as a guide for policymakers and educators to begin revisiting and reimagining instructional materials in light of the proposed methodology.

The topic of family is essential for beginner language learners (Bollas 2021; Nemi Neto 2018). To introduce the family vocabulary, I present some pictures of families that do not fall into the traditional, heteronormative family archetypes in Figure 1: my sister and her girlfriend, my lesbian sister and my gay brother, single parents, gay couples, fur family, chosen family, among others. The use of visuals is an entry point for them to learn vocabulary, to practice describing and presenting a third person, and ultimately, to reinterpret social realities and notions of a family

¿Cómo es tu familia?

Fig. 1: Describing and presenting people in the third-person: diverse families. Photo sources: Left photo by Eloisa May P. Hernandez; top right photo by Marianne Lorraine Samiling; bottom right photo by the author. Additions made by the author.

through another language. This method might also foster language awareness by comparing Spanish to their first and second languages (e.g., Tagalog and English).

Verb conjugations can also incorporate gender perspectives. For example, I adapted a text from a reference book, *Etapas plus – Editorial Edinumen*, to describe the daily routine of Turing, a Filipina drag queen, through the simple present tense, i.e., *presente de indicativo*, in Figure 2. Interestingly, some students knew Turing from the local edition of RuPaul's Drag Race. Being represented, respected and recognized, LGBTQIA+ people can connect with the learning materials and can build affective ties with the language, which may facilitate comprehension and interest. In a similar vein, non-LGBTQIA+ students can benefit from this by seeing representations beyond the cisgender and heterosexual examples. It helps them to relativize their perspectives and view the world differently (Gray 2021).

We can also introduce texts written by Filipinos, women, BIPOC (black, indigenous, and people of color), and queer identities while detaching from canon work written by white men (Tarrayo 2022). Typically, Hispanic figures have often been represented by white men in the likes of Pablo Picasso, Rafael Nadal, and Miguel de Cervantes. To challenge this prevailing narrative, I introduce women in the Hispanic world alongside the communicative goal of writing biographies using the past tense, *pretérito indefinido*. This material, which includes pictures of Hispanic women along with brief descriptions, is sourced from *Profe de ELE*, an online website that offers a repository of creative digital materials in teaching ELE, which I gladly recommend

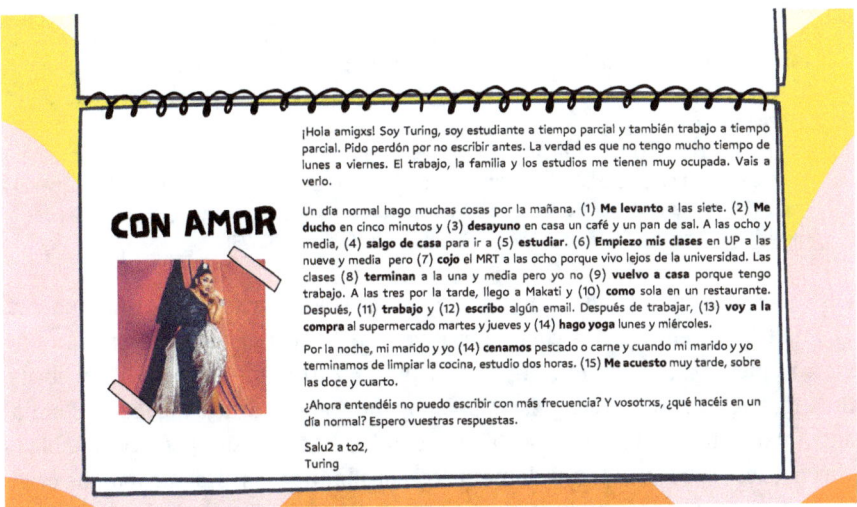

Fig. 2: Describing one's daily routine: a day in the life of Turing. This text is inspired by and adapted from a reading activity of an e-mail, found on page 27 of the Spanish learning book *Etapas Plus A1.2* (Hermira et al. 2010). Photo source: Turing Quinto.

(Profe de ELE 2025). I highly recommend exploring their site, as their materials are valuable for promoting more inclusive and diverse methods and materials in teaching Spanish. Three example introductions are given in the following (English translations by the author):

Gislenne Zamaoya (1971) es una arquitecta y empresaria mexicana. Con 36 años comenzó su transición de hombre a mujer. Hace diez años fundó su estudio de arquitectura. Actualmente compatibiliza su trabajo como arquitecta con el activismo a favor de los derechos del colectivo LGTBIQ+.
Gislenne Zamaoya (1971) is a Mexican architect and entrepreneur. At the age of 36 she began her transition from man to woman. Ten years ago she founded her architecture studio. She currently combines her work as an architect with activism in favor of LGTBIQ+ rights. (Profe de ELE 2025)

Matilde Hidalgo (1889-1974) fue una médica y activista ecuatoriana. Fue la primera mujer bachiller en Ecuador. Debido a su sexo, le negaron la inscripción en la Universidad Central de Ecuador. Tuvo que trasladarse a la Universidad de Azuay para estudiar medicina. Logró el derecho a voto de las mujeres en Ecuador en 1924.
Matilde Hidalgo (1889-1974) was an Ecuadorian physician and activist. She was the first woman to obtain a bachelor's degree in Ecuador. Because of her sex, she was denied enrollment at the Central University of Ecuador. She had to transfer to the University of Azuay to study medicine. She advocated and achieved women's right to vote in Ecuador in 1924. (Profe de ELE 2025)

> *Mariana Enríquez (1973) es una escritora argentina. Creció influida por los relatos y las supersticiones de su abuela. Empezó a escribir relatos y novelas de terror con veinte años. Actualmente sus libros están traducidos a varios idiomas y es una de las grandes referentes del relato de terror en español.*
> Mariana Enríquez (1973) is an Argentine writer. She grew up influenced by her grandmother's stories and superstitions. She started writing horror stories and novels when she was twenty years old. Nowadays, her books have been translated into several languages, and she is one of the great referents of horror stories in Spanish. (Profe de ELE 2025)

Lastly, learning to talk about household chores is a favorite topic of A2 students. The unit is paired with the communicative goal of making and responding to favors, requests, and petitions. Drawing inspiration from the *Profe de ELE* website, the unit begins with the song *Así Bailaba* by the Spanish artists Rigoberta Bandini and Amaia. This is a version of a children's song that tells a story of a girl unable to play because she is tied to her domestic responsibilities. One fragment of the original lyrics reads, *Lunes antes de almorzar, una niña fue a jugar, pero no pudo jugar porque tenía que lavar* 'Monday before lunch, a girl went to play, but she could not play because she had to wash'. In contrast, the revised version subverts this narrative, *Lunes antes de almorzar, una niña fue a lavar pero no pudo lavar porque tenía que bailar* 'Monday before lunch, a girl went to wash, but she could not wash, because she had to dance'. The edited version challenges social expectations that confine girls to chores such as washing dishes, cleaning the houses, caring for siblings, and sweeping. The use of the song not only enriches students' vocabulary but also encourages them to critically engage with the language as a means for confronting and questioning harmful gender stereotypes.

Another example is a major project my department colleagues and I are working on, which follows the same guidelines. Currently, we are developing a comprehensive and culturally-sensitive textbook-cum-workbook[1] for A1 Filipino learners of Spanish (Blázquez-Carretero et al. forthcoming, 2025). The project is an exciting endeavor aimed at capturing unique realities of learning Spanish in the Philippine contexts. The design and content of the learning material have undergone rigorous evaluation and review by partner Philippine institutions and universities, have been informed by research with students, and have been carefully crafted by authors with rich and extensive experiences in teaching Spanish in the Philippines, ensuring its relevance and impact. Aligned with queer-decolonial pedagogy, the textbook boldly integrates gender and decolonial perspectives, offering a model for educators and policymakers aiming to adopt similar approaches in their classrooms.

---

[1] This project has been funded by the UP Diliman – Office of the Vice-Chancellor for Research and Development through the Outright Research Grant (242402 ORG).

4.2 Queer decolonial pedagogy beyond language studies

The materials mentioned above illustrate how language classrooms serve as fertile sites for engaging with broader social discourses. However, queer-decolonial pedagogy extends beyond linguistics and language education, inviting educators in various fields to reflect and critically examine their current models and curricular materials. Many of these teaching practices are shaped by Western traditions, middle-class perspectives, and formally-educated contexts (Sifuentes 2021). For instance, in STEM (i.e., Sciences, Technology, Engineering, and Mathematics) fields, such an approach challenges notions of objectivity, questioning biases and 'unbiases' in scientific research. The use of the approach also entails investigating and exploring histories and knowledge systems with indigenous and queer epistemologies. In the social sciences and humanities, the pedagogy could amplify voices of marginalized racial, classed, and gendered identities. Open discussions could also encourage students to meaningfully connect their lived realities and identities to theories.

Equally important is the role of educators as facilitators of knowledge. As carriers of codes and values, we have the academic obligation to cultivate queer-friendly spaces in the classroom, from the ways we make our classes a caring and safe space, to how we thoughtfully curate our reading lists. In the case of language teaching, our position creates the impression that we are experts by virtue of knowing the language and knowing how to teach it. By recognizing that we have epistemic knowledge on a certain topic, we acquire the authority – the status of truth that gives us the power to formalize, create, and regulate discourses within our educational settings (Hall 2001). We use this power responsibly.

4.3 Pedagogical challenges

Admittedly, reimagining new grammatical gender systems and implementing alternative materials in the classroom will involve a long process of unlearning and relearning certain theoretical handles on linguistics and didactics. When I first encountered the GIL variants, I attempted to transform binary variants to inclusive ones. It felt more like a careful and conscious mental exercise, rather than the traditional method of doing it effortlessly. This may, likewise, produce discomfort in learners and teachers alike who have been acquiring and learning the language for many years. Additionally, GIL users receive backlash from language academies that work 'to cleanse, fix, and enhance the language' and weaponize academic freedom to justify policies against genderqueer people (UNDP and USAID 2014). Purists argue that such forms are linguistically invalid and inherently binary, and are only

for women (Licata and Papadopoulos 2021). GIL may also generate strong reactions that might not align with teachers' and students' personal ideologies (Tarrayo 2022). Educators who are welcoming of the idea may also feel shame and stigma in introducing GIL variants in academic spaces, as its adoption may run counter to their academic training given that they are not standardized yet. What students learn in GIL classrooms might also conflict with what they encounter in standardized language exams (e.g., DELE and SIELE) that test their fluency in language, commonly necessary when applying for school programs and employment. In effect, they may stick to feminine and masculine forms, their safest resort. The curriculum's strong gender binary orientation springs from the influence of larger institutions that work to control and 'purify' the language.

5 Moving forward

In this study, I examined the linguistic development of Spanish and historicized its teaching in the Philippines, arguing that a queer-decolonial approach in language instruction is particularly fitting in this context. By theorizing how language shapes gendered realities, we see the importance of gender-inclusive language and queer-affirming pedagogies in enriching the sociolinguistic and communicative competence of Filipino students of Spanish. Its use across social domains may (re)shape the linguistic landscape, positioning Spanish as a liberatory space for communication and identity expression. At the same time, it fosters the development of skills and resources that challenge gender norms, disrupt colonial institutions, and drive meaningful social changes.

Moving forward, the development and implementation of gender-inclusive language frameworks in the classroom are ongoing and therefore not perfect. It is essential that such pedagogy be approached with flexibility, allowing for adaptation and growth rather than rigid adherence to a set standard (Sifuentes 2021). To conclude, I call for scholars, teachers, and relevant key players and institutions to design a foreign language curriculum with a focus on a more grassroots understanding of Filipino learners of Spanish in light of the queer-decolonial approach. Moreover, it is equally important for teachers to actively participate in gender sensitivity training to fully grasp the principles behind these new conventions. It is to remind them that discomfort is normal; and the politics of integrating gender perspectives in Spanish language classrooms springs from the belief that genderqueer lives matter. When we care about the genderqueer, we also care about how they are recognized in the classroom, using methods and materials that affirm their identities.

Behind the signifiers are the signified. Language change is reflected in discourse and as more people use and accept new forms, we develop practices that cultivate the values of respect, acceptance, and social justice. If we accept that language is made and imagined, then we also believe that it can be remade and reimagined. This study is my love letter to the many students I will encounter in the many semesters and school years that will come. You can be whoever and whatever you want to be in this classroom.

References

Achugar, Mariana and Silvia Pessoa. 2009. Power and place: Language attitudes towards Spanish in a bilingual academic community in Southwest Texas. *Spanish in Context* 6(2). 199–223.
Argüelles, Belen. 1964. El estado presente de la enseñanza y aprendizaje del idioma español en Filipinas. *Presente y futuro de la lengua española* 1. 281–296.
Bautista, Luna. 2004. *La enseñanza del español en Filipinas*. Madrid: Biblioteca virtual redELE.
Blázquez-Carretero, Miguel, Jevic Anjin Cruel, Clara López-Pasarín, Justine Marielle Porras, Jeff Roxas and Anna Marie Sibayan-Sarmiento. forthcoming, 2025. *Spanish textbook-workbook for filipinos (working title)*.
Blázquez-Carretero, Miguel, Ma. Luisa Young and Anna Marie Sibayan-Sarmiento. 2023. Essay. In *Enseñar español en Filipinas: De idioma oficial a lengua extranjera*, vol. 2, 149–182. Atlas del ELE. Geolingüística de la enseñanza del español en el mundo.
Bollas, Angelos. 2021. A critical discussion of inclusive approaches to sexualities in ELT. *ELT Journal* 75(2). 133–141. https://doi.org/10.1093/elt/ccaa075.
Butler, Judith. 1990. *Gender trouble: Feminism and the subversion of identity*. New York: Routledge.
Cabling, Kristine, Naidyl Isis Bautista, Anna Marie Sarmiento, Frances Antoinette Cruz and Jillian Loise Melchor. 2020. Foreign language policy and pedagogy in the Philippines: Potentials for a decolonial approach. *Social Transformations: Journal of the Global South* 8(2). 185. https://doi.org/10.13185/3382.
Cornwall, Andrea and Susie Jolly. 2006. Introduction: Sexuality matters. *IDS Bulletin* 37(5). 1–11. https://doi.org/10.1111/j.1759-5436.2006.tb00295.x.
Coyol-Morales, Isabel. 2023. Lengua, juventud y globalización: El estudio del español en los jóvenes filipinos universitarios del siglo xxi. Online Seminar held in UP Diliman Department of European Languages.
Endo, Hidehiro, Paul Chamness Reece-Miller and Nicholas Santavicca. 2010. Surviving in the trenches: A narrative inquiry into queer teachers' experiences and identity. *Teaching and Teacher Education* 26(4). 1023–1030. https://doi.org/10.1016/j.tate.2009.10.045.
Foucault, Michel. 1972. *The archaeology of knowledge and the discourse on language*. New York: Pantheon Books.
Galvan-Guijo, Javier. 2021. El español en filipinas. In *El español en el mundo*, 599–612. Anuario Instituto Cervantes 2021.
Garcia, J. Neil. 2013. Nativism or universalism: Situating LGBT discourse in the Philippines. *Kritika Kultura* 48–68. https://doi.org/10.13185/kk2013.02003.

Gray, John. 2021. Addressing LGBTQ erasure through literature in the ELT classroom. *ELT Journal* 75(2). 142–151. https://doi.org/10.1093/elt/ccaa079.

Hall, Stuart. 2001. Foucault: Power, knowledge and discourse. In Stephanie Taylor Mary Wetherell and Simeon Yates (eds.), *Discourse, theory and practice*, 72–81. London: Sage Publications.

Heredero, Carmen. 2007. Las mujeres también cuentan. las mujeres y el lenguaje: Un amor no correspondido.

Hermira, Sonia Eusebio, Beatriz Coca del Bosque, Elena Herrero Sanz, Macarena Sagredo Jerónimo and Isabel De Dios Martín. 2010. *Etapas plus A1.2 - libro del alumno*. Madrid: Editorial Edinumen.

Kircher, Ruth and Lenna Zipp. 2022. An introduction to language attitudes research. In Ruth Kircher and Lenna Zipp (eds.), *Research methods in language attitudes*, 1–16. Cambridge: Cambridge University Press.

Licata, Gabriella and Ben Papadopoulos. 2021. *Refuting language academies' rejections of nonbinary grammatical gender*. Paper presented at the 95th annual meeting of the Linguistic Society of America, San Francisco, CA.

Nemi Neto, João. 2018. Queer pedagogy: Approaches to inclusive teaching. *Policy Futures in Education* 16(5). 589–604. https://doi.org/10.1177/1478210317751273.

Nissen, Uwe Kjær. 2002. Gender in Spanish. In Marlis Hellinger and Hadumod Bußmann (eds.), *Gender across languages: The linguistic representation of women and men*, 251–279. Pfaffenweiler: Centaurus.

Paiz, Joshua M. 2017. Queering ESL teaching: Pedagogical and materials creation issues. *TESOL Journal* 9(2). 1–20.

Papadopoulos, Ben. 2021. A brief history of gender-inclusive Spanish. *Deportate, Esulli, Profughe* 48. 40–48.

Penny, Ralph. 2009. *A history of the Spanish language*. Cambridge: Cambridge University Press.

Profe de ELE. 2025. Mujeres con historia. https://www.profedeele.es/actividad/mujeres-con-historia. Accessed: 12 March 2025.

Puar, Jasbir K. 2017. *The right to maim*. New York, USA: Duke University Press. https://doi.org/doi: 10.1515/9780822372530.

Rodao, Florentino. 1997. Spanish language in the Philippines: 1900–1940. *Philippine Studies* 45(1). 94–107.

Sales, Marlon James. forthcoming, 2025. *Hispanism as counterhegemony: Spanish-language nationalism in the US-occupied Philippines*.

Sibayan-Sarmiento, Anna Marie. 2018. How multilingual Filipinos learn Spanish as a foreign language: Some crosslinguistic considerations. *Philippine Humanities Review* 20(1). 1–13.

Sifuentes, Mauro Eugenio. 2021. Queer-decolonial pedagogy: Undoing binaries through intergenerational learning. *Journal of Homosexuality* 69(12). 2066–2083. https://doi.org/10.1080/00918369.2021.1987750.

Tarrayo, Veronico N. 2022. Gender-fair language in English language teaching: Insights from teachers in Philippine higher education institutions. *Language and Education* 37(4). 483–499. https://doi.org/10.1080/09500782.2022.2071624.

Tarrayo, Veronico N. and Aileen O. Salonga. 2022. Queering English language teaching: Insights from teachers in a Philippine state university. *Critical Inquiry in Language Studies* 20(4). 360–385. https://doi.org/10.1080/15427587.2022.2112532.

UNDP and USAID. 2014. Being LGBT in Asia: The Philippine country report. Tech. rep. United Nations Development Programme (UNDP) and United States Agency for International Development (USAID) Bangkok.

University of the Philippines Center for Women's and Gender Studies. 2021. Memorandum no. OVCAA-MTTP 21–029: Guidelines on affirming transgender and gender non-conforming (TGNC) students' names, pronouns, and titles. https://cws.up.edu.ph/?p=2060. Accessed: 25 July 2024.

D. Hunter

Morphosyntax and me: The reflections of a non-binary linguist on English gendered language

Abstract: Modern English is broadly considered a language without a grammatical gender system; however, there are cases of gender marking for some words harkening back to earlier forms of the language that did have grammatical gender. Mostly due to this lack of grammatical gender, intersections of language and gender where English is concerned have focused on pronoun use in the third person, as it is common and explicitly gendered. That said, there is still research to be done in those nouns and adjectives that still carry vestigial gender which has survived from past English varieties. The way that English-speaking individuals in the gender non-conforming community approach and interact with these pieces of gendered language has not yet been studied. This work is a self-reflection on the way I, as an English-speaking non-binary individual, have felt when this leftover gendered language is used towards me. Differing levels of dysphoria are caused by different words, which leads me to a conclusion that some words may be more inherently gendered than others. Further investigation through the lens of a distributed morphology framework reveals that there may be a difference in my dysphoria depending on where the gender feature attaches to the lexeme. This contribution explores this from a personal reflective perspective, as opposed to a generalizable one.

Keywords: distributed morphology, English, gender, lavender linguistics, non-binary, transgender linguistics

1 Introduction

In the intersection of language studies and gender studies, there has been much discussion and debate about inclusive forms for non-binary individuals, how to use them, and what impacts they may have (Anderson 2022; Fuentes and Gómez Soler 2023; Heritage 2022; Knisely 2021; Miles-Hercules 2024; Steele 2018; Zimman 2018; Zimman and Brown 2024). Non-binary people do not identify with masculine or feminine categorizations, especially as these categories have been defined by a Western and patriarchal society (Steele 2018: 1; Matsuno and Budge 2017: 1). Non-binary in-

---

D. Hunter, Department of Linguistics, University of Arizona, e-mail: deethelinguist@gmail.com

dividuals fall underneath what is referred to as the trans umbrella. The trans umbrella refers to individuals with identities other than cisgender: broadly including non-binary, agender, transgender, genderfluid, and many other identities. This is also referred to sometimes as broadly "genderqueer". It may also refer to gender-non-conforming (GNC) which more specifically includes the genderqueer community as those who do not fit neatly into a binary gender category of men or women.

Many languages have terminology that relies on a binary gender system to refer to people. When gendered terminology refers to people, this is social or semantic gender, which is distinct from grammatical gender. Grammatical gender is assigned to inanimate objects on an arbitrary basis. Grammatical gender is a function of the agreement system of a language, and while it is usually aligned with terms that refer to people, it is a function of syntax and not the actual characteristics of the item.

Grammatical gender and social or semantic gender are inherently linked concepts. Where semantic or social gender exists, however, grammatical gender necessarily follows (Corbett 1991). A person's semantic gender will force the grammatically realized gender feature to align with it. Semantically, however, there is sometimes a mismatch between the grammatical gender options and the social and semantic gender expression of any given person. This type of mismatch in gender from concept to utterance (or writing) also arises in bilingual code switching, which has been analyzed in López (2020: 46–75) utilizing the same frameworks employed here. It is in this space of mismatch that new forms may arise, particularly in social situations wherein there is significant pressure to do so.

There is a body of research which investigates emerging forms for nonbinary individuals who speak languages with binary grammatical categories (Fuentes and Gómez Soler 2023; Knisely 2021; Stetie and Zunino 2022). Silva and Soares (2024: 1) edited an entire volume which addresses this issue specifically spanning French, Italian, Portuguese, and Spanish. This body of work deals with active language change which directly impacts the gender non-conforming community, and is most of what one finds on a cursory exploration of the linguistics of gender non-conforming morphology.

Contrasting that body of research, this auto-ethnographic exploration seeks instead to contend with the discomfort (also known as dysphoria) that I, a nonbinary person, feel when encountering gendered terminology in English, as sparse as it may be. Self-reflection, especially as I have further embraced and explored my gender identity, has revealed that some terminology is more likely to cause gender dysphoria than others. As an introspective person and an incorrigible linguist, the possibility of a deeper structural reason driving these differences is enticing. The following essay examines my personal relationship with gendered language and how I rationalize it utilizing a distributed morphology framework (Halle and Marantz 1993).

This is a reflection, which utilizes a linguistic theoretical lens in a somewhat unconventional way. It is not meant to be a generalizable study which once and for all categorizes the way that non-binary people interact with gendered language. Should others resonate with the explorations I make here and find a sense of self through the academic lenses I am using, I welcome them and their interpretations. That said, I am also aware of the nature of this work and its deeply personal implications, which might result in only personal truth. In the next two sections, I detail the theoretical lenses of gender and language with which I am initiating this analysis. The section after those looks at specific words and diagrams my proposal for how gender attaches to those words before a conclusion that details the application of this work for me and my purposes.

2 Gender studies and queer theory background

The intersection of language and gender goes beyond the mechanics of grammatical gender and agreement systems. As a linguist, it is easy to analyze everything through only that lens, but queer studies have a lot to add to the study of gendered language. Utilizing both fields for an analysis is not a new proposal. Preceding me by a whole decade, Barrett et al. (2014) presented an analysis that combines the two worlds. This section examines some of the gender studies-based work that is related to my proposed theory and examines the way this informs my proposal.

Due to its lack of grammatical gender, English users do not have much interaction with gendered morphology and thus gendered language studies of English users are rarer than studies concerning users of languages with robust grammatical gender systems. Much of the scholarly work that has been done to examine the way the English language has functioned for non-binary and gender-nonconforming individuals focuses on medical scenarios (Kosher et al. 2023; Matsuno and Budge 2017; Ross et al. 2022; Warth et al. 2023). While valid and interesting studies, there are limitations here. A few of these studies look at gender-inclusive language from the perspective of the non-binary individuals themselves – as opposed to those cisgender professionals interacting with them – which does approach more relevance. Warth et al. (2023) and Kosher et al. (2023) both found that gender-neutral terminology was important. Warth et al. (2023), which looked at gender in medical settings, found that medical professionals' misuse of gendered terminology towards patients was deeply upsetting to a portion of participants, but others found little issue with it.

Non-binary studies that center linguistics and language above the discomfort of medical situations are much rarer. Cordoba (2022) evaluates some of the work that has been done so far, including the queer theorists who started to establish trans studies – in particular Stryker – and the work they have done at the intersections of language and gender. Moon (2019) evaluates how different emotional language can impact trans individuals, and the way gendered language can be disorienting. This type of disorientation is similar to that which Moon (2019) describes as "feelings of discomfort are a way of understanding that named gender and practices/experiences do not match" (Moon 2019: 75). Moon's (2019) findings showcase the range across an online forum, with no single consensus on the way that language and gender interact. Though still sparse, the existing literature further establishes that gender and dysphoria are deeply individual things that do not widely apply to all people in the same way. Wide exploration and survey of the gender nonconforming community is difficult in light of our relative vulnerability in the face of rising persecution, especially from Anglophone governments such as that of the United States of America and the United Kingdom.[1]

Some of the literature (Kosher et al. 2023; Moon 2019; Warth et al. 2023) has examined the way that language impacts non-binary people and the way they react to it; however, this work is missing an exploration of the language innovation that non-binary individuals have introduced. Barrett et al. (2014) is the first piece I have found which takes the revolutionary view of 1990s Judith Butler and expands those ideas on gender towards formal theoretical linguistics. This stands in opposition to a field of study which has previously only focused on queer theory and linguistics as an intersection confined to functional linguistics. Functional linguistics is generally concerned with the way language is used and the way that language users are influenced on a variety of levels, while formal linguistics has been concerned with the internal cognitive mechanisms driving language (Barrett et al. 2014). For those who see gender as an external performance, it would make sense to only concern oneself with the functional side of the field, but as someone with a rich internal gender and cognitive linguistic system, I find that these two play together more than the extant research would suggest. This is where Barrett et al. (2014) and I differ in approach. Barrett sees the language ideologies of formal linguistics and queer theory as being inherently oppositional, and argues that there are many ways that the ideologies of the two fields are incompatible. The inherent binarity of language proposed by Chomsky (1993) becomes the tool through which I am able to analyze my own lack of adherence to a different binary. While I do agree that queer theory and queer

---

[1] I have chosen intentionally not to include citations here about this growing hate due to the traumatizing nature of extensive citation on these points both for myself as the author and potentially affected readers.

linguists themselves bring new and necessary insight to formal linguistics, the respective frameworks are not inherently oppositional.

Queer theory examines language through a lens of how it is used to enforce, create, critique, and reestablish normativity (Barrett et al. 2014; Butler 2011). In my experience of language being used to refer to non-binary individuals, it is this standard of normativity that defines what is and is not acceptable. As a community, my peers in gender nonconformity and myself negotiate meaning where it is needed. The 'standard' language is being consistently reformed and shaped within communities, and then expanding its acceptance beyond into mostly cis-normative spaces. This is a process that over time builds to a point of normativity even for those outside of the group. This can be seen with the new prevalence of gender-neutral language earning mention in diversity training (Tarrayo 2024; University Wire 2024; Woolley and Airton 2020). Since normativity itself is socially determined, LGBTQIA+ communities and the smaller subset of gender non-conforming communities have the power to determine within their communities what gender constructs and language are and are not valid. Then, some subset of those constructs and language bleeds into other communities until it is widely accepted.

With this language acceptance is also the power to change the implications and meaning of language (Barrett et al. 2014). Combined with the specific linguistic theory to be detailed below, I have developed my own ideas about the interplay between language and gender. The frames of Barrett et al. (2014) and Butler (2011) both neglect the differentiation of I-language and E-language. I-language is the idea that each person has their own unique language system (Isac 2008), while E-language refers to the shared language that we use to communicate with each other. I-language and what one might call I-gender identity are two concepts that can interact and complement each other, and allow for the combination of formal linguistic theory with queer theory.

3 Morphosyntax background

Queer linguists are not an enigma, and in my personal experience there is more diverse representation in the field than I have seen in, say, anthropology or second language acquisition. That said, the study of queer-focused linguistics is somewhat young. My citations list here only reaches back to the nineties, despite linguistics itself having a much larger history. Queer linguistics studies are commonly referred to as *lavender linguistics*, which is also the title of the annual conference on this issue. This term seems to have been coined by William Leap around 1993[2] with the first conference of this title, according to his CV. The explorations of this new subdiscipline have focused on a variety of topics including gay men's vocal prosody (Munson and Babel 2007), pronoun reference (Conrod 2020), language innovation in Mandarin (Shiau 2015), the psycholinguistic study of gender bent professions (Gygax et al. 2008), and plenty of other factors. This work is not revolutionary in the field in terms of examination of gender non-conforming language, or any of the minutia therein. However, the theoretical perspective that I am undertaking in a linguistic sense necessitates some light introduction, just as the gender theory above did.

In the tradition of linguistics I was taught in a heavily Chomskian syntactically oriented department, the structure of language is generally understood in one specific way. The theory of minimalist syntax was the basis of my education on language structure. Minimalist syntax asserts that the grammar of a language comes together in a particular process of two lexemes combining to create a syntactic head, and then continuing to do so in order to create entire sentences (Chomsky 1993). Minimalist syntax also goes hand in hand with Universal Grammar, which assumes that all people have an innate aptitude for language that can execute that minimalist syntax (Chomsky 1993). Furthermore, the lens of distributed morphology posits that the same structure applies further down to the formation of words, and can help to model the way that certain features of words, such as gender, attach to the root of a word. The difference in the location of the syntactic attachment for these features is the main point of my analysis.

The distributed model assumes an ignorant[3] version of the language that only handles structure and has no sense of meaning or sound (Halle and Marantz 1993). Within this, it becomes clear that the base of words that are plugged into these structures have some identity outside of their meaning or sound. These bits are called roots (Harley 2014). Roots are often represented by numbers within the root sign, such as $\sqrt{146}$. For this work, I will label roots with an all-capitalized version of the lexical item in question for the easiest reading of the given examples such as $\sqrt{CAT}$. Halle and Marantz (1993) also describe different pieces called features that are introduced at various parts of this process. Some of these features exist in what is referred to as List 1.

List 1 is made up of the things that are inherent to the root, which is again ignorant to pronunciation and meaning. It is only syntactically relevant, such as a count

---

[2] https://www.nottingham.ac.uk/conference/fac-arts/english/lavlang24/why-lavender.aspx, accessed: 12 February 2025.

[3] While typically this is referred to as "blind", in response to a reviewer's comment which mentioned that the term was insensitive to those with disabilities, I have changed it. Those familiar with this theory will be familiar with the explanation that still utilizes that language.

or mass distinction (Harley 2014). I argue that gender exists as an inherent feature of these roots for some words, while being alienable and detachable for others. Other information in this list includes grammatical details that are relevant to the syntax such as count or mass distinctions (Harley 2014). Through the merge process of syntax, which combines two things into a higher syntactic head, roots can also take on affixes which give them new features. The features that are inherent to a root do not change, but rather the word takes on new affixes – either pronounceable or not – which change the features, and those features slot into their place and agreement within the rest of the sentence's syntactic structure.

Morphosyntactic explorations of the relationship between semantic gender and grammatical gender have not been looked at through a distributed morphology lens except for the work of Kramer (2015, 2016, 2020, 2023, 2024) and Steriopolo (2024). Other syntactic explorations of gender are not as relevant, since this piece seeks to explicitly use a distributed morphology lens to contextualize and justify my own dysphoria. In a paper that utilized this sort of analysis in a generalizable way, those other explorations into English gender such as a social indexical approach (Needle and Pierrehumbert 2018) or the Natural Framework approach (Dressler and Doleschal 1990) would need to be refuted before a new presentation was introduced. This is not a paper which seeks to do so, and is instead a reflection that utilizes this specific lens. If the reader is seeking to be convinced of this particular lens, then I would highly recommend a deep look at Punske's (2023) book, Harley (2014) on roots, and Bobaljik (2017) for an introduction to the framework and the arguments in the field.

For the purposes of gender itself as a feature, Kramer's explorations in particular reflect a very similar examination to the one I propose. Kramer's (2024) piece on gender is the one which most closely aligns with my own work. It is also her first piece which is not explicitly about the gender of Aramaic, but rather is about the nature of language overall (Kramer 2024: 79). As I will exemplify in the next section, Kramer proposes that gender attaches to a root along with other features through a category-defining nominalizing head *n* creating a syntactic piece, *n*P, which is a noun. In her work, she uses an example from Aramaic, as is given in Example (1).

Like my own proposal, Kramer (2024: 80) suggests that here *n* happens to contain gender features but does not necessarily need to. These features may be semantically interpretable, like in the case of a sentient and animate noun like *mist* above, or they may be uninterpretable in the case of purely grammatical gender such as the feminine agreement triggered by a word like *table* (Kramer 2024: 80). Kramer also argues that a word meaning something like *wife* can only be interpreted in the context of a [+FEM] feature. If this is indeed the lens one undertakes, that does provide a solid basis for the discomfort associated with those types of lexemes when applied to a non-binary person such as myself. It is a forcible semantic gender to pair with the grammatical aspect.

(1) Aramaic example by Kramer (2024).

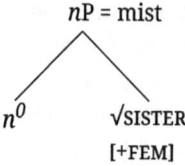

nP = mist

n^0 √SISTER
       [+FEM]

Building off of the types of concepts that Kramer (2024) outlines, Steriopolo (2024) examines the way that gender and language mismatch work in a distributed morphology framework. Steriopolo (2024) shows some cases wherein the opposite of the expected grammatical gender will be used to refer to a person who is exhibiting traits generally associated with a different semantic gender than their assumed sex (Steriopolo 2024: 389). This can also be used to show the attitude of the speaker towards the subject of the gender mismatch, either positive or negative (Steriopolo 2024: 391). When handling gender mismatches, Steriopolo (2024) suggests a double n head system, which would allow this discrepancy and also maintain what is seen as a necessary gender feature for people. Example (2) shows this aforementioned double n as it is presented by Steriopolo (2024: 394).

(2) Example for the double n head system by Steriopolo (2024).

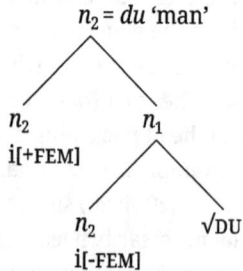

n_2 = *du* 'man'

n_2 n_1
i[+FEM]

        n_2 √DU
        i[-FEM]

There are a few things about this analysis which are not in line with my own analysis, nor with Kramer's analysis presented above. The first of this is the presentation of '√*du*'. While not explicitly stated by Steriopolo (2024), the way that this is presented assumes there are phonological features inherent to the root, which is not the consensus in the field presently, as Harley (2014) established. This could simply be a notation difference, however, and since Steriopolo (2024) makes no explicit reference to it, I will leave it alone for now. Furthermore, Steriopolo (2024) notes interpretable features with an *i-* preceding the feature in question. This is interesting since all the features above are supposed to be interpretable rather than uninterpretable, compared to Kramer's assertion that such a mismatch would yield an uninterpretable feature (Kramer 2024: 81). However, both of these analyses fail to recognize a situation wherein the gender mismatch might exist as a result of misgendering of an individual. It is always purposeful and meaningful when it happens in Steriopolo's (2024) work, and entirely impossible for Kramer (2024). However, with the eye of a genderqueer person, there are cases wherein, regardless of the agreement measures higher in the syntax or a person's traits, the mismatch would be socially rich and also full of hurt. This is where my analysis expands on these existing works.

The examples from both Kramer (2024) and Steriopolo (2024) work from languages which have extensive gender systems. Within the much more limited context of English gendered terminology, the function of these gender features may be different, on both the social level that Steriopolo (2024) describes and the purely syntactic one that Kramer (2024) addresses. Nevertheless, these are the extant examples of distributed morphology's interpretation of gender that my analysis can draw from.

4 Theoretical proposal and examples

I come to this research with the privilege of not finding myself constantly barraged with gendered language in most of my day-to-day interactions. English affords its users' freedom from gender in most situations, despite the relative gender obsession of American society in which I exist. There is, of course, still the obvious pressure of pronouns which are always weighing on every interaction with more than myself and one other participant, but that is beyond the scope of this work. In one-on-one interactions I am very rarely misgendered, and I rarely interact in group settings which call for pronoun reference.

Pronouns have been examined left and right by a variety of individuals (Bradley et al. 2019; Cheesebrough 2022; Conrod 2020, 2022; Hekanaho 2022; Hord 2016; Konnelly et al. 2022; Saguy and Williams 2022) to the point where I even have an easily readable explanation of why adherence to someone's preferences matters in my email signature. Societally – at least in the society of the white, western, academic machine – the issue of pronouns is mostly settled. Most academics know how to handle this and do so with varying levels of grace. If they struggle, there are multiple different trainings that universities pay for in order to explain pronouns and gender diversity to their faculty and staff. These existed even at my first institution, which was in the middle of a very conservative part of the United States. This is not to say that no one ever gets anyone's pronouns wrong, or that it is not a sticking point for some impassioned individuals who think they have something to prove. I've certainly been on the receiving end of those attitudes before; however, there is at a minimum a performance of institutional support if I ever felt compelled to confront someone who maliciously got them wrong all the time.

The metric of gendered pronouns, however, can be useful as a baseline from which to compare my reactions to other cases of misgendering. An entirely uncorrected *she* or *her* in conversation leaves me with a level of discomfort akin to second-hand embarrassment.[4] I would rate it like the feeling of watching someone overestimate their vocal abilities at a karaoke bar. An unpleasant thing you will think about for a while, but not disruptively so. It is of note that this is about the uncorrected pronoun slip, corrected slips are much less discomforting, like gently informing someone at the library that you have booked the study room they're using. These common encounters in daily life leave me with metrics by which to measure others.

There are a few different kinds of gendered terminology in English. Some words take on morphological bits which make them gendered like *-(r)ess* or *-ette*. Some words have gendered meanings that seem to be lacking morphological motivation for the trait. Some words apply to a broader spectrum of genders despite their inherently gendered nature such as *mailman*. Terms in this type of category were heavily explored and alternatives were offered in the second-wave feminism of the 1990s, and continuing to modern contexts (Archer and Kam 2022; Erdocia 2022; Horvath et al. 2016; Koeser et al. 2015; Medel 2022; Vergoossen et al. 2020).

4.1 Inalienable gender

Some words have gender inherent to them. There is no clear way to extract, retool, or otherwise change the gender of the lexical item without simply creating an entirely different lexical item. It is my understanding that cisgender individuals feel the same way about their genders. It is an inherent part of who they are, and there would be no way to be themselves without it. Transgender individuals – in the more

---

4 As a relatively feminine presenting non-binary person, I do not often face an uncorrected *he* or *him* and thus do not have enough context with which to use such examples as comparisons here. Since this is a personal reflection, I will not attempt to make those comparisons.

traditional transgender sense wherein one chooses an established gender different from the one associated with their assigned sex – have also expressed this relationship to gender. Such a relationship with the concept is beyond me, which I believe is related to why these words are so discomfiting.

Words with these ties tend to be very relationally oriented. *Bride, wife, aunt, mother, sister*, and *queen*[5] all exist as examples of words that I argue have inalienable gender. In a previous time and climate, the less relationally tied term *nurse*[6] would have been a good example. Luckily, society now accepts your ability to provide certain types of medical care regardless of your genitalia or social presentation. Example (3) illustrates my proposal for how such inherent gender features are syntactically introduced on the n^0 which categorizes the root as a noun.

(3)   Example for the introduction of inherent gender features.

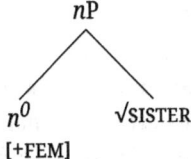

(4)   Example for the alternative attachment of inherent gender features.

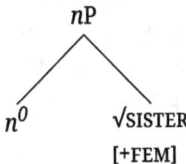

There are other features, such as [+COUNT] for the count/mass distinction, that also live under n^0, but those are not relevant here, so I have not included them. This is a work meant to be as accessible as syntactic theory can be to those uninitiated.

---

5 I am excluding examples of *queen* in relation to drag or more broadly in a "Yas queen!" exclamation in queer culture that is broadly a genderless compliment or encouragement. Future work may seek to use a similar type of study in order to gain answers as to what is happening in those specific cases.

6 Though *male nurse* is a term I have often heard used. This may be a case of a sort of beyond lexical boundary prefix for some people's I-languages. These people can only refer to a nurse who happens to be a man as a *male nurse* and refer to nurses who are women as just *nurses*.

The [+FEM] feature is generated below the first categorizing nP, and the gender in this case is so closely tied to the root it cannot be abandoned with the result of an interpretable lexeme. Another possible proposal here is that the [+FEM] feature is attached to the root itself, meaning that it is even further inalienable, as is demonstrated in Example (4).

There is relative debate about what types of information might be carried by roots in the field of distributed morphology (Acquaviva 2009; Arad 2005; Harley 2014). Generally, I ascribe to the view that there are no features on roots that Harley supposes, but my analysis is not dependent upon this point.

Either analysis leaves us with a lexically determined gender feature. Words that have [-FEM] would also be mapped in the same way as the [+FEM] examples above. Readers unfamiliar with the field may wonder why there is not a [+MASC] feature. This is due to the bigender system exhibited by English gendered words, and maximal efficiency of a system. There is no need for a [+MASC] feature when the [±FEM] will do.

In the case of these words with inalienable gender, the discomfort of being misgendered with them is equal to, and often more than, uncorrected pronoun misgendering. Some words in these categories are harder to contend with than others, though there may be other more socially-driven reasons for this. *Aunt* and *sister* are the least personally egregious of these examples to me, while *wife* is probably the worst. My levels of discomfort within the categories I have set out here may be due to the roles ascribed to those words more than their morphosyntactic constructions. There is a lot of expectational baggage attached to the gendered role of a *wife* or *mother* societally, and that baggage feels particularly contrary to my perception of self, while the roles of *sister* or *aunt* are not as heavily steeped in gendered expectations and thus are far less upsetting.

4.2 Morphological gender

Some lexical items may acquire gender features through processes that augment the base form outside of nP. In these cases, there is extra syntactic distance between the root and its gender in surface form. This terminology can be further subdivided into two different categories. There are lexical items that always take a suffix that indicates their gender such as *waiter*, *waitress*, *actor*, or *actress*. These terms have surface forms for [-FEM] features in addition to [+FEM] forms. This is illustrated in Example (5).

Other terms have null suffixes for the [-FEM] feature such as *bachelor*, *bachelorette*, *hero*, *heroine*, *prince*, or *princess*. These terms and their forms are different from the third category (discussed in Section 4.3), which defines masculine terms as defaults. There is a gender-based syntactic head on these roots following their nominalization, and that just happens to not have a pronounceable surface form in some cases. This conception fits well with other ideas of null morphology, including concepts of null plurals, such as in the case of terms like *sheep* (Harley 2014). For gender, this is demonstrated in Example (6) below.

(5) Example for words which always take a suffix that indicates their gender.

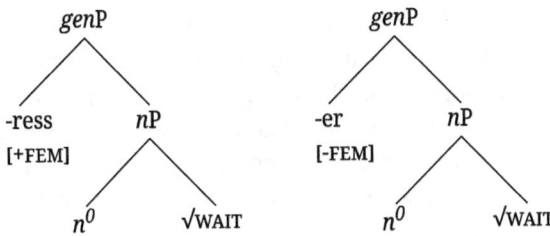

(6) Example for words with a gender-based syntactic head on their roots.

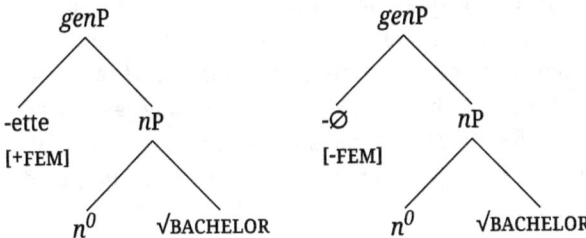

Although I have defined these two sources for gender attachment, Figures (5) and (6), differently, the levels of discomfort that are attached to them are the same. I believe that this is the case because gender attachment happens within the same node, which I have deemed here *genP*, for gender phrase. The word gender is lowercase as this is not a part of the syntax of the overall sentence, but rather of the word itself, which will plug into the rest of the syntax. Some theories might also put it under some type of an Agree head, and that would also be acceptable to my theory here. This discomfort is much less than in the case of intrinsically gendered words like those in Section 4.1. The additional syntactic distance weakens the blow of gender in a semantic sense, with the result that the term causes less dysphoria.

It is an item of note, that there is also societal baggage with these terms. While being referred to as a *bachelorette* is gendered, in the context it is used it does not often come with too many stringent gender roles, just alcohol and partying. However, other terms like *princess*, are most commonly used as unwanted pet names towards me,[7] and come with gendered implications that make me exceedingly uncomfortable.[8]

4.3 Masculine default gender

The final and third set of terms here are ones that I will not dwell on heavily. Understanding what is happening with them is rooted more in feminist literature and ideologies (Formanowicz et al. 2013; Giora 2003; Mavisakalyan 2015; Talbot 2001). These terms are technically masculine, but in their use, they refer to people of all genders. Terms like this are mostly tied to professions. Some examples include *mailman* and *fireman*. Both of these terms can be used to refer generally to the person who performs those duties.

There are non-gendered versions of these terms such as *mail carrier* and *firefighter*, but they tend to be used alongside the seemingly gendered language. I do not believe that these terms have a *gen*P, and conversely also do not have a gendered n^0 or root feature of gender. This is in contrast to *man* which is inherently gendered, but in my perspective loses this quality when it compounds in cases such as *fireman* and *mailman*. More exploration on this topic might reveal some differences depending upon the profession being described and its socially gendered context, such as for terms like *handyman*. While interesting, that concept is one best abled for exploration in a different paper. Example (7) illustrates my proposed non-gendered interpretation of *mailman*.

(7)   Non-gendered interpretation of mailman.

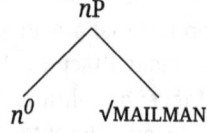

---

7 I am unfortunately entirely lacking in royal heritage.
8 This could also be compounded with a general distaste for the kind of person (usually a man) who just calls strangers *princess*.

Though I am not in a profession that uses these seemingly gendered terms, I can speculate that they would not bother me.[9] I do think they are problematic in that they perpetuate ideologies that presume only men are in those roles, but I do not have a personal issue with them in a dysphoric sense. I think of the gender of these words as like the idea of the "everyman" in literature where *man* refers to any person. While outdated and commonly replaced with *everyone* in a modern sense, this type of broad application of *man* is not meant to be gendered, and I have not embodied it in my lexicon as such.

5 Conclusion

My conception of gender is deeply associated with the idea of performance and costume. I can put on femininity or masculinity, but none of these traits are inherent to my being. Sometimes it is beneficial to me to don the costume of femininity or masculinity in accordance with the situation at hand. I am more than willing to leverage gender for my own benefit. Being more expressly feminine in some contexts, especially those where I know that being explicit about my non-binary identity would be unacceptable, inherently benefits me. In the current political contexts where I feel as if I have to hide my identity for safety, this is even more so.

None of this changes the fact that who I exist as at a core is not a gendered being. In this way, language which is inalienably tied to gender is more discomforting than language which is not. Alienable gender morphology allows for the flexibility that I experience in my identity to be reflected in the language I use. The view of gender as it attaches to words in distributed morphology allows me to provide a furtherment of the framework that calls into question List 3 semantic information. How is meaning affected by the structure of words? Of sentences?

This work also establishes itself among linguistic papers as something personal, something reflective. It is narrative and personal and inconcrete. It follows in the footsteps of gender and queer studies research that cares about the personal, while using the theoretical methodologies of linguistics. It is a parallel of my own lives and how they come together, and hopefully will be a starting point of further mixing between those two worlds.

I have given a strong, but inherently personal, case that syntactic distance has an effect on the semantic gender of a lexeme. The more of this distance there is,

---

[9] A reviewer of this work commented that they would be bothered by these terms in German. This is the exact type of interesting discussion that I believe this work will spark.

the less dysphoria a lexeme will cause. This is true, at least, for my own personal I-language.

In this examination, I have given several cases of possible attachment for the gendered features of English. They are farther away from the root when they are attached under *gen*P instead of under the n^0 node. This distance has a direct impact on the way that I as a non-binary person interact with the language presented. Future work would do well to survey a broader population of non-binary people and see if words felt more or less likely to instigate feelings of dysphoria. The application of these terms and their gender binding in other languages would also be a valid direction for further study. As was addressed in the introduction, there is boundless room for scholars to explore these concepts.

References

Acquaviva, Paolo. 2009. Roots and lexicality in distributed morphology. *YPL2 - Issue 10 (May 2009) Special Issue - York-Essex Morphology Meeting (YEMM)* .

Anderson, Catherine. 2022. Pronouns and social justice in the linguistics classroom. *Journal of Language and Sexuality* 11(2). 251–263. https://doi.org/10.1075/jls.20024.and.

Arad, Maya. 2005. Roots: Where syntax, morphology, and the lexicon meet. In Maya Arad (ed.), *Roots and patterns: Hebrew morpho-syntax*, 1–23. Springer. https://doi.org/10.1007/1-4020-3244-7_1.

Archer, Allison M. N. and Cindy D. Kam. 2022. She is the chair(man): Gender, language, and leadership. *The Leadership Quarterly* 33(6). 101610. https://doi.org/10.1016/j.leaqua.2022.101610.

Barrett, Rusty, Lal Zimman, Jenny Davis and J. Raclaw. 2014. The emergence of the unmarked. In *Queer excursions: Retheorizing binaries in language, gender, and sexuality*, 195–223. New York: Oxford Academic. https://doi.org/10.1093/acprof:oso/9780199937295.003.0010.

Bobaljik, Jonathan David. 2017. Distributed morphology. *Oxford Research Encyclopedia of Linguistics* https://doi.org/10.1093/acrefore/9780199384655.013.131.

Bradley, Evan D., Julia Salkind, Ally Moore and Sofi Teitsort. 2019. Singular "they" and novel pronouns: Gender-neutral, nonbinary, or both? *Proceedings of the Linguistic Society of America* 4. 36:1–7. https://doi.org/10.3765/plsa.v4i1.4542.

Butler, Judith. 2011. *Bodies that matter: On the discursive limits of sex*. London: Routledge. https://doi.org/10.4324/9780203828274.

Cheesebrough, Julia. 2022. A gamble on gender: Perceptions of the singular "they" pronoun among college-age students. *Global Insight: A Journal of Critical Human Science and Culture* 3. https://doi.org/10.32855/globalinsight.2022.002.

Chomsky, Noam. 1993. A minimalist program for linguistic theory. In Ken Hale and Samuel Jay Keyser (eds.), *The view from the building: 20 essays in linguistics in honor of Sylvain Bromberger*, 111–176. Cambridge: The MIT Press. https://doi.org/10.7551/mitpress/10174.003.0005.

Conrod, Kirby. 2020. Pronouns and gender in language. In Kira Hall and Rusty Barrett (eds.), *The Oxford handbook of language and sexuality*, Oxford: Oxford University Press. https://doi.org/10.1093/oxfordhb/9780190212926.013.63.

Conrod, Kirby. 2022. Abolishing gender on D. *Canadian Journal of Linguistics/Revue canadienne de linguistique* 67. 216–241. https://doi.org/10.1017/cnj.2022.27.

Corbett, Greville G. 1991. *Gender*. Cambridge: Cambridge University Press. https://doi.org/10.1017/CBO9781139166119.

Cordoba, Sebastian. 2022. *Non-binary gender identities: The language of becoming*. London: Routledge. https://doi.org/10.4324/9781003120360.

Dressler, Wolfgang U. and Ursula Doleschal. 1990. Gender agreement via derivational morphology. *Acta Linguistica Hungarica* 40(1/2). 115–137.

Erdocia, Iker. 2022. Language and culture wars: The far right's struggle against gender-neutral language. *Journal of Language and Politics* 21(6). 847–866. https://doi.org/10.1075/jlp.21050.erd.

Formanowicz, Magdalena, Sylwia Bedynska, Aleksandra Cisłak, Friederike Braun and Sabine Sczesny. 2013. Side effects of gender-fair language: How feminine job titles influence the evaluation of female applicants. *European Journal of Social Psychology* 43(1). 62–71. https://doi.org/10.1002/ejsp.1924.

Fuentes, Ronald and Inmaculada Gómez Soler. 2023. Instructors' navigation and appropriation of gender-inclusive Spanish at a U.S. university. *Current Issues in Language Planning* 24(5). 534–553. https://doi.org/10.1080/14664208.2022.2150499.

Giora, Rachel. 2003. Theorizing gender: Feminist awareness and language change. In Bettina Baron and Helga Kotthoff (eds.), *Gender in interaction: Perspectives on femininity and masculinity in ethnography and discourse*, 329–347. Amsterdam, Philadelphia: John Benjamins. https://doi.org/10.1075/pbns.93.17gio.

Gygax, Pascal, Ute Gabriel, Oriane Sarrasin, Jane Oakhill and Alan Garnham. 2008. Generically intended, but specifically interpreted: When beauticians, musicians, and mechanics are all men. *Language and Cognitive Processes* 23(3). 464–485. https://doi.org/10.1080/01690960701702035.

Halle, Morris and Alec Marantz. 1993. Distributed morphology and the pieces of inflection. In Ken Hale and Samuel Jay Keyser (eds.), *The view from the building: 20 essays in linguistics in honor of Sylvain Bromberger*, 111–176. Cambridge: The MIT Press.

Harley, Heidi. 2014. On the identity of roots. *Theoretical Linguistics* 40(3-4). 225–276. https://doi.org/10.1515/tl-2014-0010.

Hekanaho, Laura. 2022. A thematic analysis of attitudes towards English nonbinary pronouns. *Journal of Language and Sexuality* 11(2). 190–216. https://doi.org/10.1075/jls.21025.hek.

Heritage, Frazer. 2022. Politics, pronouns, and the players: Examining how videogame players react to the inclusion of a transgender character in World of Warcraft. *Gender and Language* 16(1). 26–51. https://doi.org/10.1558/genl.20250.

Hord, Levi C. R. 2016. Bucking the linguistic binary: Gender neutral language in English, Swedish, French, and German. *Western Papers in Linguistics* 3(1).

Horvath, Lisa K., Elisa F. Merkel, Anne Maass and Sabine Sczesny. 2016. Does gender-fair language pay off? The social perception of professions from a cross-linguistic perspective. *Frontiers in Psychology* 6. 2018. https://doi.org/10.3389/FPSYG.2015.02018.

Isac, Daniela. 2008. *I-language: An introduction to linguistics as cognitive science*. 1st edn. Oxford: Oxford University Press.

Knisely, Kris Aric. 2021. A starter kit for rethinking trans representation and inclusion in French L2 classrooms. In E. Nicole Meyer and Eilene Hoft-March (eds.), *Teaching diversity and inclusion: Examples from a French-speaking classroom*, 22–33. New York: Routledge. https://doi.org/10.4324/9781003126461-3.

Koeser, Sara, Elisabeth A. Kuhn and Sabine Sczesny. 2015. Just reading? How gender-fair language triggers readers' use of gender-fair forms. *Journal of Language and Social Psychology* 34(3). 343–357. https://doi.org/10.1177/0261927X14561119.

Konnelly, Lex, Bronwyn M. Bjorkman and Lee Airton. 2022. Towards an engaged linguistics: Nonbinary pronouns as a site of advocacy in research and teaching. *Journal of Language and Sexuality* 11(2). 133–140. https://doi.org/10.1075/jls.21024.kon.

Kosher, Rowena B. D., Lauren C. Houghton and Inga T. Winkler. 2023. Manstruation: A cyberethnography of linguistic strategies of trans and nonbinary menstruators. *Social Science & Medicine* 328. 115974. https://doi.org/10.1016/j.socscimed.2023.115974.

Kramer, Ruth. 2015. *The morphosyntax of gender.* Oxford, England: Oxford University Press.

Kramer, Ruth. 2016. Syncretism in paradigm function morphology and distributed morphology. In Daniel Siddiqi and Heidi Harley (eds.), *Morphological metatheory*, 95–120. Amsterdam, Philadelphia: John Benjamins. https://doi.org/10.1075/la.229.04kra.

Kramer, Ruth. 2020. Grammatical gender: A close look at gender assignment across languages. *Annual Review of Linguistics* 6. 45–66. https://doi.org/10.1146/annurev-linguistics-011718-012450.

Kramer, Ruth. 2023. The morphosyntax of imperative agreement in Amharic. *Journal of Afroasiatic Languages and Linguistics* https://doi.org/10.1163/18776930-01501003.

Kramer, Ruth. 2024. An exoskeletal approach to grammatical gender. *Linguistic Approaches to Bilingualism* 14(1). 79–84. https://doi.org/10.1075/lab.23056.kra.

López, Luis. 2020. *Bilingual grammar: Toward an integrated model.* Cambridge: Cambridge University Press. https://doi.org/10.1017/9781108756181.

Matsuno, Emmie and Stephanie L. Budge. 2017. Non-binary/genderqueer identities: A critical review of the literature. *Current Sexual Health Reports* 9(3). 116–120. https://doi.org/10.1007/s11930-017-0111-8.

Mavisakalyan, Astghik. 2015. Gender in language and gender in employment. *Oxford Development Studies* 43(4). 403–424. https://doi.org/10.1080/13600818.2015.1045857.

Medel, María López. 2022. Non-sexist language in vacancy titles: A proposal for drafting and translation in international organisations. *Journal of International Women's Studies* 23(5). Article 5. https://vc.bridgew.edu/jiws/vol23/iss5/5.

Miles-Hercules, Deandre. 2024. (Trans)forming expertise: Transness, equity, and the ethical imperative of linguistics. In Anne H. Charity Hudley, Christine Mallinson and Mary Bucholtz (eds.), *Inclusion in linguistics*, Oxford: Oxford University Press. https://doi.org/10.1093/oso/9780197755303.003.0005.

Moon, Igi. 2019. 'Boying' the boy and 'girling' the girl: From affective interpellation to trans-emotionality. *Sexualities* 22(1–2). 65–79. https://doi.org/10.1177/1363460717740260.

Munson, Benjamin and Molly Babel. 2007. Loose lips and silver tongues, or, projecting sexual orientation through speech. *Language and Linguistics Compass* 1(5). 416–449. https://doi.org/10.1111/j.1749-818X.2007.00028.x.

Needle, Jeremy M. and Janet B. Pierrehumbert. 2018. Gendered associations of English morphology. *Laboratory Phonology* 9(1). https://doi.org/10.5334/labphon.134.

Punske, Jeffrey P. 2023. *Morphology: A distributed morphology introduction.* Hoboken: John Wiley & Sons.

Ross, Lori E., David J. Kinitz and Hannah Kia. 2022. Pronouns are a public health issue. *American Journal of Public Health* 112(3). 360–362. https://doi.org/10.2105/AJPH.2021.306678.

Saguy, Abigail C. and Juliet A. Williams. 2022. A little word that means a lot: A reassessment of singular they in a new era of gender politics. *Gender & Society* 36(1). 5–31. https://doi.org/10.1177/08912432211057921.

Shiau, Hong-Chi. 2015. Lavender Mandarin in the sites of desire: Situating linguistic performances among Taiwanese gay men. *Language & Communication* 42. 1–10. https://doi.org/10.1016/j.langcom.2015.01.005.

Silva, Gláucia V. and Cristiane Soares. 2024. *Inclusiveness beyond the (non)binary in romance languages: Research and classroom implementation*. Oxon, New York: Taylor & Francis.

Steele, Ariana J. 2018. Enacting new worlds of gender: Nonbinary speakers, racialized gender, and anti-colonialism. In Kira Hall and Rusty Barrett (eds.), *The Oxford handbook of language and sexuality*, Oxford University Press. https://doi.org/10.1093/oxfordhb/9780190212926.013.74.

Steriopolo, Olga. 2024. Gender discrepancies and evaluative gender shift: A cross-linguistic study within distributed morphology. In Stela Manova, Laura Grestenberger and Katharina Korecky-Kröll (eds.), *Diminutives across languages, theoretical frameworks and linguistic domains*, 387–414. Berlin, Boston: De Gruyter. https://doi.org/10.1515/9783110792874-016.

Stetie, Noelia Ayelen and Gabriela Mariel Zunino. 2022. Non-binary language in Spanish? Comprehension of non-binary morphological forms: A psycholinguistic study. *Open Library of Humanities* https://doi.org/10.16995/glossa.6144.

Talbot, Mary M. 2001. Feminism and language. In *The routledge companion to feminism and postfeminism*, London: Routledge 2nd edn. https://doi.org/10.4324/9780203011010.

Tarrayo, Veronico N. 2024. Using the third-person singular pronoun they in academic writing: Perspectives from English language teachers in Philippine universities. *Language Awareness* 33(3). 625–648. https://doi.org/10.1080/09658416.2023.2256652.

University Wire. 2024. *Center for sexual and gender diversity celebrates international pronouns day*. Carlsbad, United States: Uloop, Inc.

Vergoossen, Hellen Petronella, Emma Aurora Renström, Anna Lindqvist and Marie Gustafsson Sendén. 2020. Four dimensions of criticism against gender-fair language. *Sex Roles* 83(5). 328–337. https://doi.org/10.1007/s11199-019-01108-x.

Warth, Rieka Von der, Gloria Metzner, Mirjam Körner and Erik Farin-Glattacker. 2023. Exploring communication preferences of trans and gender diverse individuals—a qualitative study. *PLOS ONE* 18(8). e0284959. https://doi.org/10.1371/journal.pone.0284959.

Woolley, Susan W. and Lee Airton. 2020. *Teaching about gender diversity: Teacher-tested lesson plans for K-12 classrooms*. Toronto, Canada: Canadian Scholars.

Zimman, Lal. 2018. Transgender language, transgender moment: Toward a trans linguistics. In *The Oxford handbook of language and sexuality*, Oxford: Oxford University Press. https://doi.org/10.1093/oxfordhb/9780190212926.013.45.

Zimman, Lal and Cedar Brown. 2024. Beyond pronouns 101: Linguistic advocacy for trans-inclusive language in the college classroom. In Anne H. Charity Hudley, Christine Mallinson and Mary Bucholtz (eds.), *Inclusion in linguistics*, Oxford: Oxford University Press. https://doi.org/10.1093/oso/9780197755303.003.0016.

Notes on contributors

Martina Abbondanza is a psycholinguist currently focusing on gender processing. Her research examines the effects of new gender-inclusive language strategies on language processing, with particular attention to agreement mechanisms.

Julia Elisabeth Blessing-Plötner, Nazire Cinar, Nguyet Minh Dang, Henrike Hoffmanns, Aaron Luther, Imran Peksen, and **Tomma Lilli Robke** are students at Heinrich Heine University Düsseldorf, Germany. Under the guidance of their course instructor and co-author, Dominic Schmitz, they explored the intersections of language and gender in a linguistics course on methodological approaches.

Jens Fleischhauer is a research associate at the Institute of Linguistics at Heinrich-Heine-University Düsseldorf, Germany, and works on the morphosyntax of Bantu languages, complex predicates, and the language of the political extreme right.

D. Hunter is a research associate at the University of Arizona, USA. They work primarily on language revitalization with Celtic-language communities, focusing on language policy and effective community partnerships. Their other work focuses on queerness and linguistic insight.

Zaal Kikvidze is a professor in the Department of General Linguistics at Akaki Tsereteli State University, Kutaisi, Georgia. His research focuses on sociolinguistics, language and gender, cognitive linguistics, corpus linguistics, history of lexicography, and Kartvelian (South Caucasian) languages.

Francesca Panzeri is a professor of Philosophy of Language at the Department of Psychology of the University of Milan – Bicocca, Italy. Her research focuses on the relationship among language, communication and thought.

Samira Ochs is a researcher and doctoral candidate at the Leibniz Institute for the German Language in Mannheim, Germany. Her research focuses on gender and language, queer linguistics, and corpus-linguistic methods.

Marina Ortega-Andrés is a postdoctoral researcher at the Department of Linguistics and Basque Studies at the University of the Basque Country (UPV/EHU), Spain. She is a member of the research group HiTT Hizkuntzalaritza Teorikorako Taldea. Her research focuses on lexical semantics-pragmatics, intergroup communication, and language cognition.

Jeff Roxas is an Assistant Professor of Spanish and Gender and Sexuality Studies in the Department of European Languages, University of the Philippines – Diliman, Philippines. They find pleasure and power in reading and writing research on language and gender, foreign language pedagogy, and migration and sexuality.

Jan Oliver Rüdiger holds a PhD in German Linguistics, specializing in software development for large-scale text analysis. Since 2020, he has been a senior researcher at the Leibniz Institute for the German Language in Mannheim, Germany, focusing on text and data mining as well as corpus and computational linguistics. His work includes the development of specialized software tools for the Digital Humanities.

Dominic Schmitz is a postdoctoral researcher in the English Language and Linguistics department at Heinrich Heine University Düsseldorf, Germany. His research focuses on the interaction between gender and language, as well as on the relationship between form and meaning. He also explores discriminative learning, the nature of prominence in compounds, morphophonetics, psycholinguistics, and sound symbolism.

Viktoria Schneider is a PhD student in the English Language and Linguistics department at Heinrich Heine University Düsseldorf, Germany. Her main area of research is the semantics of word-formation processes in the CRC Project C08 'The semantics of derivational morphology'.

Simon David Stein is a postdoctoral researcher in the English Language and Linguistics department at Heinrich Heine University Düsseldorf, Germany. His research primarily focuses on language attitudes: Why do people have such strong feelings about languages and their varieties? His work also includes research on morphophonetics and psycholinguistics, as well as on how attitudes are reflected in popular media.

Dila Turus is a PhD Student in General Linguistics at the Institute of Linguistics at Heinrich Heine University Düsseldorf, Germany. Her research focuses on corpus-based studies of causative light verb constructions and, inter alia, their alternation-like relationship to lexically corresponding simplex verbs.

Sol Tovar holds an MA in English Linguistics from the University of Regensburg, Germany, and a degree in TESOL from Universidad Nacional de Mar del Plata, Argentina. She is currently a doctoral candidate at the University of Heidelberg, Germany. Her research focuses on discursive and teaching practices around language, gender and sexuality.

Laura Vela-Plo is a researcher at the HiTT Hizkuntzalaritza Teorikorako Taldea research group in linguistics and a lecturer at the Philology and History Department at the University of the Basque Country (UPV/EHU), Spain, in the area of Spanish language.

Lena Völkening is a PhD student in linguistics at the University of Oldenburg, Germany. She also works as a translator and author and has published a book on gender-fair language aimed at non-academic audiences.

Index

androcentrism 34, 174, 177

bias
- bias transfer 115, 122, 124, 140, 142
- cognitive bias 177, 178, 192
- female bias 22, 179, 180
- feminine bias 179
- gender bias 97, 112, 113, 115, 129, 146, 174, 178, 186, 207
- male bias 2, 35, 102, 112, 113, 115, 128, 141, 142, 159, 177, 181, 186
- sexist bias 177, 192
- social desirability bias 117, 162

construction grammar 12, 15, 24, 26

deadnaming 86
discriminative learning
- linear discriminative learning (LDL) 101, 102
- naive discriminative learning (NDL) 100
distributed morphology 224, 226, 227, 230, 233
distributional semantics 99, 101

feminism
- (queer-)feminism 34
- feminist efforts 36
- feminist language movements 205
- feminist language reforms 175
- feminist linguistics 32, 56, 182, 205
- feminist literature and ideologies 232
- second-wave feminism 228

gender 1, 32, 84
- conceptual gender 1, 2
- covert gender 146
- gender gap 11, 18
- gender roles 1, 151
- gender star 11, 13, 17, 23, 36, 131
- gender stereotypes 2, 63–66, 150, 174, 177, 200
- gender transfer 112
- gender-fair 2, 160, 174, 200
- gender-inclusive 1, 2, 11, 13, 17, 18, 22, 24, 32, 36, 129, 159, 200
- gender-neutral 2, 32, 35, 97, 112, 128, 145, 159, 200
- gender-sensitive 12
- genderless 145, 157
- grammatical gender 1, 2, 23, 33, 157, 204
- lexico-semantic gender 1, 2
- natural gender 1, 2, 128, 157
- pronominal gender 95, 127, 160
- transgender, trans umbrella 220
generic masculine 11, 55, 100, 111, 115, 128, 147, 158–161, 169, 178

misgendering 83–86, 227, 228, 230

relativism 175, 179

singular *they* 97, 112, 200

www.ingramcontent.com/pod-product-compliance
Lightning Source LLC
Chambersburg PA
CBHW061711300426
44115CB00014B/2642